PRAISE FOR THE FIRST EDITION OF

HOSTELS FRANCE & ITALY

"The only upbeat hostel resource for France and Italy . . . Paul Karr's guides give hostelling a colorful new dimension."

—*Big World* magazine

"Students and European travelers on a budget will enjoy this amusing guide . . . [and] will want to bring it with them on their trips."

—*American Reference Books*

HELP US KEEP THIS GUIDE UP TO DATE

Every effort has been made by the authors and editors to make this guide as accurate and useful as possible. However, many things can change after a guide is published—establishments close, phone numbers change, facilities come under new management, etc.

We would love to hear from you concerning your experiences with this guide and how you feel it could be improved and kept up to date. While we may not be able to respond to all comments and suggestions, we'll take them to heart and we'll also make certain to share them with the authors. Please send your comments and suggestions to the following address:

The Globe Pequot Press
Reader Response/Editorial Department
P.O. Box 480
Guilford, CT 06437

Or you may e-mail us at:

editorial@globe-pequot.com

Thanks for your input, and happy travels!

HOSTELS SERIES

HOSTELS FRANCE & ITALY

The Only Comprehensive, Unofficial, Opinionated Guide

SECOND EDITION

Paul Karr
and Martha Coombs

The Globe Pequot Press
Guilford, Connecticut

Cover design, text design, and maps by M. A. Dubé
Contributing freelancers: Wes Ingwersen, Yasmin Mistry, and Piran Montford
Other assistance: Evan Halper

Library of Congress Cataloging-in-Publication Data

Karr, Paul.
Hostels France & Italy : the only comprehensive, unofficial, opinionated guide / Paul Karr and Martha Coombs. — 2nd ed.
p. cm. — (Hostels series)
ISBN 0-7627-0869-7
1. Tourist camps, hostels, etc.—France—Guidebooks. 2. Tourist camps, hostels, etc.—Italy—Guidebooks. I. Title: Hostels France and Italy. II. Coombs, Martha. III. Title. IV. Series.

TX907.5.F7 K37 2001
647.9444'06—dc21 00-051064

Printed on recycled paper
Manufactured in the United States of America
Second Edition/First Printing

CONTENTS

ACKNOWLEDGMENTS

Paul Karr thanks Martha once again for companionship and editorial assistance. Martha thanks Senja St. John and Richard Coombs for guidance and support.

From both of us, thanks to the following hostel professionals, who went far beyond the call of duty: Sylvie and Guillaume at FUAJ; Anita, Claudia, and Simona at AIG; and Mimi, Ilse, Nicola, Daniella, and Giuseppe at their respective hostels. All gave patient answers to our frequent questions.

We both again thank friends and family—the Karr, Coombs, Couture, and Bottinger families in New Hampshire; Tom Paquette, Chris Allen, Frank Dean, Megan Seibel, and Carolyne Conrad in New England; and our good friends Judy Purdy, Jan Neubauer, Chris Aubry, Mary Lopez, Bob Atkins and Ros Robinson among others.

Thanks to the hostelling organizations AYH (in the U.S.), AIG (in Italy), and FUAJ (in France) for continuous encouragement and assistance; to Kemwel Holiday Auto Rentals, a terrific rental company; and to Canada 3000, the lowest-cost airline in North America and staffed by some fine people besides.

Rail Europe and Eurostar—which are two different companies, by the way—get our hearty thanks for lots of information and assistance and for making rail travel a real pleasure.

And thanks, finally, to a world (literally) of new friends met or made on the road. So many of you have taught us about your corner of the world or otherwise made this work enjoyable and useful.

Thank you all.

HOW TO USE THIS BOOK

What you're holding in your hands is the first-ever attempt of its kind: a fairly complete listing and rating of all the hostels we could find in France and Italy. Dozens of hostellers from countries all over the globe were interviewed in the course of putting this guide together, and their comments and thoughts run throughout its pages. Who knows? *You* might be quoted somewhere inside.

We wrote this guide for two pretty simple reasons:

First, we wanted to bring hostelling to a wider audience. Hostels continue to grow in popularity, but many North American travelers still don't think of them as options when planning a trip. We wanted to encourage that because—at its best—the hostelling experience brings people of greatly differing origins, faiths, and points of view together in a convivial setting. You'll learn about these people, and also about the place in which the hostel is situated, in a very personal way that no textbook could ever provide.

Second, we wanted very much to give people our honest opinions of the hostels. You wouldn't send your best friend to a fleabag, and we don't want readers traveling great distances only to be confronted with filthy kitchens, nasty managers, or dangerous neighborhoods. At least, we thought, we could warn them about potentially unsafe or unpleasant situations ahead of time.

On the other hand, of course, we would also tip our friends off to the truly wonderful hostels—the ones with treehouses, cafes, free breakfasts; the ones with real family spirit. So that's what we've done. Time after time on the road, we have heard fellow travelers complaining that the guidebooks they bought simply listed places to stay but didn't rate them. Well, now we've done it—and we haven't pulled a single punch or held back a bit of praise.

How we wrote this book

The authors, along with a cadre of assistants, fanned out across France and Italy with notebooks and laptops in hand during the spring, summer, and fall of 2000. Sometimes we identified ourselves in advance as authors; sometimes we just popped in for surprise visits. We counted rooms, turned taps, tested beds. And then we talked with managers and staff.

Before we left, we also took the time to interview plenty of hostellers in private and get their honest opinions about the places they were staying or had already stayed.

The results are contained within this book: actual hosteller quotes, opinions, ratings—and more.

What is a hostel?

If you've picked up this book, you probably know what a hostel is. On the other hand, a surprising number of people interviewed for this book weren't sure at all what it means.

So let's check your knowledge with a little pop quiz. Sharpen your pencils, put on your thinking caps, and dive in.

1. A hostel is:

- **A.** a hospital.
- **B.** a hospice.
- **C.** a hotel.
- **D.** a drunk tank.
- **E.** none of the above.

(correct answer worth 20 points)

2. A hostel is:

- **A.** a place where international travelers bunk up.
- **B.** a cheap sleep.
- **C.** a place primarily dedicated to bunks.
- **D.** all of the above.

(correct answer worth 20 points)

3. You just turned 30. Word on the street has it that you'll get turned away for being that age. Do you tell the person at the hostel desk the grim news?

- **A.** No, because a hostel is restricted to students under 30.
- **B.** No, because a hostel is restricted to elderly folks over 65.
- **C.** No, because they don't care about your midlife crisis.

(correct answer worth 10 points)

4. You spy a shelf labeled FREE FOOD! in the hostel kitchen. What do you do?

- **A.** Begin stuffing pomegranates in your pockets.
- **B.** Ask the manager how food ended up in jail.
- **C.** Run for your life.

(correct answer worth 5 points)

5. Essay question. Why do you want to stay in a hostel?

(extra credit; worth up to 45 points)

Done? Great! And the envelope, please . . .

1. **None of the above.** The word *hostel* is German, and it means "country inn for youngsters" or something like that. In French, it's called an *auberge de jeunesse,* and in Italy, it's called an *ostello;* if you ever get lost, look for signs with those words on them.
2. **All of the above.** You got that one, right?
3. **C.** No age limits or restrictions here!
4. **A.** Free means free.
5. Give yourself 15 points for every use of the word "friends," "international," or "cool," okay? But don't give yourself more than 45. Yes, we mean it. Don't make us turn this car around right now. We will. We mean it.

What? All you wrote was "It's cheap"? Okay, okay, give yourself 20 points.

So how did you do?

100 points:	Born to be wild
80–100:	Get your motor runnin'
40–80:	Head out on the highway
20–40:	Lookin' for adventure
0–20:	Hope you don't come my way

Don't be embarrassed if you flunked this little quiz, though. Hostel operators get confused and blur the lines, too. You'll sometimes find a campground, retreat center, or college setting aside a couple bunks—and calling itself a hostel anyway. In those cases we've used our best judgment about whether a place is or isn't a hostel.

Also, we excluded some joints—no matter how well-meaning—if they (a) exclude men or women, (b) serve primarily as a university residence hall (with a very few special exceptions), or (c) serve you a heavy side of religious doctrine with the eggs in the morning.

In a few cases our visits didn't satisfy us either way; those places were either left out, set aside for a future edition, or briefly described here but not rated.

The bottom line? If it's in this book, it probably is a hostel. If it isn't, it's not, and don't let anyone tell you otherwise. There. 'Nuff said.

Understanding the Ratings

All the listings information in this book was current as of press time. Here's the beginning of a sample entry in the book, from a hostel in rural Provence. It's a fairly typical entry, except that the hostel isn't in a city:

FONTAINE-DE-VAUCLUSE AUBERGE DE JEUNESSE

Chemin de la Vignasse, Fontaine-de-Vaucluse, Vaucluse, 84800

Phone Number: 04–90–20–31–65
Fax Number: 04–90–20–26–20
Rates: 65 francs per HI member (about $11 US)
Credit cards: None
Beds: 50
Private/family rooms: Yes
Kitchen available: Yes
Season: February 15 to November 15
Office hours: 7:30 to 10:00 A.M.; 5:00 to 11:00 P.M.
Lockout: 10:00 A.M. to 5:00 P.M.
Affiliation: H!-FUAJ
Extras: Laundry, bike rentals, camping, breakfast, catered meals for groups, grill

First things first. See those little pictures at the bottom of the listing? Those are icons, and they signify something important we wanted you to know about the hostel. We've printed a key to these icons on the facing page.

The overall hostel rating consists of those hip-looking thumbs sitting atop each entry. It's pretty simple: Thumbs up means good. Thumbs down means bad.

We've used these thumbs to compare the hostels to one another. Only a select number of hostels earned the top rating of one thumb up, and a few were considered unpleasant enough to merit a thumb down. You can use this rating as a general assessment of a hostel.

Often we didn't give any thumbs at all to a hostel that was a mixed-bag experience. Or maybe, for one reason or another—bad weather, bad luck, bad timing, remoteness, an inability to get ahold of the staff, or our own confusion about the place—we just didn't feel we collected enough information to properly rate that hostel for you.

That said, here's a key to what these ratings mean:

Cream of the crop; recommended

So-so

Bad news; not recommended

KEY TO ICONS

- Attractive natural setting
- Ecologically aware hostel
- Superior kitchen facilities or great cafe/restaurant
- Offbeat or eccentric place
- Superior bathroom facilities
- Romantic private rooms
- Comfortable beds
- A particularly good value
- Wheelchair-accessible
- Good for business travelers
- Especially well suited for families
- Good for active travelers
- Visual arts at hostel or nearby
- Music at hostel or nearby
- Great hostel for skiers
- Bar or pub at hostel or nearby
- Editors Choice: among our very favorite hostels

The rest of the information is pretty much self-explanatory:

Address is usually the hostel's street address; occasionally we add the mailing address if it's different from the street address.

Phone number is the primary phone number.

Fax number is the primary fax number.

Note that all the phone and fax numbers are written as dialed from *within France or Italy.*

E-mail is the staff's e-mail address, for those who want to get free information or (sometimes) book a room by computer.

Web site (the example hostel didn't have one) indicates a hostel's World Wide Web page address.

Rates are the cost per person to stay at the hostel—when all the currency converting's said and done, expect to pay somewhere around $15 per person, more in cities or popular tourist areas. For private or family rooms we've listed the total price for two people to stay in the room; usually it's higher than the cost of two singles, sometimes considerably so. Single or triple room rates will vary; ask ahead if you're unsure what you'll pay.

Note that these rates sometimes vary by season or by membership in a hostelling group such as Hostelling International (HI); we have tried to include a range of prices where applicable. Most HI member hostels, for instance, charge $2.00 to $4.00 extra per day if you don't belong to one of Hostelling International's worldwide affiliates.

A few hostels might charge you about $1.00 to supply sheets or towels if you haven't brought your own. (Sleeping bags, no matter how clean *you* think they are, are often frowned upon.) Finally, various local, municipal, or other taxes might also add slightly to the rates quoted here.

Credit cards can be a good way to pay for a bed in a foreign country (you get the fairest exchange rates on your home currency). We have noted whether cards are accepted by the hostels. That usually means Visa, MasterCard, or American Express. More and more hostels are taking them, and even if we haven't indicated that they are accepted, things may have changed. When in doubt, call ahead and ask.

Office hours indicate the hours when staff are at the front desk and answer the phones—or at least would consider answering the phones. Although European custom is to use military time and all bus and train schedules read that way, we've used "American" time throughout this book. Keep in mind that nothing is carved in stone, however. Some hostel staffs will happily field calls in the middle of the night if you're reasonable, while others can't stand it. Try to call within the listed hours if possible.

A good rule to follow: The smaller a place, the harder it is for the owner/manager to drag him/herself out of bed at four in the morning just because you lost your way. Big-city hostels, however, frequently operate just like hotels. Somebody's always on duty, or at least on call.

Keep in mind that France and Italy are notorious for their lax attitudes toward time and punctuality. It could take the staff forever to answer the phone, the front desk might open late and close ten minutes early, or staff might be tucking into the daily three-hour lunch. Don't knock it; adapt and deal. It's just their way.

Season indicates what part of the year a hostel is open—if it's closed part of the year. We've made our best effort at listing the seasons of each hostel, but schedules sometimes change according to weather or a manager's vacation plans. Call if you're unsure whether a hostel will be open when you want to stay there.

Private rooms or family rooms are rooms for a couple, a family with children, or (sometimes) a single traveler. Sometimes it's nice to have your own room on the road: It's more private, more secure, and your snoring won't bother anyone. They're becoming more common in Europe, but are still hard to snag. Book months ahead for one if you're going to a popular place like Florence or Paris. Really!

Kitchen available simply indicates whether the hostel allows hostellers to cook in a kitchen or not. In North America and the U.K., almost every hostel has a kitchen—but the situation changes drastically in France and Italy. Probably half of all French hostels have some sort of kitchen setup; just as many serve a delicious meal instead, so take advantage and fill 'er up.

Italy is another case, as usual. Strict national health laws regulate who can set foot in a kitchen and what they can wear; as a result, almost none of the hostels there let you use the kitchen. That can be frustrating, especially after weeks of pizza and pasta on the road. Oh, well. For what it's worth, the hostels most likely to have kitchens are located in the extreme south of Italy (like Sicily, Puglia and Calabria) and the extreme north of Italy, near the Alps. Go figure.

Affiliation indicates whether a hostel is affiliated with Hostelling International or not. For more information about what these organizations do, see "A Word about Affiliations" (page 11).

Extras list some of the other amenities that come with a stay at the hostel. A dollar sign in parentheses after an item indicates that you must pay more for it. However, some—but not all—will be free; there's an amazing variety of services and almost as big a variety in managers' willingness to do nice things for free. Laundries, on the other hand, are never free; and there's always a charge for meals, lockers, bicycle or other equipment rentals, and other odds and ends. Some hostels maintain free information desks, and a few will pick you up at rail stations and the like.

Lockout and **Curfew:** Many hostels have hours during which you are locked out of the place; in other words, you're not permitted on the premises. Many also have a curfew; be back inside before this time, or you'll be locked out for the night.

With each entry we've also given you a little more information about the hostel to make your stay a little more informed—and fun. Here's the last part of the hostel entry that began above:

Best bet for a bite:
Super U
Insiders' tip:
Great weekend market in l'Isle-sur-la Sorgue
Gestalt:
Fontaine of youth
Hospitality:
Cleanliness:
Party index:

What does all that stuff mean?

Best bet for a bite tells you where to find food in the area. Usually we'll direct you to the cheapest and closest supermarket. But sometimes, in the interest of variety—and good eatin'— we'll point you toward a surprising health food store, *a trattoria* or a farmers' market rich with local color, or even a fancy place well worth the splurge.

Insiders' tip is a juicy secret about the area, something we didn't know until we got to the hostel ourselves.

What hostellers say relates what hostellers told us about a hostel—or what we imagine they would say.

Gestalt is the general feeling of a place—our (sometimes humorous) way of describing what it's about.

Safety describes urban hostels only; the example hostel is not in a big city, so there's no safety rating. If it had been, we would have graded it based on both the quality of the neighborhood and the security precautions taken by the hostel staff, using this scale:

No worries

Keep an eye out

Dial 911

Hospitality rates the hostel staff's friendliness toward hostellers (and travel writers):

Smile city

Grins & growls

Very hostile hostel

Cleanliness rates, what else, the general cleanliness of a place. Bear in mind that this can change—rapidly—depending on the time of year, turnover in staff, and so forth. So use it only as a general guide.

Spic-and-span

Could be cleaner . . . .

Don't let the bedbugs bite

The **party index** is our way of tipping you off about the general scene at the hostel:

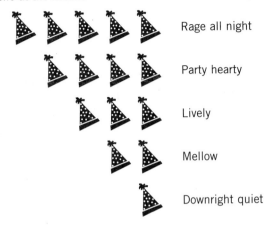

Rage all night

Party hearty

Lively

Mellow

Downright quiet

How to get there:

By bike: From village, ride across bridge along route de Cavaillon to junction with route Touristique de Gordes. Turn left and follow signs to hostel.

By bus: From Avignon, take bus to Fontaine-de-Vaucluse.

By car: From Paris, take A7 to Avignon exit; continue on D22 to D24, then follow D24 to Fontaine-de-Vaucluse. From south of France, take A7 to Cavaillon exit, and take D24 to Fontaine-de-Vaucluse.

By train: Isle-sur-Sorgue station, 5 miles away; call hostel for transit route. From Avignon station, take bus to Fontaine-de-Vaucluse.

How to get there includes directions to many hostels—by car, bus, train, plane, or even ferry. Subway directions are given in big cities if applicable. Often these directions are complicated, however; in those cases, managers have asked (or we recommend) that you call the hostel itself for more precise directions.

A SHORT HISTORY OF HOSTELLING

Hostelling as we know it started around 1907, when Richard Schirmann, an assistant schoolteacher in Altena, Germany, decided to make one of the empty classrooms a space for visiting students to sleep. That was not a completely unique idea; Austrian inns and taverns had been offering reduced rates and bunk space to students since 1885. But Schirmann would develop much grander plans. He was about to start a movement.

His idea was to get students out of the industrial cities and into the countryside. Schirmann was a strong believer that walking and bicycling tours in the fresh air were essential to adolescent development and learning. But such excursions were impossible without a place to spend the night. His logic was simple: Since rural schoolhouses were deserted during weekends and holidays, why not make use of those spaces?

The caretakers of the school he chose agreed to serve as houseparents, and some fast ground rules were established. Students were responsible for piling up the tables and benches in the classroom and laying out thin straw sacks on the floor. At some ungodly early morning hour, the students were to restack the straw mats and reorganize the classroom as they found it. Boys and girls slept in separate rooms but were treated as equals. Detractors cried scandal, wondering aloud what was going on in these schoolrooms after dark.

The experiment worked, sort of. Altena became a haven for student excursions into the countryside, but finding shelter in other communities proved to be difficult. Sometimes the situation would become dire. Late one night in the summer of 1909, Schirmann decided it was time to expand his movement beyond Altena. His goal was to establish a network of hostels within walking distance of one another. Beginning in a schoolhouse with straw mats, Schirmann eventually acquired the use of a castle. It still stands—the Ur-hostel, if you will—in Altena, and it's still used as a hostel, believe it or not.

After World War I the movement really began to spread. By 1928 there were more than 2,000 hostels worldwide. Today tens of thousands of hostellers stay at HI-affiliated hostels each year, hailing from everywhere from Alaska to Zaire. Thousands more stay at independent hostels.

The goal of a single association of hostels located within a day's walk of one another will probably never be realized. Still, you're likely to find a promising brew of cultural exchange and friendship over pots of ramen noodles and instant coffee almost anywhere you go.

In that sense, perhaps, Richard Schirmann's dream has been realized after all.

A Word about Affiliations

A majority of hostels in this book are affiliated with Hostelling International (HI); the rest, we've labeled independent hostels.

FUAJ (the Federation Unie des Auberges de Jeunesse, 27, rue Pajol, 75108 Paris; telephone 0144–898–727) is France's branch of Hostelling International. The organization is part of the International Youth Hostel Federation, which has 5,000 member hostels in seventy countries. Member hostels are held to a number of regulations, such as maximum number of beds per shower, even a minimum amount of space that must exist between top bunks and the ceiling. To get into a FUAJ hostel you must have an HI membership card (see below).

FUAJ hostels are generally okay, and they tend to have surprising extras: Most serve tasty meals at a low cost, and many have bars and/or discos! Since these hostels exist primarily for the French traveler, fun is the rule. In places like the Alps, they even run lots of fun outdoor programs like hikes and ski excursions, great for seeing the outdoors and also meeting other (usually French) hostellers.

On the downside, things tend to get messy. Young Franco hostellers are often too busy hurrying off to the next wine tasting or rave to clean up after themselves. Also, these hostels are energy-conservative to the max: Many have push-button faucets and push-button lights that go off in a few seconds. We appreciate the environmental sentiments, but it still takes getting used to.

BVJ, MIJE, and FTJ are three organizations that run large "foyers" around France. Many have age requirements, however—usually you've gotta be twenty-six or younger to get in, such as in the three great BVJ joints in Paris—so there are very few listed in this book. (Our policy, you'll recall, is not to shut anybody out.)

UCRIF (27, rue de Turbigo, 75002 Paris; telephone 01–4026–5764) is an independent nonprofit French group that runs a series of "Gites D'Etape"—roughly translated, "rustic getaway lodges"—around France. Formed in 1979, its lodgings always include dormitories but are a little more geared toward outdoorsy pursuits than some FUAJ hostels.

AIG (Associazione Italiana Alberghi per la per Gioventu, via Cavour 44, Roma; telephone 06–487–1152) is Italy's Hostelling International affiliate. AIG has converted an amazing number of beautiful villas into pretty good hostels. These are mostly clean and well run, some in locations you can't believe until you see them. Meals at night are almost always offered for a charge. And AIG has lined up some pretty spiffy discounts with local merchants around Italy—for slightly reduced prices on Internet time, train tickets, shoes, whatever. Practice asking about them at each joint as you check in.

The only drawbacks to AIG's hostels are the nonproximity of these villas to the cities and towns (count on half an hour by public transport for most). Also, virtually every one of these hostels kicks you out very early for the entire day. And they're strict about it.

In most AIG and FUAJ hostels, a breakfast is usually included for free—but it ranges from skimpy to substantial. Don't plan on huge meals here. Dinner tends to be pasta and bread, maybe salad and wine at a better place.

Many of the giant HI urban hostels in France and Italy are purpose-built facilities owned by AIG or FUAJ itself, often resembling well-equipped college dormitories. Some of these HI-owned hostels have developed impressive educational programs that incorporate volunteers from the local community and so forth.

The bulk of the HI hostels, however, are still independently owned. These joints are as varied in personality as their owners are. A common thread that runs through them is a respect for the educational dimension of hostelling. Owners reiterate that hostels offer more than just a cheap sleep; they often join HI out of respect for the organization and its goals.

In France there's another kind of place: the so-called *auberges vertes* (green hostels), which are small, simple, and rural—sometimes resembling nothing more than a spare bedroom or two in someone's rustic home. It goes without saying that your freedom (and partying) can be strictly limited at such places, but we've found some of them are great if you can abide by the rules and enjoy getting to know your hosts. You'll definitely get more attention at these places.

INDEPENDENTS are what we call all the others. Some owners opt not to join either organization. Membership costs are high, and they feel the return on such an investment isn't enough. Such a decision—in and of itself—does not reflect on the quality of the hostel. It would be foolish to write a hostel off simply because it is not affiliated.

Things are more laid-back—usually. Liquor isn't always officially off-limits at these places, for instance. (In HI joints in France and Italy, you must often buy alcohol at the hostel bar or restaurant or forget about it.) The independent Italian hostels do the lockout thing, too, but it's not quite as common or ironclad. On the other hand, there's no guarantee of quality, and the standards, upkeep, noise level, and beer flow tend to vary wildly from place to place.

A bunch of independent hostels in Italy are run by church organizations such as convents. These places obviously have stricter lockouts, curfews, and alcohol rules than anyone else in this book. Most also ban unmarried couples from sharing a bed. As a result, we have banned them from this book.

HOW TO HOSTEL

Hostelling is, generally speaking, easy as pie. Plan ahead a bit and use a little common sense, and you'll find check-in goes pretty smoothly.

Reserving a Bed

Getting a good bunk will often be your first and biggest challenge, especially if it's high season. (Summer is usually high season, but in some areas—the French and Italian Alps, for instance—winter is the toughest time to get a bed. And popular cities like Florence or Paris seem to be busy almost year-round.) Hostellers often have an amazingly laissez-faire attitude about reservations; many simply waltz in at midnight expecting a bed will work out.

Sometimes it does. Sometimes it doesn't.

Almost every Hostelling International abode takes reservations of some form or another, so if you know where you're going to be, use this service. Be aware that you might need a credit card number to hold a bed, and other hostels require you to send a deposit check. You might also need to show up by a certain hour, like 6:00 P.M., to get in. Some HI hostels are also affiliated with the worldwide International Booking Network.

Independent hostels may be either more strict or more lax about taking solid reservations. Note that in France and Italy, they're often much faster to fill up than HI joints because of the popularity of no-rules places.

If you can't or won't reserve, the best thing to do is get there superearly. Office opens at 8:00 A.M.? Get there at 7:00. No room, but checkout ends at 11:00? Be back at 11:05 in case of cancellations or unexpected checkouts. The doors are closed again till 4:30 in the afternoon? No problem. Come back around 4:00 with a paperback and camp out on the porch. That's your only shot if you couldn't or wouldn't reserve ahead, and hostellers are somewhat respectful of the pecking order: It really is first-come, first-served. So come first.

Paying the Piper

Once you're in, be prepared to pay for your night's stay immediately—before you're even assigned a bunk. Take note ahead of time which hostels take credit cards, checks, and so forth. Learn the local currency, and don't expect every little hostel to change your 100,000 lire note for a couple bucks' worth of laundry.

You will almost always be required to give up your passport and (if you have one) Hostelling International card for the night. Don't sweat it; it's just the way it's done over there, and in fact they have good reasons. In Italy, for example, the police require hospitality outfits to tell them who's staying each night. Also, if an emergency happens (nah, no chance), the passport might help hostel staff locate your significant others.

Remember to pay ahead if you want a weekly stay, too. Often you can get deep discounts, though the downside is that you'll almost never get a partial refund if you decide you can't stand the place and leave before the week is up.

If you're paying by the day, rebook promptly each morning; hostel managers are very busy during the morning hours, keeping track of check-ins, checkouts, cleaning duties, and cash. You'll make a friend if you're early about notifying the manager of your plans for the next day. On the other hand, managers hate bugging guests all morning or all day about whether they'll be staying on. Don't put the staff through this.

All right, so you've secured a bed and paid up. Now you have to get to it. This may be no easy task at some hostels, where staff and customers look and act like one and the same. A kindly manager will probably notice you bumbling around and take pity. As you're being shown to your room, you're also likely get a short tour of the facilities and a briefing on the ground rules.

You might need to pay a small amount if you lose your room key—usually about 20 francs or 8,000 lire (about $5.00 US), sometimes more. On checkout, you'll get your card and passport back.

Knowing the Ground Rules

There's one universal ground rule at every hostel: You are responsible for serving and cleaning up after yourself. And there's a corollary rule: Be courteous. So, while you're welcome to use all the kitchen facilities, share the space with your fellow guests—don't spread your five-course meal out over all the counter space and rangetop burners if other hungry folks are hanging around waiting. And never ever leave a sinkful of dirty pots and pans behind. That's bad form.

Hostel guests are almost always asked to mark their name and check-in date on all the food they put in the refrigerator. Only a shelf marked FREE FOOD (*GRATUIT* or *LIBRE* in France; you won't find free food in Italy) is up for grabs; everything else belongs to other hostellers, so don't touch it. Hostellers might get very touchy about people stealing their grub. Some of the better-run hostels have a spice rack and other kitchen essentials on hand. If you're not sure whether something is communal, ask. Don't assume anything is up for grabs unless it is clearly marked as such.

Then there's the lockout, a source of bitter frustration among non-European hostellers. Almost every hostel in France and Italy, even the big-city joints, kicks everybody out in the morning and doesn't let them back in until the afternoon or early evening. Lockouts tend to run from around 9:30 A.M. (which is ungodly, we say, but pretty typical) to 5:00 or 6:00 P.M., during which time your bags might be inside your room—but *you* won't be. A few places let you back in around 2:00 or 3:00 P.M. Ooooooh, the generosity.

The practice has its pros and cons. Managers usually justify a lockout by noting that it forces travelers to interact with the locals and also allows their staff to "meticulously clean" the rooms. The real reason is usually that the hostel can't or won't pay staff to hang around and baby-sit you all day. On the upside, these hostels never become semiresidential situations stuffed with couch potatoes, like many U.S. hostels, so maybe the lockouts solve that problem.

Curfews are also very common; usually the front doors lock between 11:00 P.M. and midnight, and they won't give you a key. Big-city joints generally have some system in place to let you get in twenty-four hours: a guard, a numbered keypad, a room key that also opens the main door. But check first.

In the reviews we've tried to identify those hostels that enforce lockouts. Usually you wouldn't want to be hanging out in the hostel in the middle of the day anyway, but after several sleepless nights of travel—or when you're under the weather—daytime downtime sure is appreciated. So beware. Note that even if we haven't listed a lockout or a curfew, it might exist. These things change. Assume that you will get kicked out at 9:30 A.M. for the day and—except in big cities—will need to be back by midnight.

Finally, some hostels also enforce a maximum limit on your stay—anywhere from three days, if the hostel is really popular, to about two weeks. Savvy budget travelers have learned how to get around this unfortunate situation, of course: They simply suck it up and spend a night at the "Y" or a convenient motel—then check back into the cheaper hostel first thing in the morning. But *we* didn't tell you to do that. Uh-uh.

Etiquette and Smarts

Again, to put it simply, use common sense. Hostellers are a refreshingly flexible bunch. All these people are able to make this system work by looking after one another; remember, in a hostel you're a community member first and a consumer second. With that in mind, here are some guidelines for how to act:

- The first thing you should do after check-in is get your bed made. When you're assigned a bed, stick to it. Don't spread your stuff out on nearby bunks, even if they are empty. Someone's going to be coming in late-night for one of 'em, you can bet the backpack on it.
- Be sure to lock your valuables in a locker—or in a safe if they've got one. Good hostels offer lockers as a service; it might cost a little, but it's worth it. Bring a padlock in case the hostel has run out or charges an arm and a leg.
- Set toiletries and anything else you need in a place where they are easily accessible. This avoids your having to paw through

your bag late at night, potentially disturbing other guests from their slumber. The same goes for early-morning departures: If you're taking off at the crack of dawn, take precautions not to wake the whole place.

- If you're leaving early in the morning, try to make all arrangements with the manager before going to bed the night before. Managers are usually accommodating and pleasant folks, but guests are expected to respect their privacy and peace of mind by not pushing things too far. Dragging a manager out of bed at four in the morning—or for some other trivial matter—is really pushing it.
- Be sure to mind the bathroom. A quick wiping of the shower floor with a towel after you use it is common courtesy.
- Finally, be sure to mind the quiet hours. Some hostels have curfews, but very few force lights-out. If you are up after-hours, be respectful. Don't crank the television or radio too loud; don't scream in the hallways late at night. (Save that for the beach, and annoy people staying in much nicer digs.)

Packing

Those dainty hand towels and dapper shaving kits and free soaps you get at a hotel won't be anywhere in sight at the hostel. In fact, even some of the base essentials might not be available—kitchens are *not* a given in France or Italy, for instance. You're on your own, so bring everything you need to be comfortable.

There are only a few things you can expect the hostel to supply:

- A bed frame with a mattress and pillow.
- Shower and toilet facilities.
- A common room with some spartan furniture.
- Maybe a few heavy blankets.

Some of the more chic hostels we've identified in this guide may be full-service. But they are the exceptions to the rule.

Bring stuff like this to keep your journey through hostel territory comfortable:

- If you're traveling abroad from the United States, you obviously need a passport. Unlike U.S. hostels, a Euro-hostel will often take your passport as collateral when you check in. Don't get nervous; this is extremely common. It's the equivalent, over there, of taking down your driver's license number when you write a check. However, in the unlikely event that someone loses your passport, make sure you've got backup copies of the issuing office, date, and passport number—in your luggage and also back home.
- Hostelling International membership cards are a good thing to have on hand. They can be purchased at most member HI hostels or back home before you go. This card identifies you as a certified superhosteller and gets you the very cheapest rate for

your bed in all HI (and also some unaffiliated) hostels. With discounts of $2.00 to $4.00 per night, these savings can add up fast. Cost of membership is $25 for adults ages 18 to 54 and $15 if you're over age 54. Kids under age 18 are members for free.

Sometimes that membership card gets you deals at local restaurants, bike shops, and tours, too. Again, it will be easier to deal with the front desk at some of the more cautious hostels (even nonmember ones) if you can flash one of these cards.

- Red Alert! Do not plan on using a sleeping bag in most hostels. A good number of places simply won't allow it—problems with ticks and other creatures dragged in from the great outdoors have propelled this prohibition into place.

The alternative is a sleepsack, which is basically two sheets sewn together with a makeshift pillowcase. You can find them at most budget travel stores or make your own. Personally, we hate these confining wraps and rarely get through the night in one without having it twist around our bodies so tight that we wake up wanting to charge it with attempted manslaughter. Our preferred method is to bring our own set of sheets, though that might be too much extra stuff to pack if you're backpacking.

Some hostels give you free linen; most that don't will rent sheets for about $1.00 to $2.00 per night. You don't get charged for use of the standard army-surplus blankets or the musty charm that comes with them.

- Some people bring their own pillows, as those supplied tend to be on the frumpy side. In France, especially, they resemble rolled-up sausages; and they're about as comfortable. Small pillows are also useful for sleeping on trains and buses.
- We definitely suggest earplugs for light sleepers, especially for urban hostels—but also in case you get caught in a room with a heavy snorer.
- A small flashlight is a must, not only for late-night reading but also to find your bed without waking up the entire dorm.
- A little bit of spice is always nice, especially when you have had one too many plates of pasta. You'll find the cost of basil and oregano in convenience stores way too high to stomach once you're on the road. Buy it cheap before you leave and carry it in jars or small plastic bags.
- Check to see which hostels have laundry facilities. Most won't, and then you'll need to schlep your stuff to the local laundromat—*buanderie* in France, *lavanderia* in Italy. It'll be expensive, so bring lotsa money.
- Wearing flip-flops in the shower might help you avoid a case of athlete's foot.
- Be sure your towel is a quick-drying type. Otherwise you'll wind up with mildew in your pack—and in your food.

TRANSPORTATION

Take a careful look at your transportation options when planning a hostel journey. You should be able to hop from city to city by bus or train without a problem, but you could have trouble getting to rural hostels without a car.

GETTING TO FRANCE AND ITALY

BY PLANE

The airline business is crazy: great deals and rip-off fares come and go with a regularity that is frightening to behold. Supply, demand, season, the stock market, and random acts of cruelty or kindness all appear to contribute to the quixotic nature of fares.

As a result, there is no one piece of simple advice we can give you, other than this: Find a darned good travel agent who cares about budget travelers, and trust your agent with all the planning. You can cruise the Internet if you like, and you might find an occasional great deal your agent doesn't know about. Just make sure the sellers are reputable before giving out that credit-card number.

A couple tips:

- **Charters are the cheapest way to go,** though it's no-frills all the way. From the United States check out the option of going via a connecting flight from Luxembourg (on Icelandair), Brussels (via MartinAir), or Frankfurt (that's Lufthansa, though it's more expensive) rather than flying directly to Rome or Paris.
  From Canada, Canada 3000 offers the cheapest charter flights to France. They fly from Montreal, Toronto, Halifax, and other cities. In summer there are lotsa flights, but they're superpopular, so book early. Other cheap flights to France from Canada can be had on Nouvelle Frontieres or Air Transat.
- **Cheap-ticket brokers** (also called consolidators or bucket shops) are a great bet for saving money, but you have to be fast on your feet to keep up, as the deals appear and disappear literally daily. London and New York are major centers for bucket shops. Both *The Rough Guide* and *Lonely Planet* series of guidebooks include expanded material on the best hubs, connections, and consolidators from everywhere from Australia to Ireland.
- **Flying as a courier** comes highly recommended by some folks who've tried it. Others are nervous about it. It works this way: You agree to carry luggage for a company in exchange for a very cheap round-trip ticket abroad. You must be flexible about your departure and return dates, and you can't change those dates once assigned to you—and you usually can bring only carry-on luggage.

There isn't nearly as much demand for couriers from smaller destinations to, say, Europe as there is from places like New York or Los

Angeles; but it's still worth a shot. Check out *The Courier Air Travel Handbook* by Mark Field (Perpetual Press: Seattle, 1996) for courier company listings. Also check out the Web site: www.courier.org.

BY TRAIN

There's only one way to get to the continent from England by train: Eurostar. They've got a monopoly on the sub-Chunnel service that takes you from England to France in three hours, but they run it well. You'll never get onto a faster or more efficiently run train.

Eurostar likes to advertise that you can have breakfast in Westminster and lunch in Montmartre, and you really can—without the delays of airport check-in and checkout and with pretty minimal customs and immigration formalities.

Of course you pay extra for the privilege. Tickets run from £99 (about $180 US) off-season, booking in advance) to much more if you book on short notice or travel during a summer weekend. And—bummer—buying a one-way ticket isn't any cheaper than purchasing a round-tripper. So you might as well go whole hog.

Always check ahead for price information. Book ahead by fifteen days and you might save as much as 50 percent! It's easiest to book ahead through your travel agent at home, but Eurostar also has offices in Paris's Gare du Nord and London's Waterloo Station.

GETTING AROUND FRANCE AND ITALY

BY PLANE

Planes, within Europe, used to be fantastically expensive. However, times are changing: A raft of cut-rate short-hop airlines have sprung up—like Go!, Easyjet, British Midland, Ryanair, Debonair and Virgin Express—to fly you from places like Edinburgh to places like Milano. Check out the papers and travel agents for the latest-breaking deals, and be prepared to sometimes fly into or out of a weird airport like East Midlands to save the dough.

Also be on the lookout for smaller airlines within the two countries (like Air One Compagnia in Italy, which zips around to Naples, Milan, Rome, and Bologna and over to London and Greece). Prices are in constant flux, so you never know what you might save by checking around.

BY TRAIN

Trains are still king in Europe. Sure, the car dominates everyday life for locals, but when you're a tourist you just can't beat the iron horse.

France's train system is one of the world's best—especially the TGV superfast bullet trains that blast you from Paris out into the countryside at upwards of 100 miles an hour. TGV trains always cost a little extra, and you must reserve a ticket at least ten minutes before departure. It's a pittance, usually about 20 francs (about $4.00 US) per ticket, for the reservations.

Italy's trains are a little different. It's dirt-cheap to ride by rails, even long-distance (you pay according to distance, by the way); just don't expect things to be smoothly organized. Schedules, stations, arrival times . . . all are subject to potential change, so plan ahead to avoid missing connections—and always have a backup plan in case things go wrong. Sometimes they do.

Tickets and Passes

What to buy? If you're going to be doing lots of short city-to-city hops, just buy tickets each day; it's cheaper. In Italy, buy *kilometric tickets* for these short journeys from tobacco shops in small Italian towns, which might not have manned train stations. For short hops in France, you buy one-way ("sample") or return ("ray-tour") tickets at the train stations. Buy all fast-train tickets at big stations in either country, remembering that Italy's fast trains cost extra—the surcharge can be 15,000 lire or more (about $9.00 US) per person.

Always remember to punch your train ticket before you get on the train. There will be a yellow (in Italy) or orange (in France) machine in every station that stamps the current date and time on the ticket's magnetic strip, giving you twenty-four hours to use it or lose it.

Eurail passes can be key. If you need to blow through France or Italy in a hurry, get a regional pass; if you're seeing these countries as part of a through-Europe tour, get the Eurail. In our experience, these passes are a great deal for covering big distances. You can purchase these through Rail Europe at (800) 438–7245 or www.raileurope.com.

Sure, they're not cheap, but they're super convenient and cover almost everything. If you do get the Eurail pass, you've gotta play by the rules: Wait until the first day you're gonna use it, then go to the station early and have it validated (stamped) by a ticket agent. Write the current date into the first square (it should have a "1" beneath it) and remember to put the day first (on top), European-style.

Now it gets easier. Just show your pass to ticket agents when you want to reserve a seat on a train (which is crucial in summer season, on weekends, and during rush hours). That smiling person will print you out a seat reservation, which you show to the conductor. You must reserve seats before the train arrives, and since you'll probably have no idea where or when that will be, it's best to reserve a day or two ahead.

If you can't or won't get a reservation, just show your pass to the conductor. Sometimes he'll let you get on anyway.

Finally, don't fold, bend, or otherwise mangle the long cardboard pass (and that can be difficult to achieve while fumbling for your money belt at the station as the train whips in). That might invalidate the whole thing.

The cost of these passes depends on a few things: one, how long you're traveling, two, how much comfort you want and three, your age. First-class passes, which few hostellers buy, cost 50 percent more and give you a little more legroom.

In 2000, it costs as little as $388 for two weeks (actually fifteen days) of unlimited riding; the price rises as high as $1,089 for three months of rides. (You can also buy other lengths of time.) If you're older than twenty-six, you *must* buy a first-class pass, which costs $554 for two weeks of unlimited riding, $890 for a month, and $1,558 for three months.

However, if you're like us—you like to stay a few days in each town—get a Flexipass instead. This allows you to choose ten or fifteen days in a two-month period to ride the rails. It costs either $458 (ten days) or $599 (fifteen days) per person if you're under twenty-six. If you're older than twenty-six the price goes up to $654 (ten days) or $862 (fifteen days)—but, hey, at least you can always sit in first class.

And new for 2000, Eurail has introduced a shorter, more flexible option called the Eurail Selectpass. It's good for first class train (and ferry) travel in any three bordering countries for five, six, eight, or ten days in a two-month period. Prices range from $328 a person for five days to $476 for ten days—the days do not have to be consecutive. For those twenty-five and under, the pass is an even better deal at $230 to $334.

Also remember that two people traveling together get about a 15 percent discount no matter the pass as long as they buy the passes at the same time. Ask for the Saverpass.

France and Italy also have their own individual country passes. The France Railpass is simple as pie: it gives you three days of travel in a month for $180 to $210; there's no discount for age. You can add extra days for $30 a pop.

Italy's Railpass is available in many different permutations, similar to the Eurailpass. It costs anywhere from $199 (second class, eight days) up to $522 (first class, thirty days); or get a flexible pass, which costs from $159 to $239 for four days in a month, $223 to $334 for eight days in a month, and $286 to $429 for twelve days in a month. Again, there's no discount here for younger hostellers.

Whew.

Remember that trains don't run as frequently on weekends; Saturday is usually the worst day to travel within France or Italy. International trains and sleeper cars usually run seven days a week, and Fridays and Sundays are feast or famine; check schedules and think like a local. If you want to go to the Italian beaches or the south of France, for example, lots of trains will be running from the cities to the country on Friday afternoon. Sunday, everyone's either going to the beach or going home.

BY BUS

Buses can be a cheaper ride than the train or more expensive, depending on local whims. They're extremely useful in parts of Italy where trains simply don't go—reasonably on time, scenic, with lots of locals riding alongside you happy to give advice or opinions or soccer scores.

It might take you all day to make connections, but most bus drivers are helpful and knowledgeable. As a bonus, they'll sometimes let you off where you want to go, even if there isn't an actual scheduled bus stop there. They are also quite accustomed to hostellers asking "Where's my stop?" and handle the situation calmly and professionally. Usually. In small towns, though, anything goes.

In France you buy short-distance tickets from the drivers and long-distance tickets at the stations. In Italy, you get tickets for long-distance buses at a bus station and tickets for city buses at tobacco shops (called *tabbachi*), not from drivers.

Always remember to punch your ticket on the bus; there will be a machine on every French and Italian bus that stamps the current date and time on the ticket's magnetic strip. Most are good for one hour.

Finally, Eurolines is a good company running comfortable long-distance buses around Europe for very competitive rates, including to and from England to France and Italy and to points between. In Italy contact Eurolines Italia in Florence (via G.S. Mercadante 2b, Firenze 50144; telephone 055–357–110). In France look up Eurolines France (28, avenue du Général-de-Gaulle, Paris; telephone 01–49–72–51–51).

BY CAR

Renting a car is definitely the most expensive way to see Europe, and yet it has advantages: You can cover the hamlets a whole lot quicker, you have complete freedom of movement, and you get that cool feeling of the wind and rain rushing past your ears.

Just bring your wallet: Rentals in France go for a good $60 US a day, and that might or might not include heavy taxes and insurance. Rent or lease long-term through a company such as Kemwel (800–678–0678; www.kemwel.com), which books long-term rentals for a fraction of the daily rate if you book ahead from your home country. (They also do short-termers, too, but you save more with a seventeen-day lease.) You won't use as much gas as in the U.S. because it's a smaller car, but it'll cost—something like $3.00–$4.00 a gallon at last check.

Speeds and distance in France and Italy are always measured in kilometers. Just to remind you, one kilometer is about three-fifths of a mile, and 100 miles equal roughly 160 kilometers. Here are some common speed limits you might see on road signs, with their U.S. equivalents:

40 kph = 25 miles per hour
100 kph = 62 miles per hour
50 kilometers away = 31 miles away

Stop signs are round and red and, surprisingly, they say STOP in English. Can't get much clearer than that. Streetlights are also simple: Red means stop, yellow means slow down, green means go. A green or blinking green arrow means go ahead and turn left; a yellow arrow means slow down.

Never turn right at a red light; it's illegal in France. The French hate it, and police won't take kindly to it either.

Gas is measured in liters, and there are roughly four liters to the U.S. gallon. Gas prices are listed per liter, so multiply by four and then convert into home currency to estimate the price per gallon you'd pay back home—you'll be shocked at how much it is. Want a bike yet?

PHONES AND MONEY

PHONES

Two words: *phone card.*

Dealing with French and Italian pay phones can be frustrating, so don't bother pumping change unless you're truly desperate. Instead, buy Telecom Italia and France Telecom phone cards at tobacco shops or other small markets and stick 'em into the slots in the phones. (In Italy, push it in hard and all the way with the magnetic strip facing up; in France, push it in more easily with the little computer chip facing up.) Local calls won't eat up much of these cards, but long-distance calls within a country will; figure about ten or fifteen minutes per card at most.

Don't bother trying to call Mom and Dad back home with these cards. Instead, get a phone card from the USA or your home country before you arrive. It'll be cheaper and easier, though a few phones might block your phone card.

You dial differently depending on whether you are in the country or not. *Inside the countries, dial the numbers just as they are printed in this book.*

To call from North America to FRANCE: Dial 01–133 and DROP THE FIRST ZERO from all numbers in this book.

To call ITALY from North America: Dial 01–139 and add the numbers just as they appear in this book. *DO NOT* drop the first zero; this is a recent change.

MONEY

You'll need it, that's for sure. Things can get a little pricey in cities like Paris or Florence, especially if you're sick of pizza.

First, remember this: Always get money from an ATM if possible rather than changing money. If you must change, use a big bank instead of a tourist office, train station, bureau de change, or small bank; their rates are all terrible, and they figure you won't know the difference. Try to spend all your change before you leave one country for another unless you're coming back, since you can't exchange coins—only bills.

The Euro won't be used for cash transactions until 2002. Credit card charges might, however, appear in Euros on your bill at some places—although the final result will still be converted back to dollars or your home currency on your monthly statement.

The money takes a little getting used to. In France you'll carry lots of change and some squarish bank notes. Five francs are roughly equal to one U.S. dollar, so those 100-franc notes are worth a twenty back home. Fifties are worth about the same as a $10 bill. *Note:* The dollar was worth about 5–6 francs during the writing of this book, so prices expressed in U.S. dollars are approximate—but they're pretty darned close. Check the current exchange rates before your departure.

French change is pretty easy to figure out. Most useful are the ten-franc coins, which have a gold rim and a silver center and are worth about two bucks; many vending machines take them. (Try to forget that bottle of water is costing you so much.) One-, five-, and ten-franc coins are pretty obvious—they're all about the same size, but the numbers are clearly printed. The teeny half-franc is worth about 10 cents US Centimes are like cents, only worth a whole lot less; don't keep 'em around.

In Italy you carry bills with big numbers and lots of zeroes. *Definitely* take the time to get to know your cash, because you could easily get duped. The toughest part is telling a 50,000-lire note from a 5,000-lire note or a 100,000 from a 10,000 or a 1,000 in a hurry. So remember: *Size matters.* These bills are all slightly different sizes, and the bigger the bill, the more it's worth.

There are about 1,600 lire to the dollar (the rate fluctuates, of course; prices in this book are based on rates that fluctuated between 1,600 and 1,700 lire per dollar), so that pale-green 100,000-lire note is worth about $60 US—enough for a hostel night and a dinner, about what you'd spend in a typical day on the road probably. The maroon-purplish 50,000-lire note is worth about $30. The longer, thinner blue 10,000-lire notes are the most useful for everyday purchases, though they're worth only about $6.00 US. The green 5,000-lire notes are a bit smaller and worth about three bucks. And the smallest, reddish-pink 1,000-lire notes are worth about 80 cents each.

Italian change is worth very little in American; it's useful for short phone calls and almost nothing else. So don't carry too much around, because it's heavy. For the record, a 200-lire coin is worth about 12 cents (use it for local phone calls), the gold and silver two-tone 500-lire coin counts for about 30 cents, and there are two kinds of 100-lire coins worth about 6 cents each. The 50-lire coins are worth perhaps 3 cents, yet are as big and heavy as American quarters.

When you pay in Italy, wait an extra half-minute for all your change . . . sometimes merchants are *very* slow to count it out and give it all back. They tend to do it in two stages, so if you grab the first pile they put down, you might have cheated yourself out of lots of dough.

Finally, note that you might have trouble with some Italian ATMs if you use the Plus system. Just keep hunting. Banco Toscana is one that will work with Plus, and BNL is another—but if you're outside Tuscany, it could take a while to find one. It's better to get a card that works on the Cirrus system, which is much more heavily used in Italy.

SPEAKING FRENCH AND ITALIAN

Contrary to popular belief, you can get by with just a smattering of the local language in France and Italy—and people won't hate you for trying. Except maybe sometimes in Paris. But keep at it; many rural French and Italians hardly speak English, either, and this might be your only chance to forge a meaningful bond while getting the right bus tickets, too.

Hereforth, a short primer.

Bon courage! E buona fortuna!

FRANÇAIS (FRENCH)

WHAT THEY SAY	HOW THEY SAY IT (approximately)	WHAT THEY MEAN
oui	we	yep
non	no!	nope
peut-etre	put ed	maybe
un	uh	one
deux	do	two
trois	twa	three
quatre	cat	four
billet/billets	B.A.	ticket/tickets
premiere classe	premier class	first class
deuxieme classe	do-zyem class	second class
autobus	aw toe booze	bus
non fumer	naw foo may	non-smoking
passe d'Eurail	pass door rail	Eurail pass
train	tren	train
quai/voie	kay/vwa	platform/track
voiture	vwa-choor	car number of a train
voiture-lit	vwa-choor leet	sleeping car of a train
place	plass	seat
pardon	par don	excuse me/I'm sorry
de Nice	de niece	from Nice
a Paris	ah, pear "E"	to Paris
je voudrais	zhuh food ray	I'd like...
j'ai besoin de	J.B. swan, duh	I need...
merci	mare "C"	thank you
merci bien	mare CBN	thanks a lot!
bonjour	bon shoe	good morning, good afternoon
bon soir	bon swar	good evening, good night
au revoir	oh, vwar	good-bye
a bientot	ah, be in tote	see ya soon
de rien	darien	you're welcome
monsieur	miss yew	sir
madame	ma damn	m'am
madamoiselle	madam was hell	miss
mesdames	may damn	ladies
messieurs	may sure	sirs
ceci	sir see	this one
cela	sir la	that one

ITALIANO (ITALIAN)

WHAT THEY SAY	HOW THEY SAY IT (approximately)	WHAT THEY MEAN
si	see/she	yes
no	no	no
una/uno	ohh, nah/ooh,	no one
due	do "A"?	two
tre	tray	three
quattro	kwa-tro	four
biglietta/biglietti	Billy eta/Billy A.T.	ticket/tickets
prima classe	preema class "A"	first class
seconda classe	sick on da class "A"	second class
non fumatori	naw foo ma tory	nonsmoking
passa di treno	passa the traino!	train pass
treno	traino	train
binario	beanario	platform
mi dispiace	me "D" spee-ah-chee	I'm sorry
grazie	Yahtzee	thank you
grazie mille	gratsy mealy	thanks a lot!
bongiorno	bon journo	good morning
buona sera	wanna Sara	good afternoon, good evening
ciao	chow	hi;bye
ciao-ciao	chow-chow	bye-bye
arrivaderci	a-riva-dare-chay	good-bye
prego	prego	you're welcome
pronto	pronto!	yes?
da Roma	d'aroma	from Rome
per Firenze	pear friends, ah	to Florence
Vorrei	vor Ray	I'd like . . .
Ho bisogno di	obi sanyo "D"	I need . . .
Questa	quest-ah	this one
Quella	kwell-ah	that one

OTHER RESOURCES

There's surprisingly little out there about hostelling and hostels—that's why you're reading this, right?—but we did find a few sources. Most simply list phone numbers and addresses.

Remember that hostels are constantly opening, closing, renovating, being sold, and changing their policies. So not everything written in a guidebook will always still be true by the time you read it. Be smart and call ahead to confirm prices, availability, and directions, rather than rolling into town depending on a bed—and getting a nasty surprise like a vacant lot instead. We know; it has happened to us.

But there are a few Web sites worth checking out. Twirl your browser to these coordinates:

www.hostels-aig.org
This is the home page of AIG, Italy's Hostelling International–affiliated chain of hostels. Pages are pretty good, if only in Italian. AIG's handbook is better, however; pick it up at any hostel.

www.fuaj.org
In French only, this is the page of FUAJ, France's HI-related hostel organization. Depending on your browser, the mapping function can be great or maddening to use; but at least you can get some basic info—if you read French.

members.aol.com/Atomev
members.aol.com/Atomev/hostels_canada.html
Yup, it's the official *Hostels USA* page! Plus its companion page, *Hostels Canada.* That's us. Not a whole lot of dazzling graphics here—but, hey, you'll get to know us a little better. And that's worth something, 'cause we're a couple of great folks. Never fear, though: More features are sure to come in the near future.

The prices and rates listed in this guidebook were confirmed at press time. We recommend, however, that you call establishments before traveling to obtain current information.

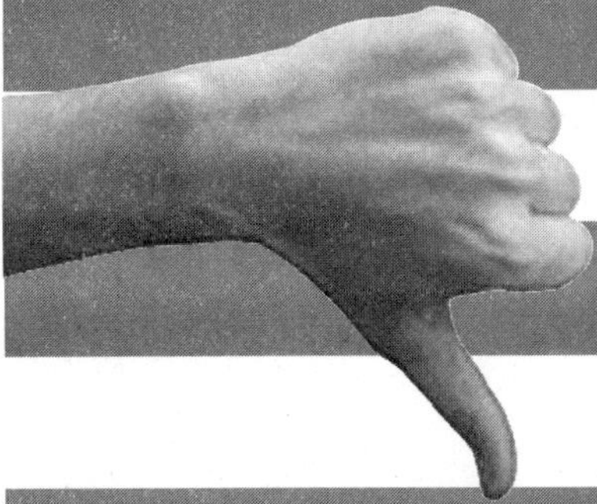

The Hostels

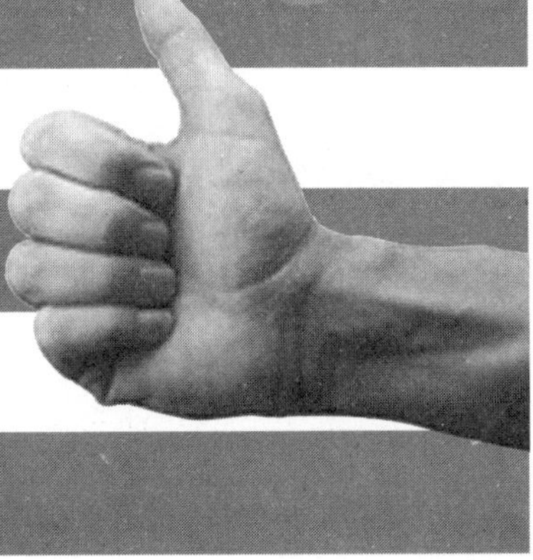

PARIS AND ÎLE DE FRANCE

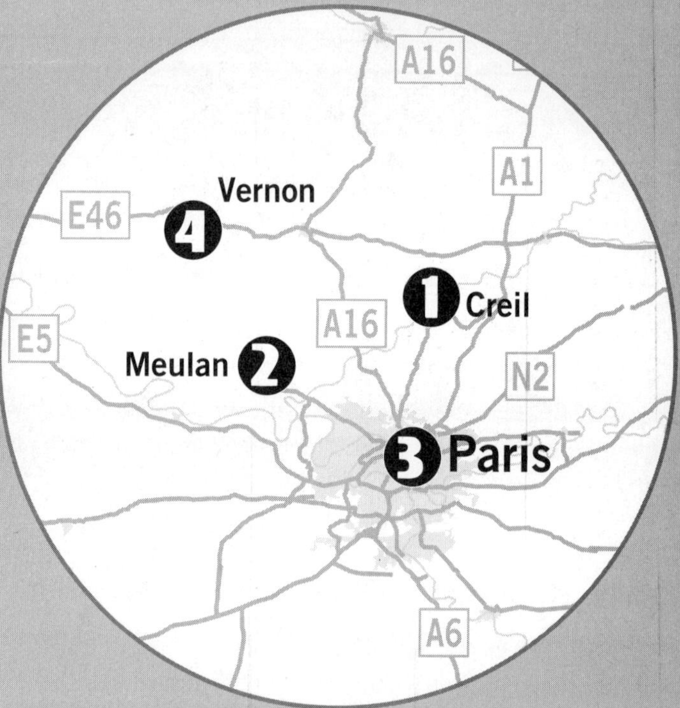

Page numbers follow town names.

PARIS AND ÎLE DE FRANCE

PARIS

Paris, City of Lights: Practically every other European traveler begins or ends a European adventure here, so it's not really surprising that there are more hostels concentrated in the greater Paris area than in just about any other city on the Continent. Some are okay, some are dingy; some are central, some are miles out in the burbs. We've done our level best to separate the wheat from the chaff below.

Some other hostels are located in the outskirts—the so-called Ile de France, a rich rural area surrounding the city and skirted by three rivers.

Seasons are crucial here. In winter the city's obviously pretty dead except for locals. Spring can be nice, though it doesn't warm up until April or May. Then it's really nice, possibly the best time to come. June is great but starting to push it as Americans and others on summer vacation begin arriving. July, well, forget it; this is a terrible time to visit.

August is strange: All the locals go away on vacation, so the entire city is taken over by tourists. Yet, paradoxically, three-quarters of the businesses are closed down—including many of the restaurants and other places you might have wanted to try. Museums, hotels, and banks are still open. But it's a strange time to come, almost comatose in one sense; only the early-August finish of the Tour de France shakes the city from its torpor. Sure, parking and traffic will be a bit easier, but who wants to see a city full of tourists?

September is delightful, weatherwise, and many of the tourists have gone home. But—and it's a huge "but"—this is when the French themselves visit Paris, fabricating entire conventions and conferences and every other excuse possible to come see the city without those piggish foreigners clomping all over the place. So you might actually find it harder to get a bed in September than during the height of summer; and all the tourist places and restaurants, freshly reopened, will be quite busy.

October is a good time to come, as long as winter hasn't arrived early. If it's cold, wait till next spring! But the streets will be empty (relatively speaking), and beds will be plentiful.

Transportation

Getting into town is no problemo. A ring of train stations surrounds Paris, shuttling travelers to and from all points in Europe; all the city's train stations are on the subway.

Once here, though, parking is atrocious. Chances are you're not hauling your car into the city, but if you are—well, just don't. Get rid of it at a parking garage or lot or rental drop-off area in the burbs, or just don't rent one until you leave town. You won't need it anyway, as driving in Paris can needlessly consume hours of vital sight-seeing time.

Instead, rely on that Metro subway system—one of the world's best—and the buses that race all over the city. (Taxis are expensive and scarce except at the train stations, but they're quite useful when you need to make a desperate dash.)

Before doing anything, take time to figure out the Metro map—which can be quite confusing at first glance—and orient yourself according to line number (*ligne* in French). You need to know what stop is at the **END** of the line you're traveling in order to figure out which side of the platform to get on. Got it? Let's say you wanna take line number 5 away from town to the north. That line ends at Bobigny station. Okay! Now, in the station look for a sign with a 5 in a circle that says DIRECTION BOBIGNY. Presto, that's your line.

You can buy books of tickets (way cheaper than single tickets) at any station; ask for a *carnet*—say "un carnay"—and fork over your 52 francs. As you enter the subway, place the skinny blue ticket into the slot in the gate and then take it out again when it pops up. You'll have a few seconds to get through the gate, so be speedy, and don't push your luggage ahead of you to avoid getting it caught in the doors. That's it: In seconds you'll be elsewhere in town. Hang onto the ticket till you get off, too, since conductors will occasionally demand to see it.

The RER (suburban railway) is a related system, even more efficient (there are lots fewer stops), and your Metro ticket gets you on board at no extra cost unless you need to go outside city limits to the airports or Disneyland Paris. Check the map; you can often zip from a station to the action *much* faster using the RER. Each station also has helpful boards posting the next incoming train and where it'll be stopping, one advantage over the Metro.

We'd avoid most of the Paris buses except as a cheap sight-seeing tour. To get to the airport, use Air France buses because they have luggage compartments.

Street Smarts

Once you're here, act like a local. Don't stand in those huge above-ground lines to get into the Louvre; go late in the day, and take the underground mall stairway instead of the above-ground cattle call. Score cheap clothes at flea markets. Buy food at farmers' markets. Watch yourself at night in dimly lit alleys like in Saint-Germain or around the train stations.

The Hostels

As for the hostels: Not one of them really knocked our socks off. We'd guess that Paris is so popular you could rent out a paper bag and charge ten bucks for it, and maybe that's why. For what it's worth, the HI-affiliated hostels are cleaner and better run than almost all the independent ones—but they're much worse located.

The independents tended to be more relaxed. Too relaxed, actually. Most of them (six, to be exact) are run by the same group, called C.H.E.A.P. These hostels vary wildly in quality from pretty nice to funky/yucky; definitely check our reviews before booking into these places. All are in great locations, at least, so if you can stand the beds, you'll probably love the surroundings.

In case all the good hostels are full, there are two other sets of accommodations you might want to know about: MIJE and BVJ. (Their French names are too long to deal with just now.) We haven't included them in this book, because they discriminate based on age: You can't get in unless you're under a certain age. Since that would exclude some of our readers, we're not giving up the goods on those guys. But there's a fantastic BVJ almost under the nose of the Louvre and another in the heart of Paris's Latin Quarter; contact the organization to learn more about these and other BVJs.

Also call to learn about MIJE's network, which in Paris consists of three fine hostels for young people only in the Marais neighborhood.

ÎLE DE FRANCE

The Île de France is not actually an island, but almost: This small, elliptical area is bounded by three rivers that encircle the Paris suburbs and countryside. It's a well-loved pastoral getaway for Parisians, and it's chock-full of cute scenery, chateaus, and prices that'll make your head spin. This is not the true rural France, though it tries hard to look that way at times. Instead, for many centuries it has been the place rich people go to sip wine in country homes while Paris steams through summer. You'll see more mansions, Lombardy poplars, and expensive cars here than you can believe.

Still, there are a few budget lodgings here to help us hostellers experience the good life.

CENTRE DE FORMATION DES CADRES SPORTIFS

1, rue du General Leclerc, Creil, Oise, 60100

Phone Number: 03–44–64–62–20

Fax Number: 03–44–64–62–29
Rates: 62 francs per HI member (about $11 US)
Credit cards: Yes
Beds: 144
Private/family rooms: Yes
Kitchen available: Yes
Office hours: 8:00 A.M. to 9:00 P.M. (Monday to Saturday); 8:00 A.M. to 7:00 P.M. (Sunday)
Affiliation: HI-FUAJ

Extras: Meals ($), laundry, bike rentals, bike storage, TV, pool table, conference room, tennis, tours, outings, games, patio

Set in the valley of the Oise River, approximately 30 miles north of Paris, this hostel's pretty sporty considering there are no big mountains anywhere nearby to speak of. Plenty of common spaces and amenities make a stay here fun in and of itself; you've got meals, a game room, a television room, three dining rooms, and more.

Gestalt: Oise up?

Party index:

Tours and outings are frequently arranged and booked from this hostel—or you can rent a bike if you want to make your own ramble in the countryside.

How to get there:

By bus: Take 1 bus to Buhl or Champrelle stop.
By car: Call hostel for directions.
By train: From Creil station, walk 1 mile to hostel.

AUBERGE RELAIS RANDONÉE

10, bis rue de Gournay, Oinville-sur-Montcient, Meulan, Yvelines, 78250

Phone Number: 01–34–75–33–91

Rates: 31 to 45 francs per HI member (about $5.00 to $7.50 US)
Credit cards: None
Beds: 19
Private/family rooms: None
Kitchen available: Yes
Office hours: Twenty-four hours
Affiliation: HI-FUAJ
Extras: Laundry, camping

Another simple rustic place not too far from Paris—it's about 20 miles northwest of the city—this one has just nineteen beds in a rather plain setup. You can't get a family room, but a kitchen and laundry are available. A small campsite accommodates up to six (hopefully happy) campers, and walking local trails seems to be the main draw. What the heck, might as well try it out.

Party index:

How to get there:

By bus: Call hostel for transit route.
By car: Call hostel for directions.
By train: Meulan Hardricourt station, 3 miles away; Juziers station, 3 miles away.

PARIS HOSTELS at a glance

	RATING	PRICE	IN A WORD	PAGE
Résidence Bastille	👍	125 francs	sedate	p.46
FIAP Jean-Monnet	👍	133 to 287 francs	educational	p.43
Woodstock	👍	87 to 97 francs	hoppin’	p.48
AJ Jules Ferry	👍	115 francs	strict	p.40
AJ Leo Lagrange	👍	115 francs	quiet	p.42
Maison des Clubs UNESCO	👍	130 to 170 francs	plain	p.45
AJ Le D’Artagnan	👍	115 francs	lively	p.41
AJ Cité des Sciences	👍👎	114 francs	distant	p.37
Le Village Hostel	👍👎	117 to 147 francs	new	p.45
La Maison Hostel	👍👎	117 to 147 francs	okay	p.44
Aloha	👍👎	97 to 107 francs	small	p.35
Young & Happy	👍👎	97 to 117 francs	tiny	p.49
AIJ	👎	81 to 91 francs	chaotic	p.39
Three Ducks	👎	97 to 117 francs	dirty	p.47

ALOHA HOSTEL 👍👎

1, rue Borromée, Paris, 75015

Fifteenth Arrondisement

Phone Number: 01–42–73–03–03

Fax Number: 01–42–73–14–14
Rates: 97 to 107 francs per person (about $16 to $18 US); private/family rooms 107 to 127 francs (about $18 to $21 US)
Beds: 130
Private/family rooms: Yes
Kitchen available: Yes
Office hours: Call hostel for hours
Lockout: 11:00 A.M. to 5:00 P.M.
Curfew: 1:00 A.M.
Affiliation: None

Extras: TV, breakfast, bar

We'd place this joint in the midle of the pack among Parisian hostels: not the best, but certainly not the worst. Actually, locationwise it's got many of the rest of them beat hands-down. Plus it's fun. So it's worth a look.

Just don't expect the lap of luxury. This place, despite the high bed number, is small and *feels* small. Dorms contain two to six beds each, and although they're in surprisingly good condition, they're also kinda tight. There's one huge dorm, too. The upper-floor bunk beds are superatmospheric, beneath a sloping roof and giving views down into the hopping streets. They also have a very few double rooms; by all means try to get those if you can.

Best bet for a bite: Rue Cler

What hostellers say: "Tight quarters."

Gestalt: Hawaii five-oh

Safety:

Hospitality:

Cleanliness:

Party index:

But as for bathrooms, kitchen . . . well, they're teensie-weensie, not much space at all. We're talking just one little shower—it's in a closet that opens into a hall—and just a couple of toilets for the whole darned place. So resign yourself to waiting in lines and bumping into people constantly. You might never get that shower, but at least your dorm room likely has a sink; it could be sponge-bath city. The outdoor kitchen, as mentioned, is minuscule, and common space consists of a couple tables in the lobby.

Staff does a good job here, though, of keeping the place semiclean and trying to help you discover Paris. They'll even sell you beer and wine from the check-in desk sometimes, which oils conversation considerably. We liked the bright red gas pumps in the bar area. (Points off for the official hostel motto, though: "Fun . . . that's the point, isn't it?" Boy, is that lame.)

The real draw here, anyway, isn't the hostel but rather the neighborhood. Everyone who stays here remembers one thing about it: The Eiffel Tower is around the corner, and when you turn that corner—well—it's almost like a religious experience. You've arrived in Paris. And nearby are those quintessential Parisian cafes, produce markets, student fast-food eateries, and even a laundry and a post office. Not a bad place at all to base yourself.

Annoyingly, though, lots of Americans and Brits stay here, possibly detracting a bit from that purely French experience you wanted.

How to get there:

By bus: Call hostel for transit route.

By Metro: Take Metro to Volontaires stop, then walk west on rue de Vaugirard; turn right at rue Borromée and continue to hostel.

By plane: Two large airports outside Paris; call hostel for transit route.

By train: Call hostel for transit route.

AUBERGE CITÉ DES SCIENCES

24, rue des Sept Arpents, Le Pré Saint-Gervais (Paris), 93310

Just outside Nineteenth Arrondisement

Phone Number: 01–48–43–24–11

Fax Number: 01–48–43–26–82
E-mail: paris.cite-des-sciences@fuag.org
Web site: www.fuaj.fr/h_cite.htm
Rates: 115 francs per HI member (about $20.00 US)
Credit cards: Yes
Beds: 184
Private/family rooms: Yes
Kitchen available: Yes
Office hours: Twenty-four hours
Affiliation: HI-FUAJ
Extras: Breakfast, laundry, lockers

This place is pretty far out from central Paris—in fact, it's technically not in the city but in the suburb called Le Pré Saint-Gervais—but you might get stuck here because the rest of the hostels are all filled up. At least it's on a Metro line and quite handy to several northern Parisian rail stations. But that cuts both ways; train station neighborhoods tend not to be the greatest.

Beds here come two to six to a room, and things can get a little tight. On the plus side, they keep the common room open all day during the room lockout and maintain a laundry for which you need two-franc and ten-franc coins (frustratingly, reception doesn't always have enough change on hand) and an ironically itsy-bitsy kitchen.

Accommodations are a little sterile, if clean and adequate. Rooms in the newer of the two buildings have big, big windows with absolutely no awnings or curtains. (Don't come bopping out of the shower *au naturel* if you

Best bet for a bite: Bakery near Metro exit

Insiders' tip: Sidewalks too narrow for luggage

What hostellers say: "Your French stinks."

Gestalt: Blinded by science

Safety:

Hospitality:

Cleanliness:

Party index:

know what we mean.) These quads for families and other folks come with their own washing facilities—a sink that shoots cold water for about two seconds. The shower, also pushbutton, shoots hot water—but there's no curtain. Toilets are not included; you have to clomp down the hallway and pray the WC is free. The newer building is more crowded but also more congenial, a lot more conducive to the sort of social mixing you came here to do.

The scene here consists of people gathering in the big common room to write postcards, practice their French, and listen to live music performed by locals who tend to dress in drag. You can also make phone calls with phone cards purchased from the vending machine. Laundry facilities are located in the basement along with the gigantic storage area.

Unfortunately, there's virtually nothing to do at or around the hostel except sit at one of the outdoor tables watching the street. Pinch us. Since the neighborhood's so blah and distant, you'll need to whip out your Metro pass and ride the rails to see anything of note. At least the crowd here at the hostel tends to be lively and friendly, and staff—those who will deign to speak English with you, anyway—are okay.

Oh, and if you're into high-tech museums, the Cite des Sciences nearby does a great job of letting you touch, feel, and even smell science and nature up close and personal. Not too Parisian, but it's a cool rainy-day trip.

How to get there:

By bus: Take bus to Port de Pantin stop, then walk 200 yards to hostel.

By Metro: Take #5 line to Hoche stop.

KEY TO ICONS

- Attractive natural setting
- Ecologically aware hostel
- Superior kitchen facilities or cafe
- Offbeat or eccentric place
- Superior bathroom facilities
- Romantic private rooms
- Comfortable beds
- Editors Choice Among our very favorite hostels
- A particularly good value
- Wheelchair-accessible
- Good for business travelers
- Especially well suited for families
- Good for active travelers
- Visual arts at hostel or nearby
- Music at hostel or nearby
- Great hostel for skiers
- Bar or pub at hostel or nearby

AUBERGE INTERNATIONALE DES JEUNES

10, rue Trousseau, Paris, 75011

Eleventh Arrondisement

Phone Number: 01–47–00–62–00

Fax Number: 01–47–00–33–16
Rates: 86 to 96 francs per person (about $15 to $16 US)
Beds: 40
Credit cards: Yes
Private/family rooms: None
Office hours: Twenty-four hours
Lockout: All day
Curfew: 1:00 A.M.
Affiliation: None
Extras: Laundry, breakfast

Chaos.

That's a good word to describe this hostel, Paris's cheapest—and possibly its best located—but also the most crowded.

Most dorms contain four to eight beds, and it's majorly cramped here. The bigger the room, paradoxically, the worse it gets. The bathrooms have also seen better days. Sure, they give you free breakfast—but nobody liked it. The all-day lockout is annoying, too, though this is far from the only Paris hostel to indulge in that practice.

But the location's good, near La Bastille—once a famous French jail. But now the jail is gone and it's a hip, edgy neighborhood of bars, immigrants, and shops. (You can't hear the action from your bunk, which is a plus.) You can mail letters, stock up on grub, and take care of other errands all within a block or two. A number of cool clubs are located here, too, though they tend to specialize in bad imitation soul music.

Best bet for a bite:
Monoprix

What hostellers say:
"Another night? Umm . . . no."

Gestalt:
French fried

Safety:

Hospitality:

Cleanliness:

Party index:

How to get there:

By bus: Call hostel for transit route.

By Metro: Take Metro to Ledru-Rollin stop; walk east on rue du Faubourg St-Antoine 1 block to rue Trousseau; turn left.

By train: From Gare du Lyon, walk to Ledru-Rollin; turn and walk east on rue du Faubourg St-Antoine 1 block to rue Trousseau; turn left.

AUBERGE JULES FERRY

8, boulevard Jules Ferry, Paris, 75011

Eleventh Arrondisement

Phone Number: 01–43–57–55–60

Fax Number: 01–40–21–79–92
E-mail: paris.jules-ferry@fuaj.org
Web site: www.fuaj.fr/h_ferry.html
Rates: 115 francs per HI member (about $20.00 US); doubles 230 francs (about $39 US)
Credit cards: Yes
Beds: 99
Private/family rooms: None
Kitchen available: No
Office hours: Twenty-four hours
Lockout: Noon to 2:00 P.M.
Affiliation: HI-FUAJ
Extras: Laundry, breakfast, cafeteria ($), lockers, bicycle storage, travel agency

Best bet for a bite: Brasseries around République

What hostellers say: "Wheee!"

Gestalt: Ferry tale

Safety:

Hospitality:

Cleanliness:

Party index:

An extremely light breakfast is included at this big but not super-huge Paris hostel, which is as clean and efficient as the rest of the Hostelling International joints in and around town—and a whole lot more hoppin' than you'd expect. The joint's placed in an excellent location near two cool neighborhoods, La Bastille and the Marais. Definitely one of the better hostels in the city.

Staff is pretty strict about curfew-busting, food-snatching, or using too much water in the showers, but you can probably deal with it because it's still one of the best deals you'll find. The atmosphere, in particular, is surprisingly laid-back once you return after the lockout. Yes, people actually have fun here! Facilities include a cafeteria, laundry, and lockers. The Hostelling International office right next door serves as an information depot, travel agency, and more, so take full advantage of it.

Arrive early at the trim six-story building, though, for two simple reasons: First, they don't ever take advance reservations by phone. Second, this is always one of the first to fill up in the morning.

How to get there:

By bus: Take 75 or 96 bus to hostel.

By Metro: Take Metro to République stop; walk east along rue du

Faubourg du Temple to Boulevard Jules Ferry; turn right.

By plane: From airport, take 350 bus to hostel.

By train: Call hostel for transit route.

AUBERGE LE D'ARTAGNAN

80, rue Vitruve, Paris, 75020

Twentieth Arrondisement

Phone Number: 01–40–32–34–56

Fax Number: 01–40–32–34–55
E-mail: paris.le-dartagnan@fuaj.org
Web site: www.fuaj.fr/H_arta.htm
Rates: 115 francs per HI member (about $20 US); doubles 260 francs (about $44 US)
Credit cards: Yes
Beds: 439
Private/family rooms: Yes
Kitchen available: No
Office hours: Twenty-four hours
Lockout: Noon to 3:00 P.M.
Affiliation: HI-FUAJ
Extras: Laundry, meals ($), breakfast, bar, disco, movies, lockers, concerts, piano, climbing wall

This huge edifice is in kind of a weird area for a hostel, in a drab neighborhood that's really only close to a train station and giant Père-Lachaise Cemetery (where Jim Morrison and others now rest). So if you've come to lay flowers at the Lizard King's feet, well, this is the hostel for you. Otherwise it's just too too far from the action.

At least there are tons of activities here. They show free movies every week, host concerts, and run a bar in the basement. Did we mention the new discotheque? (Nobody dances, but that's beside the point.) All that, plus a laundry, family and private rooms, and meals. Free breakfast is included with your bed, though it wasn't as sumptuous as the staff-only lunch spread that's off-limits to hostellers.

Drawbacks? Try the attitude sometimes displayed by a hipper-than-you'll-ever-be staff, who'd rather watch you fumble for hours with unresponsive pay phones than explain that

Best bet for a bite:
Bastille area

What hostellers say:
"Got a light?"

Gestalt:
Lachaise lounge

Safety:

Hospitality:

Cleanliness:

Party index:

they don't work. The in-house cafe attempts cowboy cooking with a Tex-Mex menu that just doesn't quite cut it, and plumbing is outdated and not always in good repair. Most annoying, groups of French schoolkids tend to book the place and make a lot of noise in the halls at night.

Still, it's a good place, safe and reasonably clean. Dorms are generally three- to four-bed affairs (though there are also some eight-bedded dorms), kept fairly clean. They're a welcome change from the gargantuan dorms we'd feared when we laid eyes on the place. All the activity from below does occasionally filter upwards; try to get a top-floor bunk if you don't want noise or the omnipresent cigarette smoke hovering about.

The real trade-off here, as we said, is location; you need to hoof it to the Metro, then ride awhile, to get most places you want to be. Otherwise, this isn't a bad hostel at all.

How to get there:

By bus: Take 351 bus to rue Vitruve stop, or take 26 bus to Gare du Nord or Gare St. Lazare.

By Metro: Take #3 Metro line to Porte de Bagnolet stop; walk ⅓ mile to hostel.

By plane: From airport, take 351 bus to hostel.

By train: Euroline terminal, ½ mile from hostel.

AUBERGE LEO LAGRANGE

107, rue Martre, Clichy (Paris), 92110

Just outside Seventeenth Arrondisement

Phone Number: 01–41–27–26–90

Fax Number: 01–42–70–52–63
E-mail: paris.clichy@fuaj.org
Rates: 115 francs per HI member (about $20 US)
Credit cards: None
Beds: 338
Private/family rooms: Yes
Kitchen available: Yes
Office hours: Call hostel for hours
Affiliation: HI-FUAJ
Extras: Breakfast, lockers, bar

Breakfast is included, and so are free sheets, at this grim-looking but decent hostel on the outskirts of Paris—in fact, it's a couple blocks outside Paris, in the suburb of Clichy if you're gonna get picky about things.

Bunkrooms are thankfully small—just two to four beds in all of 'em—and FUAJ has thoughtfully provided free breakfasts, a bar, and lockers for hostellers' enjoyment. Don't forget to hang out with your new buds in the balcony chairs, either. All in all, a quiet place removed from the frenzy of most other Parisian hostels.

This is fairly close to both Montmartre and the Champs-Elysées, although you'll need to do a little fancy footwork to get there. And, as with FUAJ's other hostels, you'll need to hop Le Metro to get to downtown's chief attractions.

How to get there:

By bus: Call hostel for transit route.

By car: Call hostel for directions.

By Metro: Take #3 Metro line to Mairie de Clichy stop.

By plane: From airport, take Orlybus or Roissybus to hostel area.

By train: Call hostel for transit route.

Best bet for a bite: Try Montmartre

What hostellers say: "Far out. Literally."

Gestalt: Lagrange hall

Safety:

Hospitality:

Cleanliness:

Party index:

FIAP JEAN-MONNET

30, rue Cabanis, 75014 Paris

Fourteenth Arrondisement

Phone Number: 01–45–89–89–15

Fax Number: 01–45–81–63–91
Rates: 133 to 287 francs per person (about $23 to $48 US); doubles 376 francs (about $63 US)
Credit cards: V, MC
Beds: 500
Private/family rooms: Yes
Office hours: Call hostel for hours
Curfew: 2:00 A.M.
Affiliation: UCRIF
Extras: Cafeteria ($), laundry, club, conference rooms, game room, classes, tourist information, breakfast

If tour groups didn't get first dibs on the beds here, it would be darned near perfect. As it is, this great hostel might not have any space when you call—especially in summer—for individual hostellers. But we're including it because if they do have room, it's a great place to hang.

Clean and educational, that's what this place is. How educational? Try French classes taught right in the hostel! Plus concerts and shows in the hostel's lounge and a tourist info desk to point you the right way in the city that never sleeps. On the practical side, there's a laundry and cafeteria plus a game room for idle pursuits.

What hostellers say:
"Huge but fun."

Gestalt:
Monet, Monet

Hospitality:

Cleanliness:

Party index:

And the rooms—well, they're every bit as clean and nice as you'd expect, in configurations of from two to eight beds each; en-suite bathrooms are often present, too.

Only problem is, if it's summertime you're probably not going to get a bunk. That doesn't seem fair. But that's the way it is. So come off-season.

How to get there:

By bus: Call hostel for transit route.

By Metro: Take Metro to Glacière stop, then walk down boulevard St-Jacques to rue Ferrus; make a left, then immediate right onto rue Cabanis.

By plane: Two large airports outside Paris; call hostel for transit route.

By train: Call hostel for transit route.

LA MAISON HOSTEL

67 bis, rue Dutot, 75012 Paris

Twelfth Arrondisement

Phone Number: 01–42–73–10–10

Fax Number: 01–42–73–08–08
Rates: 97 to 107 francs per person (about $17 US); private/family rooms 107 to 127 francs (about $18 to $22 US)
Beds: varies
Private/family rooms: Yes
Extras: Breakfast

Another in the string of six well-situated C.H.E.A.P. hostels around Paris, La Maison used to be better. Now it's losing some of its gloss, but is still a doable option practically under the nose of that big iron tower some of you are going to Paris to see.

Rooms come in usually small (two- to four-bed) configurations. The dining room's nice, and a decent amount of work has gone into making this one of the two best in the C.H.E.A.P. chain.

You're not far from the Eiffel Tower, as we mentioned, and also pretty close to the Montparnasse train station if you're heading out for points south and west.

How to get there:

By bus: From station take Metro to Volontaires stop.

By train: From any station, take Metro to Volontaires stop.

LE VILLAGE HOSTEL

20, rue d'Orsel, 75108 Paris

Eighteenth Arrondisement

Phone Number: 01–42–64–22–02

Fax Number: 01–42–64–22–04
E-mail: village@levillage-hostel.fr
Rates: 117 to 147 francs (about $19 to $25 US); doubles 294 to 310 francs (about $49 to $52 US)
Beds: 95
Private/family rooms: Yes
Kitchen available: No
Affiliation: None
Extras: Breakfast, bar, Internet access, fax, terrace

So you're walking downhill off Sacre Coeur, still blown away by the church (and hordes of Americans snapping pics of it), and you turn a corner; there it is, a big blue neon HOSTEL sign. You've found the newest hostel in Paris, already a darling of certain cheapie guidebooks but one that still has kinks to work out.

The beds are good, so far, though the mostly Aussie and American crowds appear to be beating up the furniture fast. Bunks come in rooms with from two to four beds (in summer they add more to reduce your privacy, but the price is also less); some coveted doubles are available. This place has the best views and terrace in Paris, so that's definitely worth something. Management and staffing are hit or miss, while the small bar appears to be where the socializing gets done.

Hospitality:

Cleanliness:

Party index:

Internet access is available, though it's a so-so service at best. Also, though they claim to have a kitchen, it's really just a hot plate and microwave combo. So we can't consider that the real deal.

How to get there:

By Metro: Take Metro to Angers stop; walk up rue Steinkerque to rue d'Orsel and turn right; walk ½ block. Hostel is on left.

MAISON DES CLUBS UNESCO

43, rue de la Glacière, 75013 Paris

Thirteenth Arrondisement

Phone Number: 01–43–36–00–63

Fax Number: 01–45–35–05–96
Rates: 130 to 170 francs per person (about $22 to $29 US); doubles 300 francs (about $50 US)
Office hours: 7:00 A.M. to 1:30 A.M.
Curfew: 1:30 A.M.
Affiliation: UCRIF
Extras: Breakfast

This place is small and plain but certainly adequate—it's definitely better than some of the joints in town. Unfortunately, they won't take reservations, so be prepared to stand in line for a while.

Hospitality:
Cleanliness:
Party index:

Rooms normally come in quads. Also be advised that this place does a lot of tour business, so you'll undoubtedly cross paths at some point with hordes of people all dressed the same way with name tags. The hostel, like most in town, does serve breakfast.

How to get there:

By bus: Call hostel for transit route.

By Metro: Take Metro to Glacière stop, then walk 100 yards east on Boulevard Auguste Blanqui to rue de la Glacière; make a left and walk through garden to hostel entrance.

By plane: Two large airports outside Paris; call hostel for transit route.

By train: Call hostel for transit route.

RÉSIDENCE BASTILLE

151, avenue Ledru-Rollin, 75011 Paris

Eleventh Arrondisement

01–43–79–53–86

Rates: 125 francs per person (about $21 US)
Credit cards: V, MC
Beds: 170
Private/family rooms: Sometimes
Office hours: 7:00 A.M. to 10:00 P.M.
Lockout: Noon to 4:00 P.M.
Curfew: 1:00 A.M.
Affiliation: None
Extras: Internet, lockers, breakfast

Hospitality:
Cleanliness:
Party index:

One of our reviewers' favorite hostels in Paris, this place has rooms with just two to four beds each—a welcome change in a town where it's usually barracks city. And what a location! You're in the Bastille, one of Paris's hippest and most happenin' areas.

For fun, take a stroll over to the places the city's prettiest squares and quite popu with local families and their tots.

How to get there:

By bus: Call hostel for transit route.

By Metro: Take Metro to Voltaire stop; cross place Leon Blum and walk down Ledru-Rollin.

By plane: Two large airports outside city; call hostel for transit route.

By train: Call hostel for transit route.

Gestalt:
Bastille city

Safety:

THREE DUCKS TRAVELERS HOSTEL

6, place Etienne Pernet, 75015 Paris

Fifteenth Arrondisement

Phone Number: 01–48–42–04–05

Web site: www.echange.fr/3-ducks
Rates: 97 to 117 francs per person (about $16 to $20 US)
Credit cards: V, MC
Beds: 95
Private/family rooms: None
Kitchen available: Yes
Office hours: Call hostel for hours
Lockout: 10:00 A.M. to 5:00 P.M.
Curfew: 2:00 A.M.
Affiliation: None
Extras: Storage, lockers, courtyard, breakfast, sheets ($)

Beaten-down and packed with beer-guzzling North Americans, this place is Party Central—and that's about it. This is Paris's worst hostel in every way except one: If you're absolutely intent on getting bombed off your pierced butt and then hitting on some other soused hosteller in the process, then you'll love it.

But first things first. The rooms here—which contain two to eight beds apiece—are cold, cramped, and dirty. There's no heat in winter, and some beds don't even have pillows. That's right. No pillows. It's BYOP, apparently. Bathrooms are even worse, not even approaching cleanliness or hotness of water. (That's what happens when scrungy hosteller after hosteller kneels before the porcelain god at the end of a long drunk.) Management somehow gets away with locking you out of the place all day long, too, though they don't appear to use that free time to do much cleaning or upkeep.

e hostellers told us that the staff here were tough to deal , while others claim staff are helpful; it probably depends on hat you're wanting. If it's a party, then they'll help you out. Got a complaint? Tough luck. Breakfast is free but not terribly nutritious; when we stopped in, it was weak hot chocolate and a cheapo baguette. They also charge for sheets, towels—heck, everything.

What hostellers say: "Party-y-y-y!"

Gestalt: Daffy ducks

Safety:

Hospitality:

Cleanliness:

Party index:

The bar—the only reason people could possibly want to stay here—throbs all night long with bad music, making sleep all but impossible. The atmosphere resembles a twenty-four-hour hookah party, with hostellers traipsing in and out, smoking, drinking, and becoming ill from dusk till dawn.

Our call? This is about the equivalent of lying down and sleeping in the middle of the Champs Elyseés, we'd say—and sleeping in the street is about a hundred francs cheaper!

How to get there:

By bus: Call hostel for transit route.

By Metro: Take Metro to Commerce stop. Walk south on rue du Commerce toward church; hostel is on right.

By plane: Two large airports outside Paris; call hostel for transit route.

By train: Call hostel for transit route.

WOODSTOCK HOSTEL

48, rue Rodier, 75009 Paris

Ninth Arrondisement

Phone Number: 01–48–78–87–76

Rates: 87 to 97 francs (about $15 to $16 US) per person; doubles 214 francs (about $36 US)
Beds: 75
Private/family rooms: Yes
Kitchen available: Yes
Office hours: Twenty-four hours
Lockout: 11:00 A.M. to 5:00 P.M.
Curfew: 2:00 A.M.
Affiliation: None
Extras: Bar, laundry, breakfast

$

By the time we got to Woodstock . . . ah, never mind. This hostel dubs itself "The American Youth Embassy in Paris," and—as the name implies—the place is partly staffed by folks from the US of A. So it feels very American. If you're looking for the quintessential French hotel experience, you've come to the wrong place—but every so often it's comforting to bunk with those who know where you're coming from.

The bar on the ground level is the nerve center of the place, and the music blaring twenty-four hours a day creates an exciting social atmosphere (if you like rock music). Luckily, walls in the bunkrooms are thick enough to block out most of the sound waves. So the party ends when you want it to. There's a nice mix of doubles, triples, and dormitory-style rooms, all within a very fair price range for Paris. Another room is available to store your packs for the day, suitable as long as you trust your roomies.

The massive and ongoing building renovation project here created some hassles when we stopped by, such as having to walk outside to the enclosed courtyard just to take a shower and fighting the buildup of mud that was accumulating with the construction. When all's said and done, though, this should be one of the most bourgeois sleepovers in the City of Lights.

A breakfast is included with your overnight stay, itself not very American. But the hostel baguettes, jelly, coffee, and hot chocolate should give you the French jump start necessary to get through that first museum after a late night. As a bonus, the hostel's just 2 blocks from the Metro, close to the famous Sacre de Coeur church, and also just a short walk from Paris's pulsing red-light district.

Best bet for a bite:
Grocery store on corner

What hostellers say:
"Which state are *you* from?"

Gestalt:
Back to the garden

Safety:

Hospitality:

Cleanliness:

Party index:

How to get there:

By bus: Call hostel for transit route.

By Metro: Take Metro to Anvers stop, then walk across street to park with gazebo; walk through park and make a right on avenue Trudaine, then turn left on Rodier. Hostel is on left.

By plane: Two large airports outside Paris; call hostel for transit route.

By train: Call hostel for transit route.

YOUNG & HAPPY (Y&H) HOSTEL

80, rue de Mouffetard, Paris

Fifth Arrondisement

Phone Number: 01–45–35–09–53

Fax Number: 01–47–07–22–24

Rates: 97 to 117 francs per person (about $18 US); doubles 274 francs (about $46 US)
Credit cards: V, MC
Beds: 75
Private/family rooms: Sometimes
Kitchen available: No
Office hours: Call hostel for hours
Lockout: 11:00 A.M. to 5:00 P.M.
Curfew: 1:00 A.M.
Affiliation: None
Extras: Breakfast, fax

This fairly new Paris hostel tries to be good to you, but its small space and odd management practices don't quite mesh with ideal hostelling yet.

It's somewhat unclean (though, inexplicably, popular with Japanese visitors) and crams you in: The watchword here is tiny. Rooms (two to six beds apiece) are close quarters, hallways are narrow, and there's little common or eating space; a small breakfast and showers are free.

Best bet for a bite:
Crepe stands

Insiders' tip:
Mouffetard market closes for lunch

Gestalt:
Young and restless

Safety:

Hospitality:

Cleanliness:

Party index:

The real draw here is the surrounding area, which is fairly cool—if a bit distant from the central city. It's yet another Parisian neighborhood of shops, bars, and student hangouts where real Parisians live. Come to the Mouffetard market, the city's oldest, where farmers and others hawk their goods. It's not the best market in the city, not by far, but if you want a quickie introduction to the market phenomenon (and you like fresh fruit), check it out.

At press time, a kitchen and more common space were reportedly in the works here. We'll reserve further judgment, then, until this additional work is done.

How to get there:

By bus: Call hostel for transit route.

By Metro: Take Metro to Monge stop; follow rue Ortolan to rue Mouffetard.

By train: Call hostel for transit route.

VERNON AUBERGE DE JEUNESSE

28, avenue de l'Île-de-France, Vernon, Eure, 27200

Phone Number: 02–32–51–66–48

Fax Number: 02–32–21–23–41
Rates: 48 francs per HI member (about $8.00 US)
Credit cards: None

Beds: 24
Private/family rooms: Yes
Kitchen available: Yes
Season: April 1 to September 30
Office hours: 7:00 to 10:00 A.M.; 6:00 to 10:00 P.M.
Affiliation: HI-FUAJ
Extras: Breakfast ($), garden, camping

As a base for visiting Giverny, this hostel, approximately 40 miles northwest of Paris, is perfectly positioned; hence, it gets busy, so book ahead. But boy, it's worth it as a base outside frenetic Paris. Everything's clean and roomy, and the staff is friendly for a change.

Even the campground's nice, with twenty sites and access to the good hostel showers for a fee.

Gestalt: Giverny more

Hospitality:

Cleanliness:

Party index:

How to get there:

By bus: Take 3 bus to Folenrue stop.

By car: Call hostel for directions.

By train: Vernon station, 1 mile away; from station walk 1 mile along road marked PARIS to hostel.

LOIRE VALLEY AND REGION

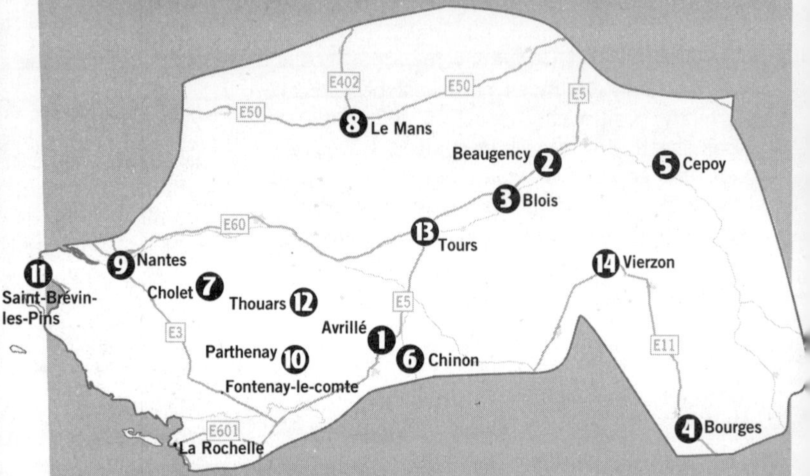

Page numbers follow town names.

LOIRE VALLEY AND REGION

The Loire Valley is classic France—the first image that comes to mind when you're sitting on that plane dreaming about what the country's gonna look like a few hours after the jet lag kicks in. One continuous carpet of elegant stone chateaux (castles), long-necked swans gliding along slowly moving rivers, and orderly gardens constructed in true French style—from paths and mazes of carefully sculpted hedges—this area helps you escape the hard thrum of Paris and ease into a more relaxed sight-seeing pace.

It isn't cheap, though: Accommodations and food can cost a lot in those precious little towns. Fortunately, many of the hostels here don't stray far from the river itself; you can easily spend a couple days touring the area by bike or train and jump hostel to hostel. (Buses don't regularly make runs through the valley, so they're not the best option around here. A car can certainly get you to the really off-the-beaten-path towns, but keep in mind that renting in France can be notoriously expensive.)

Where to begin? Most folks start in the big city of Orléans, the two hostels in smaller Blois, or the university city of Tours, and end their sight-seeing somewhere around Angers or in semi-interesting Nantes, a gateway to or from Brittany—which in summer has three hostels for some reason. In between, there are more castles than you can shake a stick at; everyone's got a personal favorite, so we won't recommend any here. Just dive in. The most famous ones are in Blois, Chambord, and Chenonçeaux—but you'll have to claw through swarms of snapping cameras while there.

You might try, instead, to construct a route to lesser known chateaux in little towns like Chapelle-aux-Choux or Azay-le-Rideau; no hostels, but their castles are darn good. There are small hostels in places like Beaugency (no castle, but a nice bridge) to help you get away from the tourist masses.

Finally, though they don't have castles, two other cities in the general Loire area might merit a detour from the riverside: Le Mans and Cholet. The former's known for its medieval character and twenty-four-hour car racing; the latter is famous as a place to get designer clothing cheap.

AUBERGE DE JEUNESSE AVRILLÉ-LANGEAIS

Rue des Tilleuls, Avrillé, Indre et Loire, 37340

Phone Number: 02–47–24–96–00

Fax Number: 02–47–48–26–59
Rates: 51 francs per HI member (about $9.00 US)
Credit cards: None
Beds: 35
Private/family rooms: Yes
Kitchen available: Yes
Season: July 1 to August 31 (for individuals)
Office hours: 5:00 to 10:00 P.M.
Affiliation: HI-FUAJ
Extras: Laundry, meals ($), shuttle

This Loire-area hostel isn't huge, but it comes through with a shuttle to and from a train station 10 miles away. Other pluses here include a laundry and meal service. Groups are allowed only during the deep of winter and early spring, so you're in luck there, too, if you hate sharing the common space with tons of young'uns.

Party index:

How to get there:

By car: Take the A10 or N10 in the direction of Tours; N152, direction Langeais; then D57 and 70, direction Avrillé.

By bus: Call hostel for transit route.

By train: From Langeais station, 10 miles away, call hostel shuttle for pickup.

HAMEAU DE VERNON

152, route de Chateaudun, Beaugency, Loiret, 45190

Phone Number: 02–38–44–61–31

Fax Number: 02–38–44–14–73
Rates: 51 francs per HI member (about $9.00 US)
Credit cards: None
Beds: 110
Private/family rooms: Yes
Kitchen available: Yes
Season: March 1 to December 31
Office hours: Call hostel for hours
Affiliation: HI-FUAJ
Extras: Meals ($), camping, bike rentals, courtyard

Situated in a lovely complex of buildings in Loire-side Beaugency, this is a nice place. The staff here appears to have a healthy appreciation for flexibility in rules; it's a fairly relaxing FUAJ joint, none of the usual admonitions to get in early, get up early, and get out early.

Gestalt: Beaugency bridges

Party index: 🎉🎉

There are five couples' rooms plus sixteen dorms, all about the same size (five to eight beds apiece). While here you can rent a bike, camp in the campground, and buy breakfast, lunch, or dinner to take out to the hostel's courtyard.

While you're out exploring the turf and stretching your legs, head down to rue de l'Evêque, where a bridge spans the Loire with more than twenty arches.

How to get there:

By bus: Call hostel for transit route.
By car: Take A10, exit Beaugency.
By train: From Beaugency station, walk 1 mile to hostel.

AUBERGE LES GROUETS 👍

18, rue de l'Hotel Pasquier, Blois, Loir-et-Cher, 41000

Phone Number: 02–54–78–27–21

E-mail: bloise@fuaj.org
Rates: 41 francs per HI member (about $7.00 US)
Credit cards: None
Beds: 48
Private/family rooms: None
Kitchen available: Yes
Season: March 1 to November 15
Office hours: 6:45 to 10:00 A.M; 6:00 to 10:30 P.M.
Lockout: 10:00 A.M. to 6:00 P.M.
Curfew: Yes
Affiliation: HI-FUAJ
Extras: Breakfast, bike storage

About 4 miles outside actual Blois, this hostel is rustic and simple but is nice in a quiet way. It's a farmhouse with flowers and such around it, so that's soothing. Bunks are plain, housed in just two bunkrooms that are way too big.

Gestalt: Blois, Blois, Blois

Party index: 🎉

One other caveat: There's not a whole lot of food around here except for the free light breakfast. So you'll want to tote grub here from town and fix it in the really good kitchen.

In contrast to the plain-speaking hostel, Blois is home to a gargantuan chateau that housed self-indulgent royalty. You can self-tour the place and go ga-ga over its ornate decorations and furniture. The chateau also witnessed an assassination of a duke who had intentions to overthrow the king—but don't get any ideas, okay?

How to get there:

By bus: Take 4 bus from Blois to Les Grouets; get off at eglise (church) or auberge (hostel) stop.

By car: From Paris take A10 or N20 to Orléans then N152, direction BLOIS/TOURS.

By train: Blois station, 3 miles.

MONTLIVAULT AUBERGE DE JEUNESSE

Montlivault Village (Blois), Cedex 181, Vineuil, 41350

Phone Number: 02–54–78–27–21

Fax Number: 02–54–78–27–21
Rates: 31 to 45 francs per HI member (about $5.00 to $9.00 US)
Credit cards: None
Beds: 37
Private/family rooms: Sometimes
Kitchen available: Yes
Season: July 1 to August 31
Office hours: Call hostel for hours
Affiliation: HI-FUAJ
Extras: Bike rentals, camping, table tennis

In the pleasant Loire valley countryside, this hostel isn't directly in Blois but in the nearby village of Montlivault.

It's got a summery, casual feel—probably because it's only open in summertime—and is reasonably equipped with a hosteller

KEY TO ICONS

- Attractive natural setting
- Ecologically aware hostel
- Superior kitchen facilities or cafe
- Offbeat or eccentric place
- Superior bathroom facilities
- Romantic private rooms
- Comfortable beds
- Editors Choice Among our very favorite hostels
- A particularly good value
- Wheelchair-accessible
- Good for business travelers
- Especially well suited for families
- Good for active travelers
- Visual arts at hostel or nearby
- Music at hostel or nearby
- Great hostel for skiers
- Bar or pub at hostel or nearby

kitchen, table tennis, and small camping area. They rent bikes here, as well. Note that family rooms aren't available per se, but they will shuffle things around to create one if they're not too full.

Gestalt: Loire house

Party index: 🎉

How to get there:

By bus: Call hostel for transit route.
By car: Go in the direction of Orléans-Blois.
By train: Blois station, 6 miles away.

AUBERGE JACQUES COEUR

22, rue Henri Sellier, Bourges, Cher, 18000

Phone Number: 02–48–24–58–09

Fax Number: 02–48–65–51–46
E-mail: bourges@fuaj.org
Rates: 48 francs per HI member (about $8.00 US)
Credit cards: None
Beds: 74
Private/family rooms: None
Season: January 7 to December 17
Office hours: 7:00 A.M. to noon; 2:00 to 11:00 P.M. (weekdays) 7:00 A.M. to noon; 5:00 to 10:00 P.M. (weekends and holidays)
Kitchen available: Yes
Affiliation: HI-FUAJ
Extras: Laundry, breakfast, table tennis, TV, bar, grill, bike storage

$ 🍺

Not far from downtown Bourges, this place has some social action going with the holy trifecta of grill, hostel bar, and big common room.

Hostellers can choose from two doubles with bathrooms, four triple rooms, or ten medium-sized bunkrooms with five to eight beds each. They also serve breakfast here daily and, sometimes, lunch and dinner as well.

Bourges is officially part of Burgundy, but it really doesn't have much to do with the wine culture of the area. It's a slow town, although the Experiment Music Festival in June could feature any of your counterculture faves. Also stop in for a French-only tour of a remarkable cathedral, which withstood bombing during two world wars.

Gestalt: Bourges in the road

Party index: 🎉🎉🎉🎉

How to get there:

By bus: Take 1, 2, or 12 bus to Maison de la Culture.
By car: Go in the direction of Centre-Ville, then go toward Museum d'Histoire Nature lle, Germain 1.
By train: Bourges station, 2 miles.

Cepoy Auberge de Jeunesse

Cepoy

(photo courtesy of FUAJ)

CEPOY AUBERGE DE JEUNESSE

25, Quai du Port, Cepoy, Loiret, 45120

Phone Number: 02–38–93–25–45

Fax Number: 02–38–93–19–25
Rates: 51 francs per HI member (about $9.00 US)
Credit cards: Yes
Beds: 100
Private/family rooms: Yes
Kitchen available: Yes
Season: February 1 to December 19
Office hours: 8:00 A.M. to noon; 6:00 to 10:00 P.M.
Affiliation: HI-FUAJ
Extras: Laundry, meals ($), camping, bike rentals

Party index:

Pretty simple, this one, although big. Meal service, laundry, and a small campground—ten open-air campsites in all—are about the gist of it. Sorry about the sketchy details. It's just that we've never met a hosteller who made it out here. Yet.

How to get there:

By bus: Take bus 2; get off at Cepoy Ealise (church).

By car: From Paris take the A6 and exit at Dordives.

By train: Montargis station, 4½ miles; call hostel for transit route.

MAISON DES JEUNES

Centre Animation Accueil, rue Descartes BP233, Chinon, 37500

Phone Number: 02–47–93–10–48

Fax Number: 02–47–98–44–98
Rates: 48 francs per HI member (about $8.00 US)
Credit cards: None
Beds: 40
Private/family rooms: Yes
Kitchen available: Yes
Office hours: 6:30 to 11:30 P.M.
Lockout: 10:30 A.M. to 6:00 P.M.
Curfew: 11:30 P.M.
Affiliation: HI-FUAJ
Extras: Laundry, bike rentals, TV, cafeteria ($), table tennis, pool table

We weren't too thrilled with this place: It treated us like Boy Scouts instead of worldly wise travelers, and we can't understand why. (The place does double as a youth center, so that may explain it, but geeeez.) They charge a hefty fee for sheets, for example, and institute both the dreaded lockout and curfew.

So we don't put this place on top of our "to stay" list when we're in France. Still, if you're coming there are two quad rooms best for families, plus seven more dorm rooms of medium to large size. The television room, game room, and cafeteria are always popular places; the laundry, less so—but much more useful.

Just remember not to spill any soap, you bad little boy.

Come to think of it, maybe there's a reason for all this. Rabelais, the official "bad boy" of Chinon, is celebrated each August here in the form of the ubiquitous Renaissance Fair. (Rabelais wrote that book *Gargantua et Pantagruel,* which contained—scandalously at the time—many references to private parts and toilet humor.) Years later, hostellers are still paying the price of his insolence.

Gestalt:
Rabelais rouser
Party index:

How to get there:

By bus: Call hostel for transit route.
By car: Call hostel for directions.
By train: Call hostel for transit route.

AUBERGE LES GOELANDS

Les Goelands, 2, rue Hallouin, BP 133, Cholet Cedex, Maine et Loire, 49301

Phone Number: 02–41–62–23–57
Fax Number: 02–41–55–48–61
Rates: 72 francs per HI member (about $12 US)
Credit cards: None
Beds: 20
Private/family rooms: None
Kitchen: Sometimes
Season: Call ahead for open days
Office hours: Monday to Friday only, 8:00 A.M. to 7:30 P.M.
Affiliation: HI-FUAJ
Extras: Laundry, meals for groups, bike storage

This very small hostel is kinda tilted toward groups, what with the for-groups-only meals. But the laundry and bike shed are there for everybody.

Party index:

Cholet is perfect for discount-shopping hostellers and fashion mavens; it's considered one of the French capitals of prêt à porter (ready-to-wear) fashion. A good place to squeeze some bargains into your backpack before you head back home.

How to get there:

By bus: Take A or B bus to St. Bernadette stop.
By car: Call hostel for directions.
By train: From Cholet station, ½ mile to hostel.

AUBERGE LES PAQUERETTES

5, rue de la Casse, BP316, Cholet Cedex, Maine et Loire, 49303

Phone Number: 02–41–71–36–36
Fax Number: 02–41–62–62–22
Rates: 68 francs per HI member (about $12 US)
Credit cards: None
Beds: Varies
Private/family rooms: Yes
Kitchen available: No
Season: June 15 to September 15
Office hours: Call hostel for hours
Affiliation: HI-FUAJ
Extras: Laundry, cafeteria ($), TV, pool table, table tennis, conference rooms

Another schoolkid-oriented place, this is nevertheless a good pick if you're in Cholet during the summer. The town sits on the Atlantic coast, equidistant from Nantes, Angers, and Saumur.

Cheers for the six handicapped-accessible rooms here, the nice outdoor terrace, the game room, and the cafeteria. This place would be perfect for families as well, we'd guess.

The town has a unique sports instruction program that allows noncitizens (that would be you) to learn or practice a sport from May to September. Ask the hostel staff for more information.

Party index: 🎉🎉🎉

How to get there:

By bus: Take 1 bus to St-Pierre stop.
By car: Call hostel for directions.
By train: Near Cholet station.

AUBERGE LE FLORE

Avenue Bollée, 23, rue Maupertuis, Le Mans, Sarthe, 72000

Phone Number: 02–43–81–27–55

Fax Number: 02–43–81–06–10
E-mail: florefjt@cybercable.tm.fr
Rates: 65 francs per HI member (about $12 US)
Credit cards: None
Beds: 28
Private/family rooms: Yes
Kitchen available: Yes
Office hours: Twenty-four hours
Affiliation: HI-FUAJ, FJT
Extras: Breakfast, meals ($), laundry, bike storage, TV, table tennis, tourist information, bar, volleyball

A small place in a nice town, this hostel includes breakfast with your tab. There's a laundry, it's wheelchair accessible, and other meals are served later in the day. Room layouts include five doubles, two triples, four quads, and four wheelchair-accessible rooms containing a total of twelve beds.

Fun is heavily emphasized, too—how about a bar, television room, volleyball court, and tourist information desk? You're just a mile from downtown Le Mans, also.

Gestalt: Twenty-four hours of Le Mans

Party index: 🎉🎉🎉

But don't even THINK of trying to book this place during the twenty-four-hour Le Mans race; otherwise it's a decent possibility. If fast cars don't thrill you, you can amble through the medieval old city where Hollywood has shot a few films that required that age-old Euro-ambience you just can't get in, say, L.A. And summertime brings Les Scénomanies to Le Mans. Don't worry if you can't pronounce it; you'll still find an array of jugglers and multicultural museums and other stuff at your disposal.

How to get there:

By bus: Take 4 or 12 bus to Erpell stop; walk 50 yards to hostel.

By car: Call hostel for directions.

By train: Station is less than a mile from hostel.

AUBERGE LA MANU

2, place de la Manu, Nantes, Loire-Atlantique, 44000

Phone Number: 02–40–29–29–20

Fax Number: 02–51–12–48–42
Rates: 48 francs per HI member (about $6.00 US); doubles 174 francs (about $32 US)
Credit cards: None
Beds: 73
Private/family rooms: Yes
Kitchen available: Yes
Season: open year-round
Office hours: 11:00 A.M. to 11:00 P.M.
Lockout: 10:00 A.M. to 5:00 P.M.
Affiliation: HI-FUAJ
Extras: Meals ($), breakfast, bar, bike storage

A three-story structure with trees out front, this hostel is pretty central in Nantes and pretty well thought out. It's so nice, you'd never guess it was once a tobacco factory! Rooms are mostly quads with their own bathrooms; singles are available, too. Breakfast is included, and they serve other meals.

Gestalt:
You-go-nuts
Party index:

And get this: For socializing, one entire floor of this joint is dedicated to a bar and restaurant—a good idea unless you're sleeping right above it!

The layout is kinda drab and boring—but what would you expect from what is now also a student residence? So you'll feel like you're in college. Big deal.

Anyone who managed to keep his or her eyes open during European history class might recall Nantes's role in assigning liberty to the put-upon Huguenots—those Protestant dissenters who bucked up against the stony Catholic Church.

They eventually sailed across the big pond in search of more religious freedom to be found in the American colonies and ended up in, of all places, what is now South Carolina. And to think: It all began here in Nantes.

How to get there:

By car: From downtown go in direction of Paris on boulevard Stalingrad, then take third street on left.

By train: From Nantes Nord station, walk less than ¼ mile to hostel.

By tram: Take #1 trolley, direction BEAUJOIRE, to Manufacture stop.

AUBERGE PORT BEAULIEU

9, boulevard Vincent Gache, Nantes, Loire-Atlantique, 44200

Phone Number: 02–40–12–24–00

Fax Number: 02–51–82–00–05
Rates: 51 to 68 francs per HI member (about $9.00 to $12.00 US)
Credit cards: Yes
Beds: 66
Private/family rooms: Yes
Kitchen available: Yes
Season: June 1 to August 31
Office hours: 8:00 A.M. to 11:00 P.M.
Affiliation: HI-FUAJ, FJT
Extras: Meals ($), laundry, bar, bike rentals

The second of three Hostelling International hostels in Nantes, this one is open for even less of the summer than the hostel on place de la Manu.

There's an overabundance of single rooms here, twenty-five in all with their own bathroom facilities, plus three double rooms, a triple and four quads—again, all with bathroom facilities and definitely well suited for families. There are also two wheelchair-accessible rooms on the ground floor.

Gestalt: Nantes guilty

Party index:

They rent bikes at this one, allow kitchen use, and—of course—stock a bar to loosen up fellow hostellers. You could bring your good cheer to the Nantes Summer Festival, usually held in the beginning of July, where there's scads of francophone entertainment to choose from.

How to get there:

By bus: Take 24, 26, 28, 29, or 31 bus to Man Beaulieu stop, or take #2 trolley from place du Commerce to Vincent Gache stop.

By car: Going in direction of Beaulieu, hostel is on an island facing the Galerie Commerciale.

By train: Nantes station, 1 mile.

AUBERGE PORTE NEUVE

1, place Ste. Elisabeth, Nantes Cedex 02,
Loire-Atlantique, 44042

Phone Number: 02–40–20–63–63

Fax Number: 02–40–20–63–79
Rates: 72 francs per HI member (about $13 US)
Credit cards: Yes
Beds: 40
Private/family rooms: Sometimes
Kitchen available: Yes
Office hours: Twenty-four hours
Affiliation: HI-FUAJ
Extras: Breakfast, meals ($), laundry, TV, table tennis, pool

A grim-looking edifice, this is the third of Nantes's three hostels and the only one open year-round. It's actually okay, though, with staff including breakfast with your tab and maintaining a game room, television room, and laundry as well. Other meals are served for a fee.

KEY TO ICONS

- Attractive natural setting
- Ecologically aware hostel
- Superior kitchen facilities or cafe
- Offbeat or eccentric place
- Superior bathroom facilities
- Romantic private rooms
- Comfortable beds
- Editors Choice Among our very favorite hostels
- A particularly good value
- Wheelchair-accessible
- Good for business travelers
- Especially well suited for families
- Good for active travelers
- Visual arts at hostel or nearby
- Music at hostel or nearby
- Great hostel for skiers
- Bar or pub at hostel or nearby

Although Nantes is now associated with all things Loire-ish, it used to be the capital of Brittany. The Château des Ducs is a must-see to bring this history to life and to learn. Buy a pass that allows you to see this and five other museums for a fraction of what it would cost you to see each museum separately. The best part? All those museums are within a short walk of one another.

Party index: 2 party hats

How to get there:

By bus: Take 40 or 41 bus to Viarme stop, or take trolley from Marchix to hostel stop.

By car: Call hostel for directions.

By train: Nantes station, 1½ miles.

PARTHENAY AUBERGE DE JEUNESSE

16, rue Blaise Pascal, Parthenay, 79200

Phone Number: 05–49–95–26–32 or 05–49–94–00–71

Fax Number: 05–49–94–64–85
E-mail: periscope@district-parthenay.fr
Rates: 48 francs per HI member (about $8.00 US)
Credit cards: None
Beds: 105
Private/family rooms: Yes
Kitchen available: Yes
Office hours: 7:30 A.M. to 10:00 P.M.
Affiliation: HI-FUAJ
Extras: Breakfast ($), meals for groups, bike storage, Internet access, TV, laundry

This hostel, located in a nice area, is pretty squeaky-clean—morally at least: There's a bar but no alcohol, which kinda defeats the purpose, doncha think? Anyhow, there's also a television room, an Internet terminal, a garage for cycles, and breakfast for a small charge.

All the rooms here are small and snug: seven single rooms, twenty-eight doubles (so couples are well taken care of), and fourteen triple rooms are what they've got.

Party index: 3 party hats

How to get there:

By bus: Gare SNCF bus stop less than 1 mile away.

By car: Call hostel for directions.

By train: From Parthenay station, walk ½ mile to hostel.

Auberge la Pinede
Saint-Brévin-les-Pins
(photo courtesy of FUAJ)

AUBERGE LA PINEDE

1-3, allèe de la Jeunesse, Saint-Brévin-les-Pins, Loire-Atlantique, 44250

Phone Number: 02–40–27–25–27

Fax Number: 02–40–64–48–77
Rates: 51 francs per HI member (about $9.00 US)
Credit cards: None
Beds: 59
Private/family rooms: Yes
Kitchen available: Yes
Season: February 8 to October 10; November 1 to December 31
Office hours: 8:30 A.M. to 1:00 P.M.; 6:00 to 10:00 P.M.
Affiliation: HI-FUAJ
Extras: Meals ($), camping, bike storage

This hostel, close to Saint-Nazaire and Nantes but more rural, features a little campground—ten open-air sites and sixteen covered ones—in addition to the usual meal service, bunk beds, and family rooms.

You'll find yourself close to the fairly industrial city of Saint-Nazaire, which has undergone considerable renovation since WWII bombing nearly destroyed it. Most of the tourist stuff here revolves around museums devoted to submarines and cruise ships. However, there's also a pretty neat dolmen (a big rock with mysterious underpinnings) stuck smack dab in the middle of the city, left there no doubt by a Celtic tribe.

Gestalt: Bombshell

Party index:

How to get there:

By bus: Take P bus to La Courance stop, then walk 1 mile to hostel; or take 8 bus to campground stop and walk 150 yards to hostel.

By car: Call hostel for directions.

By train: Saint-Nazaire station, 7½ miles.

AUBERGE HECTOR ETOUBLEAU

5, boulevard du 8 Mai, BP 77, Thouars 79102

Phone Number: 05–49–66–22–40

Fax Number: 05–49–66–10–74

Rates: 51 to 68 francs per HI member (about $9.00 to $11.00 US)

Credit cards: None

Beds: 35 (summer), 19 (winter)

Private/family rooms: No

Kitchen available: No

Office hours: Call hostel for hours

Affiliation: HI-FUAJ

Extras: Restaurant ($), breakfast, TV, game room, pool table, laundry

This quite small hostel is surprisingly well outfitted considering its size, with a restaurant, game room, television, and working laundry! Free continental breakfast is also included with your bunk, which comes in one of just two medium-sized bunkrooms.

Party index:

How to get there:

By bus: Call hostel for transit route.

By car: Go in direction of Saumur Zone Industrielle.

By train: Thouars station, ⅓ mile.

TOURS AUBERGE DE JEUNESSE

Parc de Grandmont, avenue d'Arsonval, Tours, Indre-et-Loire, 37200

Phone Number: 02–47–25–14–45

Fax Number: 02–47–48–26–59
Rates: 48 francs per HI member (about $8.00 US)
Credit cards: Yes
Beds: 170
Private/family rooms: Yes
Kitchen available: Yes
Office hours: Twenty-four hours
Affiliation: HI-FUAJ
Extras: Meals ($), laundry, bike storage

They do meal service here at the big "official" Tours hostel and have a laundry and kitchen in addition to the bunkrooms.

Gestalt: Grand tour
Party index:

Tours, of course, is capital of the Loire region, so it's the place to go for university life: tons of students hanging out in bars, clubs, coffeeshops, bookstores, and the like.

How to get there:

By bus: Take 3, 6, or 11 bus to Auberge de Jeunesse stop, 200 yards to hostel.

By car: Take the A10 or the N10.

By train: Tours station, 2 miles.

VIERZON AUBERGE DE JEUNESSE

1, rue François Mitterand, Vierzon, Cher, 18100

Phone Number: 02–48–75–30–62

Fax Number: 02–48–71–19–03
E-mail: vierzon@fuaj.org
Rates: 48 francs per HI member (about $8.00 US)
Credit cards: None
Beds: 83
Private/family rooms: Yes
Kitchen available: Yes
Season: January 1 to mid-February; February 20 to December 31
Office hours: 7:30 A.M. to noon; 5:00 to 10:00 P.M.
Affiliation: HI-FUAJ
Extras: Laundry, restaurant ($), TV, karaoke, grill, garden, library, bar, store

How many hostels are snug up against a canal? Well, this one is—talk about your quintessential français location. It's near a forest, too.

Lots of social mixing goes on at this hostel: A small bar, grill, karaoke machine, and garden provide numerous opportunities to meet that lone gal (or guy) sittin' in the corner.

Party index:

How to get there:

By bus: Take Ligne Forum République bus to Pierre Debournou stop.

By car: Call hostel for directions.

By train: Vierzon station, ⅓ mile.

KEY TO ICONS

- Attractive natural setting
- Ecologically aware hostel
- Superior kitchen facilities or cafe
- Offbeat or eccentric place
- Superior bathroom facilities
- Romantic private rooms
- Comfortable beds
- Editors Choice Among our very favorite hostels
- A particularly good value
- Wheelchair-accessible
- Good for business travelers
- Especially well suited for families
- Good for active travelers
- Visual arts at hostel or nearby
- Music at hostel or nearby
- Great hostel for skiers
- Bar or pub at hostel or nearby

BRITTANY

Page numbers follow town names.

BRITTANY

Brittany is a pretty cool place to pedal away for a week. The combination of unique Breton culture and compelling scenery around here mean there's always something fairly interesting around the bend—a town with a tongue-twisting name, a great view of rocks and ocean. (As an aside, this area has tons and tons of history but gets little respect: Breton locals have traditionally been the butt of Parisians' jokes).

This is one of France's biggest provinces, yet it's not so big that you can't get around. The only problem is that public transit doesn't go everywhere you wanna be. The fast train heads from Paris in a straight line to Rennes, which is merely a jumping-off point. From there, lines head erratically out as far as the end of the land but don't branch off anywhere en route.

If you're coming from Normandy and have enough time, start near the swashbuckling, walled city of Saint-Malo and work your way west along the edge of Brittany's northern coastline by bus or bike. Circle around south and back east until you get to Nantes; then it's time to dive into the Loire valley. Most of the hostels here are located close to the coast, so you can hit lots of scenery if you travel hostel to hostel in this circular fashion. There are also some towns with hostels in the interior that might pique your historical interest.

And you can stretch that budget dollar nicely in the region by taking a sleeping bag and using the good campgrounds attached to many of Brittany's hostels.

Bear in mind that tourists don't make their ways out to the very end of the land as much, so the true Breton culture—including the actual language, which resembles Gaelic rather than French—is better preserved out there. There are also a few towns and cities with hostels in the interior—again, less touristed, more authentic, and quite historic. Hostels are very simple, but you get a good dose of local daily life.

Finally, spice your speech with a little Breton and you'll make friends fast; for starters, "demat" means "hello" and "kenavo" means "goodbye." And when you raise your glass of the famous local cider—not plain squeezed apple, but fermented apple juice that packs one heck of an alcoholic punch—say "yec-hed mat" (cheers!). Folks'll love it.

AUBERGE DE JEUNESSE BELLE-ILE EN MER

Haute Boulogne, Belle-Ile, Le Palais, 56360

Phone Number: 02–97–31–81–33

Fax Number: 02–97–31–58–38
Rates: 51 francs per HI member (about $9.00 US)
Credit cards: Yes
Beds: 93
Private/family rooms: Yes
Kitchen available: Yes
Season: January 3 to September 30; October 10 to December 24
Office hours: 8:00 A.M. to noon; 6:00 to 8:00 P.M.
Affiliation: HI-FUAJ
Extras: Meals ($), bike rentals, bar, pool table, volleyball, camping

Gestalt: Belle tower

Cleanliness:

Party index:

Located on a nice island with complete exposure to the sea, this place is clean and well run. It features forty-two doubles and three triples, all but guaranteeing privacy and quiet. There's a pool table in the game room, a really fun tropical-themed bar, and a volleyball court outside, too. The kitchen is superb. For fun, you could rent one of the hostel bikes and set out into the countryside.

Remember that this good hostel does close for three weeks in October, though.

How to get there:

By bus: Call hostel for transit route.
By car: Call hostel for directions.
By ferry: From Le Palais dock, follow signs to La Citadelle parking lot, then follow signs along small road near museum to hostel.
By train: Belle-Ile station nearby.

AUBERGE DE JEUNESSE PORT PICAIN

Port Picain, Cancale 35260

Phone Number: 02–99–89–62–62

Fax Number: 02–99–89–78–79
E-mail: cancale@fuaj.org
Rates: 51 francs per HI member (about $9.00 US)
Credit cards: Yes
Beds: 82
Private/family rooms: Yes

Kitchen available: Yes
Season: Closed January
Office hours: 9:00 A.M. to 1:00 P.M.; 6:00 to 8:00 P.M. (October to April), 8:00 A.M. to 1:00 P.M.; 5:00 to 10:00 P.M. (May to September)
Affiliation: HI-FUAJ
Extras: Camping, bike storage, meals ($), laundry, Internet access, meeting rooms

This hostel, located not too far from the dramatic monastery at Mont-Saint-Michel, faces the ocean and has its own beach. Potentially private rooms come in every size from the lone single to doubles (fourteen), triples (one), and quads (five)—and there are several larger dorm rooms, too. Two of the bedrooms are wheelchair accessible, with en-suite bathroom facilities.

Gestalt:
Can-can
Party index:

You can swim, SCUBA dive, take a sailing class, or walk a coastal footpath right in the area; the hostel also has its own campsite. There are even supposedly oysters in the waters around here.

Cancale is simply a fishing harbor and as such offers lots of opportunities to educate yourself about the local aquaculture; oysters are a specialty, and you can try them at a dégustation (tasting). Even if you can't afford to eat here, there's a restaurant housed in a mansion originally built by local pirates. Try angling for a tour if you're so inclined.

How to get there:

By ferry: From Saint-Malo ferry terminal, take bus to Cancale.

By car: Take A11 to Rennes, then take N137 and D76 to Cancale.

By bus: From Saint-Malo station, take bus to Cancale.

By train: From Saint-Malo station, take bus to Cancale; from Rennes station, take bus to Mont-Saint-Michel and onward to Cancale.

AUBERGE DE JEUNESSE PLEVENON

La ville Hardrieux-Kerivet, Cap Fréhel, Côtes-d'Armor, 22240

Phone Number: 02–96–41–48–98

Fax Number: 02–96–41–48–98
Rates: 41 francs per HI member (about $8.00 US)
Credit cards: None
Beds: 46
Private/family rooms: Yes
Kitchen available: Yes
Season: April 1 to September 30

Office hours: 8:00 P.M. to midnight (summer); 8:00 to 10:00 P.M. (rest of year)
Affiliation: HI-FUAJ
Extras: Laundry, meals ($), camping, grill, table tennis, bike rental

Located in one of Brittany's wilder corners, this hostel is remarkable mostly for its setting: It's located in parkland, not far from the ocean.

Gestalt: Caped crusader

Party index:

There are two double rooms for families, six dorm rooms of five to eight beds each, and lots of campsites (would you believe eighty-four?) for the adventurous. A grill and table tennis provide the social lube, and, yeah, they also serve meals. Kudos for the one wheelchair-accessible bedroom, too.

Brittany really pours on the wild scenery here on what is known as the Emerald Coast, and Cap Fréhel is no exception. You can access a really cool nature preserve by auto or bike or even by foot; wend your way along the striking narrow path down to a cliff, where you can see the Breton coastline from all directions. Or, to see all this from a different perspective, rent a sea kayak and glide past those enormous cliffs.

How to get there:

By bus: Take bus to Auberge de Jeunesse stop.
By car: From Fréhel or Matignon, go in direction of Plévenon.

AUBERGE MOULIN DE MEEN

Vallee de la Fontaine des Eaux, Dinan, Côtes d'Armor, 22100

Phone Number: 02–96–39–10–83

Fax Number: 02–96–39–10–62
E-mail: dinan@fuaj.org
Rates: 51 francs per HI member (about $9.00 US)
Credit cards: None
Beds: 82 (summer); 70 (winter)
Private/family rooms: Yes
Kitchen available: Yes
Office hours: Call hostel for hours
Lockout: 11:00 A.M. to 5:00 P.M.
Affiliation: HI-FUAJ
Extras: Laundry, meals ($), lockers, camping, bike storage

Thumbs up to this hostel, where a bunk in a five-bedded dorm room is a pretty darned good deal. It's an atmospheric old stone

Auberge Moulín de Meen

Dinan

(photo by Launay Bernard, courtesy of FUAJ)

mansion with ivy growing up the walls and a brook running through the property. If that doesn't grab ya, maybe the meals will. Or you could make the half-hour trot into Dinan, a cool little medieval town, to poke around.

While you're poking, you might want to detour toward the open-air farmers' market held every week. Brittany is pretty much a seafood kinda place, but you might score something from a local baker in the way of a prune tart—more delicious than it sounds, though you don't always want *this* much fiber for breakfast.

Party index:

How to get there:

By car: Call hostel for directions.

By train: Dinan station, 1½ miles away. From station, turn left on rue Clos du Hètre, go left across tracks, and follow signs.

ILE-DE-GROIX AUBERGE DE JEUNESSE

Fort du Méné, Ile de Groix, Morbihan, 56590

Phone Number: 02–97–86–81–38

Fax Number: 02–97–86–52–43
Rates: 41 francs per HI member (about $7.00 US)
Credit cards: None
Beds: 50

Private/family rooms: Yes
Kitchen available: Yes
Season: April 1 to October 15
Office hours: Twenty-four hours
Affiliation: HI-FUAJ
Extras: Breakfast ($), laundry, camping

Party index:

Tons of campsites are available at this hostel, which is open about half the year. You can choose from bunkrooms or family rooms, there's a laundry, and breakfast can be bought for a small charge.

How to get there:

By bus: Call hostel for transit route.

By car: Go in direction of Lorient, then take ferry (forty-five-minute ride).

By train: Lorient station 1½ miles.

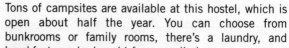

AUBERGE FERME DU GORÉE

Ferme du Gorée, Inzinzac-Lochrist, Morbihan, 56650

Phone Number: 02–97–36–08–08

Fax Number: 02–97–36–90–83
Rates: 43 to 62 francs per HI member (about $8.00 to $12.00 US)
Credit cards: None
Beds: 35
Private/family rooms: Yes
Kitchen available: Yes
Season: March 1 to October 15
Office hours: Twenty-four hours
Affiliation: HI-FUAJ
Extras: Breakfast, grill, bike rentals

Although the stone walls of this farm building date from the nineteenth century, they've been recently refurbished. It's got a nice old-country look, and the old farm implements and farm machinery scattered around the grounds don't hurt, either.

Party index:

There are two dorm rooms, eight doubles good for couples, and three singles—one of which is wheelchair accessible. And, get this, not one but two common rooms.

How to get there:

By bus: Take H or I bus to le Gorée stop.

By car: Call hostel for directions.

By train: Lorient station, 10 miles, is nearest stop; call hostel for transit route.

AUBERGE DE JEUNESSE VERTE (COUNTRY HOSTEL)

Route de Goalagorn, Beg Leguer, Lannion, 22300

Phone Number: 02–96–47–24–86

Fax Number: 02–96–37–02–06
Rates: 45 francs per HI member (about $8.00 US)
Credit cards: None
Beds: 12
Private/family rooms: None
Kitchen available: Yes
Office hours: Twenty-four hours
Affiliation: HI-FUAJ
Extras: Meals for groups, camping

Party index:

Pretty simple pickings here, just a little twelve-bed hostel without any extras—no laundry, no meals, and so on and so forth—just a place to doze. If you're looking for comforts and amenities, call Lannion's other hostel first.

How to get there:

By bus: Sundays only, take bus to Plage Goalagorn stop.
By car: Call hostel for directions.
By train: Lannion station, 2½ miles.

AUBERGE LES KORRIGANS

Lannion, 22300

Phone Number: 02–96–37–91–28

Fax Number: 02–96–37–02–06
E-mail: lannion@fuaj.org
Rates: 72 francs per HI member (about $12 US)
Credit cards: None
Beds: 68
Private/family rooms: Yes
Kitchen available: Yes
Office hours: Twenty-four hours
Affiliation: HI-FUAJ
Extras: Meals ($), breakfast, bike storage, laundry, bike rentals, bar

Linen and breakfast are free at this pretty large hostel, situated in a blocky three-story stone building. Rooms consist of three doubles, thirteen quads, and one bigger dorm room; none has its own bathroom. A kitchen and a laundry are both available here, thank goodness, and you can buy meals prepared by hostel staff if you're too tuckered to cook.

Party index:

Hostellers who brought their own two wheels can store them here; the area is awesome for exploring by bike. If you happen to come on Wednesday night, you would do well to investigate the farmers' market held every Thursday. Use the adequate kitchen and make like a French chef.

How to get there:

By bus: Take #15 bus to Gare SNCF or Monastere stop.

By car: Take RN12, direction of Paris/Rennes/Brest, and exit at Guingamp.

By train: Lannion station, 2½ miles.

AUBERGE DE TER

41, rue Victor Schoelcher, Lorient, Morbihan, 56100

Phone Number: 02–97–37–11–65

Fax Number: 02–97–87–95–49
Rates: 46 francs per HI member (about $8.00 US)
Credit cards: None
Beds: 80
Private/family rooms: Yes
Kitchen available: Yes
Season: January 4 to December 17
Office hours: Call hostel for hours
Affiliation: HI-FUAJ
Extras: Laundry, meals ($), store, bike storage

Two miles southwest of the little seaside town of Lorient, this place is basic although pretty big, so you're unlikely to get shut out—except one week a year, that is (see below). A hostel store, laundry, and meal service are all useful amenities here, but it isn't the Hilton, that's for sure.

Gestalt:
Lorient express
Party index:

August brings a lively festival to the small and sort of bland town of Lorient. It's known as the Festival Interceltique, and it's HU-U-U-U-U-U-GE compared with the size of the village. Not one, not two, but at least five thousand musicians come here to perform music, dance, and other manifestations of Celtic culture. (Didja know? Brittany is where the Celts were originally from! True, true, true.) About a quarter of a million people attend this thing, so it's absolutely imperative that you reserve your bed way-y-y-y-y ahead of time.

How to get there:

By bus: Take B2 bus to auberge (hostel) stop. On Sunday and holidays take C1 bus.

By car: From Lorient go in direction of Larmorplage Le Ter, then follow arrows to hostel.

By train: Lorient station, 2 miles away.

MANOIR-FERME DE KÉRAUFFRET

Maël Pestivien, 22160

Phone Number: 02–96–45–75–28

Rates: 41 francs per HI member (about $8.00 US)
Credit cards: None
Beds: 15
Private/family rooms: Yes
Kitchen available: Yes
Season: April to October
Office hours: 9:00 A.M. to 9:00 P.M.
Affiliation: HI-FUAJ
Extras: Meals ($), laundry, camping

This place is mostly distinguished by its fifteen campsites; otherwise, it's pretty bare-bones—just fifteen bunks and a laundry. You might want to seek something better if you've come for comfort. They do serve three meals a day for a fee here, though.

Gestalt: Maël call

Party index:

How to get there:

By bus: Call hostel for transit route.

By car: Take the RN12, then the D20.

By train: Coat Guégan station, 6 miles.

CHATEAU DE KERRAOUL HOSTEL

Paimpol, Côtes-d'Armor, 22500

Phone Number: 02–96–20–83–60

Fax Number: 02–96–20–96–46
E-mail: paimpol@fuaj.org
Rates: 48 francs per HI member (about $8.00 US)
Credit cards: Yes
Beds: 80
Private/family rooms: Yes
Kitchen available: Yes

Office hours: Call hostel for hours
Affiliation: HI-FUAJ
Extras: Meals ($), TV, kayaks, classroom, camping

This hostel's pretty good-sized, bunking hostellers up in six double rooms, three quads, and nine bigger dormitories. There's also a small campground, meal service all day long, and some sea kayaking courtesy of a local adventure outfit. Paimpol (say "pimple"—without giggling—and you're getting close to the pronunciation) isn't a superexciting place to explore, but it does enjoy proximity to walking trails and an abbey.

Gestalt:
Paimpol and circumstance
Party index:

The really fun thing to do here, though, for our money is to head to the point nearby and take a short ferry ride to the Ile de Bréhat, an island nicknamed the "isle of flowers" for its amazing flora. The Gulf Stream warms the air here enough so that mulberry and eucalyptus trees (brought back by sailors from distant lands) thrive and blossom.

How to get there:

By bus: Call hostel for transit route.

By car: Take the RN12 in the direction of Brest. Exit after Saint-Brieuc, toward Paimpol on the D7.

By train: From Paimpol station, walk 1 mile to hostel.

AUBERGE DE JEUNESSE VERTE (COUNTRY HOSTEL)

Choucan-en Brocéliande, Paimpont, Plélan-le-Grand, Ile-et-Vilaine, 35380

Phone Number: 02–97–22–76–75

Rates: 45 francs per HI member (about $9.00 US)
Credit cards: None
Beds: 24
Private/family rooms: Sometimes
Kitchen available: Yes
Season: May 1 to September 30
Office hours: Call hostel for hours
Affiliation: HI-FUAJ
Extras: Laundry, camping, breakfast ($)

Kind of inaccessible, this small place is quite simple—just a kitchen, a few bunkrooms, eight campsites, and a laundry. It's a typical French countryside hostel, really. You can buy breakfast for a small charge from the hostel staff.

Auberge de Jeunesse Verte
Plélan-le-Grand

(photo courtesy of FUAJ)

How to get there:

By bus: From Tiv, take bus 7 miles to Paimpont. Walk 4½ miles north on D773, and follow road toward Concoret; hostel is at sign on right near Isaugovet.

By car: Take RN24 Rennes-Lorient exit at Plélan le Grand and go in direction of Paimpont Concoret.

By train: Rennes station, 30 miles away, is closest stop.

Party index:

CENTRE DE VACANCES DE KERMARC'H

Plouguernevel, Rostrenen, 22110

Phone Number: 02–96–29–10–95

Rates: 45 francs per HI member (about $8.00 US)
Credit cards: None

Beds: 25
Private/family rooms: Yes
Kitchen available: Yes
Office hours: Call hostel for hours
Affiliation: HI-FUAJ
Extras: Laundry

This is more of a group place, fairly bare-bones: Think Boy Scout camp and you'll be pretty close to the feel of the place. Surprisingly, though, family rooms are available, and there's also a laundry.

Party index:

How to get there:

By bus: From Saint-Brieuc, take bus to Rostrenen.
By car: Go in the direction of Rostrenen.
By train: Saint-Brieuc station nearby.

PONTIVY AUBERGE DE JEUNESSE

Ile des Recollets, Pontivy, Morbihan, 56300

Phone Number: 02–97–25–58–27

Fax Number: 02–97–25–76–48
Rates: 51 francs per HI member (about $9.00 US)
Credit cards: None
Beds: 65
Private/family rooms: Yes
Kitchen available: Yes
Office hours: 8:00 A.M. to noon; 5:30 to 10:00 P.M.
Affiliation: HI-FUAJ
Extras: Laundry, meals ($), camping, bike storage

Another simple Bretonese hostel with a laundry, kitchen, meal service, and fifteen covered campsites. Almost all the sixty-five beds come in bunks, but the good news here is that the place was recently renovated.

Gestalt: Pontivy league

Party index:

The area used to be the home of the powerful Rohan family, Breton bigwigs who managed to maintain a stable political climate while feudal fighting surrounded them on all sides in the good old (*really* old) days. Their château still stands and is now the home of the most important classical music festival in Brittany. (Hmm. Are there a lot of classical music festivals in Brittany?)

Anyway, picnickers and nibblers will want to saunter over to the farmers' market held in town each Monday.

How to get there:

By bus: Take Rennes-Pontivy bus and stop at LaPlaine.
By car: Take the RN24 or D754.
By train: From Pontivy station, walk 1 mile to hostel.

AUBERGES LES FILETS BLEUS

45, rue du Roch Priol, Quiberon, Morbihan, 56170

Phone Number: 02–97–50–15–54

Rates: 46 francs per HI member (about $9.00 US)
Credit cards: None
Beds: 30
Private/family rooms: None
Kitchen available: Yes
Season: May 1-Sept. 30
Office hours: Twenty-four hours
Lockout: 10:00 A.M. to 6:00 P.M.
Affiliation: HI-FUAJ (HI card required)
Extras: Breakfast ($), camping

This hostel has a surprisingly large campground—forty-five sites in all, about half of them covered and half open-air—plus breakfast for a small cost. There's also an equipped kitchen for budget gourmets. Management is hospitable and appears to run a sound place.

Quiberon, as a base, helps hostellers get back to nature; it's part of a stretch of coastline known as the "wild coast," still much in its pristine glory. You also might come face-to-face with some of those much-talked-about menhirs, fairly tall rocks with Celtic religious meaning.

Gestalt: Quiberon west

Hospitality:

Party index:

How to get there:

By bus: Take 23 or 24 bus to Gare SNCF stop. Hostel is less than 1 mile.

By car: Take the A11 Paris/Rennes to E50 Rennes/Auray, then Auray/Quiberon voie rapide.

By train: Station less than 1 mile from hostel.

KEY TO ICONS

- Attractive natural setting
- Ecologically aware hostel
- Superior kitchen facilities or cafe
- Offbeat or eccentric place
- Superior bathroom facilities
- Romantic private rooms
- Comfortable beds
- Editors Choice Among our very favorite hostels
- A particularly good value
- Wheelchair-accessible
- Good for business travelers
- Especially well suited for families
- Good for active travelers
- Visual arts at hostel or nearby
- Music at hostel or nearby
- Great hostel for skiers
- Bar or pub at hostel or nearby

AUBERGE QUARTIER DE PENHARS

6, avenue des Oiseaux, Quimper, Finistere, 29000

Phone Number: 02–98–64–97–97

Fax Number: 02–98–55–38–37
Rates: 48 francs per HI member (about $8.00 US)
Credit cards: None
Beds: 54
Private/family rooms: None
Kitchen available: Yes
Office hours: 8:00 to 11:00 A.M.; 5:00 to 9:30 P.M.
Season: January 5 to December 23
Affiliation: HI-FUAJ
Extras: Meals ($), bike storage

Gestalt: Happy Quimper

Party index:

Quimper (say "camp-air" to avoid sounding stupid) sits at the far west of the Breton peninsula. And this hostel appears as stark as the surrounding scenery, offering three meals a day and not much else besides fifty bunk beds. There aren't any private rooms here, but they do serve meals for a charge.

The city plays host to the Festival of Cornoauille each year, an event that does draw tourists, and it's a big hit. When festivals aren't in swing, you can learn more about local culture at the Faienceries Quimper: a museum depicting this particular strain of Celtic people. When you've exhausted yourself silly doing that, you might be ready for a snack—try the local pastry called *kouign-ammann* (just point, don't bother trying to pronounce it) at one of the pâtisseries in town.

How to get there:

By bus: Take 1 or 8 bus to Chaptal stop.
By car: Call hostel for directions.
By train: From Quimper station, walk 1 mile to hostel.

AUBERGE MAPAR

2, rue Chantebel, BP101, Redon Cedex, Ile-et-Vilaine, 35603

Phone Number: 02–99–72–14–39

Fax Number: 02–99–72–16–53
E-mail: mapar@wanadoo.fr
Rates: 51 francs per HI member (about $9.00 US)
Credit cards: None
Beds: 20
Private/family rooms: Yes

Kitchen available: Yes
Season: June 1 to August 31
Office hours: 9:00 A.M. to 10:00 P.M. (weekdays); 9:00 A.M. to noon; 3:00 to 7:00 P.M. (weekends and holidays)
Affiliation: HI-FUAJ
Extras: Cafeteria ($), table tennis, TV, library, store, bike storage

This hostel is decked out quite well for a tiny joint, with a television room, table tennis, small hostel library, and more. A cafeteria serves meals most of the time (weekend there's no dinner, however); a laundry is also available for hosteller enjoyment, and they'll arrange private rooms for families and couples.

Party index:

How to get there:

By bus: Call hostel for transit route.
By car: Call hostel for directions.
By train: Near Redon station.

CENTRE INTERNATIONAL DE SÉJOUR

10-12, Canal Saint-Martin, Rennes, Ile-et-Vilaine, 35700

Phone Number: 02–99–33–22–33

Fax Number: 02–99–59–06–21
Rates: 72 francs per HI member (about $12 US); doubles 180 francs (about $30 US)
Credit cards: Yes
Beds: 96
Private/family rooms: Yes
Kitchen available: Yes
Office hours: 7:00 A.M. to 1:00 A.M.
Affiliation: HI-FUAJ
Extras: Breakfast, laundry, meals ($), grill, volleyball, table tennis

We're not wild about this place in an institutional brick warehouselike building, where comfort and cleanliness definitely aren't top-shelf.

The rooms here consist of six singles, eighteen doubles, six triples, and ten quad rooms. They aren't the greatest, and neither are the bathrooms. At least they've thought to build three wheelchair-accessible rooms. There was some fun stuff to do to distract ourselves from this drab place, including a volleyball net and a grill. The laundry provided hours of endless enjoyment, we'll tell ya.

Gestalt:
Rennes and skimpy
Party index:

Centre International de Séjour

Rennes

(photo courtesy of FUAJ)

Breakfast is included here if you're a Hostelling International member; if not, suck it up and pay up.

If you're still coming despite this not-so-great hostel, at least come in early July for a hoppin' event known around these parts as Les Tombées de la Nuit. It's a potluck festival featuring that artful trio of music, dance, and theater. The kicker is that most events are free, with the exception of bigger name acts. Just remember to book ahead.

How to get there:

By bus: Take 18 bus to AJ Pont St-Martin.

By car: Take Autoroute Paris/Rennes/St-Malo and exit at Beauregard, then go along road toward St-Malo and follow signs to hostel.

By train: Approximately 1¼ miles to station.

MANOIR DE LA VILLE GUYOMARD

Les Villages, Saint-Brieuc, Côtes-d'Armor, 22000

Phone Number: 02–96–78–70–70

Fax Number: 02–96–78–27–47
E-mail: saint-brieuc@fuaj.org
Rates: 72 francs per HI member (about $12 US)

Credit cards: Yes
Beds: 127
Private/family rooms: Yes
Kitchen available: Yes
Office hours: Twenty-four hours
Affiliation: HI-FUAJ
Extras: Laundry, restaurant ($) (July to August), meeting room, library, conference room, volleyball, minigolf, table tennis, bike rentals

This stone farmhouse hostel in an incredibly picturesque setting has got lots of atmosphere and a good energy about it.

You can sleep in a variety of situations, choosing from four single rooms, six doubles (four have their own bathroom facilities), ten triple rooms, or fifteen quads. Needless to say, couples and families are well taken care of here; also, this place gets bonus points for the eight wheelchair-accessible rooms with a total of fourteen beds in them.

And the services! You couldn't ask for more—bikes for rent, a laundry, a restaurant, library, minigolf course (okay, maybe that's overdoing it a bit . . .), and game room, among other amenities.

Saint-Brieuc is an excellent stopover if you want to do a little bodysurfing or sun worshipping, as there are loads of beaches around here to choose from. Or come in late October when the Rock and Art Festival is in swing, showcasing (obviously) musical and artistic impulses.

Gestalt: Saint-Brie

Party index:

How to get there:

By bus: Take 3 bus to Géant stop or Jean Moulin stop.
By car: Call hostel for directions.
By train: Saint-Brieuc station, 2 miles away.

AUBERGE DE JEUNESSE VERTE

Bourg de Saint-Guen, Mur de Bretagne, Côtes d'Armor, 22530

Phone Number: 02–96–28–54–34

Fax Number: 02--96–26–01–56
Rates: 45 francs per HI member (about $8.00 US)
Credit cards: None
Beds: 40
Private/family rooms: Sometimes
Kitchen available: Yes
Season: April 1 to October 31
Office hours: 8:00 to 11:00 A.M.; 5:00 to 10:00 P.M.
Affiliation: HI-FUAJ

Extras: Restaurant ($), TV, library, games, horses

This hostel seems good for kids and school groups, as it's outfitted with games, a television, and a library. They also have a restaurant.

Gestalt:
Guen and bear it

Party index:

Saint-Guen, a little agricultural village in central Brittany, has walking trails, horseback riding, a lake, and forests; it's off the beaten tourist path, so it's a good look at actual Bretonese workaday life.

How to get there:

By bus: From Loudéac station, take bus to Saint-Guen.

By car: Go in direction of Carhaix.

By train: Loudéac station, 11 miles.

AUBERGE PATRICK VARANGOT

37, avenue du R. P. Umbricht, BP 108, Saint-Malo Cedex, Bretagne, 35407

Phone Number: 02–99–40–29–80

Fax Number: 02–99–40–29–02
Rates: 72 francs per person (about $12 US)
Credit cards: Yes
Beds: 150
Private/family rooms: Yes
Kitchen available: Yes
Office hours: Twenty-four hours
Lockout: 10:00 A.M. to 5:00 P.M.
Affiliation: HI-FUAJ and UCRIF (HI card required)
Extras: Laundry, table tennis, meals ($), pool table, volleyball, tennis, audiovisual room, TV, lockers

All right, Saint-Malo isn't exactly thrillsville; it's more like a place to change money or rest before or after taking a ferry across the English Channel.

Gestalt:
St. Elsewhere

Party index:

But this hostel, a couple blocks from the beach, makes a decent stab at giving you a good bunk. The shower facilities do present a problem; many hostellers have complained that they tend to alternately scald and freeze you. But the hostel staff serves meals, runs a game room, maintains a laundry, and organizes activities to keep you from being bored out of your gourd. You can also play anything from table tennis to basketball here using the free hostel equipment.

Once known as a playground of corsairs—basically, pirates who played nice-nice with those in authority—the walled city of Saint-Malo has managed to maintain its fierce identity and independent spirit because of those chaps, those walls, and its remote location. It's also a popular first stop in France for travelers getting off the ferry from England.

How to get there:

By bus: Take bus 1, 2, or 5 to auberge (hostel) stop.

By car: Go to Saint-Malo from direction of Parame, then to Courtoisville. Follow arrows to hostel.

By train: Saint-Malo station, 1 mile.

AUBERGE LE TOËNO

Route de la Corniche, Trébeurden, Côtes-d'Armor, 22560

Phone Number: 02–96–23–52–22

Fax Number: 02–96–15–44–34
Rates: 48 francs per HI member (about $8.00 US)
Credit cards: None
Beds: 56
Private/family rooms: Yes
Kitchen available: Yes
Office hours: Twenty-four hours
Affiliation: HI-FUAJ
Extras: Meals (sometimes), camping, bike rentals, game room, grill

Facing the ocean, this hostel's location is its main plus. There's also a decent amount of socializing going on, what with a game room, a grill for barbecueing, and three meals a day served for a charge.

Party index:

The place consists entirely of nine dormitory rooms, but they'll also set aside space for families or couples when needed. Eighteen campsites are available, too.

For kicks, we'd rent a bicycle at the hostel and cruise the local sea towns, checking out the area's distinctive rose-colored granite. Or we'd visit the village of Gaulois for a glimpse at that prehistoric time when Celts were running around the forests of this area long before comic book artists dreamed up Asterix.

How to get there:

By bus: Take Verts bus to auberge (hostel) stop.

By car: Take A11 and then RN12.

By train: Lannion station, 6 miles.

NORTHERN FRANCE

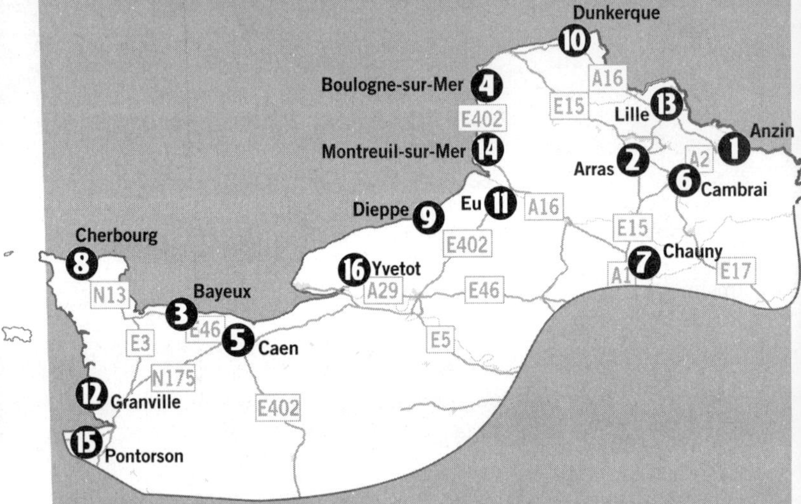

Page numbers follow town names.

NORTHERN FRANCE

Considered by some to be France's dullest area—maybe it's the proximity to England?—the north of France actually does have a few reasons to come and visit, especially if you're into history: This area suffered terribly during the second World War. And if you're taking the Chunnel from England, it's the first you'll see of La France.

The region of Normandy, for example, is a must-see to visit the beaches that were stormed by the Allies during 1944. Bayeaux and Dunkerque are the best places to see and hear all about it. A tour of the renowned cathedral and other churches at Rouen or the fantastic island monastery (accessible by land at low tide) at Mont-Saint-Michel are other options. Norman food is also quite a draw if you're a fan of rich, lactose-heavy sauces covering various meats; seafood; or apple cider with a strong kick.

Over by the Belgian border, in the Pas-de-Calais region, things do get kind of boring. But Lille is justly famous for its cathedral, and towns like Arras supply a little diversion on your way to Brussels or Amsterdam.

Hostels up here can be few and far between, though. If you're bent on exploring this region in depth, don't try to rely too heavily on the inconvenient train system. You might do well to hitch or double up on a rental car. Biking is also a great option, since the terrain is very flat.

If you've started your French voyage via Great Britain, you will most likely enter via ferry at one of the several port towns on the Norman coast. Starting at Dunkerque, we'd work our way along the coast hitting the bigger towns of Boulogne, Rouen (which is inland), Caen, Bayeux, up the Cotentin Peninsula to Cherbourg, and then on to Mont-Saint-Michel. A few lesser known cities and towns with good hostels also dot the northern interior such Vernon—where you'll find the gardens that inspired some of Monet's greatest works.

Actually, our favorite way to get here is to start or end a visit to France by taking the overnight ferry to or from Cherbourg to Rosslare or Cork, Ireland. If you're coming, it's a good way to begin using your Eurail pass (the ride is free but costs you a day of pass use). Just make sure the weather isn't too rough when you leave, or the ride might not be as much fun.

AUBERGE DE JEUNESSE ANZIN

43, rue des Martyrs, Anzin, Nord, 59410

Phone Number: 03–27–28–21–00

Fax Number: 03–27–28–21–01

Rates: 48 francs per HI member (about $8.00 US)
Credit cards: None
Beds: 40
Private/family rooms: None
Kitchen available: Yes
Office hours: 8:00 to 10:00 A.M.; 5:00 to 10:00 P.M.
Affiliation: HI-FUAJ

This place is quite simple, just forty beds in bunkrooms. No family rooms are available, and there's no kitchen, laundry, or meal service, either. At least the hostel's located in a park.

Party index:

How to get there:

By bus: Take 2 bus to Saint Amand or 3 bus toward Beauvrage to Rousseau stop.

By car: From Paris take Autoroute in direction of Valenciennes and get off at exit 7. From Brussels take Autoroute in direction of Valenciennes and get off at exit 7.

By train: Valenciennes station.

ARRAS AUBERGE DE JEUNESSE

59, Grand-Place, Arras, Pas-de-Calais, 62000

Phone Number: 03–21–22–70–02

Fax Number: 03–21–07–46–15
Rates: 48 francs per HI member (about $8.00 US)
Credit cards: None
Beds: 54
Private/family rooms: Yes
Kitchen available: Yes
Season: February 1 to November 30
Office hours: 7:30 to 10:00 A.M.; 5:00 to 11:00 P.M.
Affiliation: HI-FUAJ
Extras: Catered meals for groups, TV, bike rentals

Party index:

Right in downtown Arras, a seaside resort town in France's northern Pas-de-Calais region, this joint sees a fairly hip crowd of beachgoers. Canadians find the place especially interesting because of a war memorial nearby in Vimy that commemorates that country's fallen soldiers.

They don't serve meals here (except to big groups), but the bikes for rent, and television room do provide something to do besides walk the beach with the rest of the tourists in funny T-shirts. A biweekly farmers' market whisks you away from that torrent of tourists. Pick up some of the area's famous apples Wednesday and Saturday to munch on if the season is right, although you need to get there early in the morning for the best choice.

How to get there:

By bus: Take D bus to Grand-Place stop.

By car: Take Autoroute A1 to Arras Est exit, then take the A26 and follow in direction of LesPlaces.

By train: From Arras station, walk ½ mile to hostel.

INTERNATIONAL FAMILY HOME HOSTEL

39, rue Gal de Dais, Bayeux, 14400

Phone Number: 02–31–92–15–22

Fax Number: 02–31–92–55–72
Rates: 51 to 68 francs per HI member (about $9.00 to $12.00 US)
Credit cards: Yes
Beds: 140
Private/family rooms: Yes
Kitchen available: Yes
Office hours: Call hostel for hours
Curfew: 11:00 P.M.
Affiliation: HI-FUAJ
Extras: Laundry, meals ($), breakfast, bike rentals, camping, TV, conference room

There are three single rooms here, sixteen doubles, seven triples, and six quads—two of which have en-suite bathrooms—plus fourteen bigger dorm rooms. In addition, two wheelchair-accessible rooms have been outfitted, and there are thirty open-air campsites on the hostel property.

Gestalt: Blue Bayeux

Hospitality:

Party index:

Superb gathering and dining areas make socializing a snap: There are four common areas, for example, plus a restaurant. Other amenities include a laundry, television room, bikes for hire, and a conference room if you happen to need one. Finally, you're very central to Bayeux, a must-see town for World War II buffs or anyone else interested in this riveting chapter of world history. Our only quibbles: It's not the friendliest hostel in France (despite the name), and some of the beds and furniture here are getting worn. If you can handle that, this place is a worthwhile stopping place.

Besides the war memorials, the other big draw to town is a tapestry located in the Centre Culturel depicting the whole story of William the Conquerer (he of 1066, Battle of Hastings fame).

How to get there:

By bus: Take bus vert to AJ stop.
By car: Call hostel for directions.
By train: Bayeux station is adjacent to hostel.

BOULOGNE-SUR-MER AUBERGE DE JEUNESSE

Place Rouget-de-Lisle, Boulogne-sur-Mer, 62200

Phone Number: 03–21–99–15–30 or 03–21–99–15–35

Fax Number: 03–21–99–15–39
E-mail: boulogne-sur-mer@fuaj.org
Rates: 72 francs per HI member (about $12 US)
Credit cards: Yes
Beds: 134
Private/family rooms: Yes
Kitchen available: Yes
Office hours: 8:00 A.M. to 1:00 A.M. (April to August); 8:30 to midnight (September to March)
Affiliation: HI-FUAJ
Extras: Restaurant ($), breakfast, bar, TV, VCR, karaoke, pool table, game room, patio

This place looks vaguely like a concrete rocketship from the outside, but inside there's no denying the interplanetary fun taking place.

Insiders' tip:
Hosteller discount at local bowling alley

Gestalt:
Toney Boulogne

Party index:

It's a pretty new hostel, so facilities are in good repair. They've got a bar, karaoke machine, restaurant, television room with movies on tape, pool table—everything you need to mix and mingle, meet and greet. Breakfast is always free, too. Group rooms are an especially good discount here, coming with en-suite bathroom and an alarm clock; two wheelchair-accessible rooms are available.

For kicks, most hostellers head off to the huge aquarium here called "NAUSICAA" (not to be confused with nausea). We prefer to wander around the backstreets of this fishing town, where fresh fish can be bought all over the place FOB (fresh off the boat) at extremely early morning hours. This is a classic walled city with a cathedral, so there's also that to do, and there's a beach nearby popular with windsurfers and walkers. You can take whatever you dig up at the Wednesday/Saturday farmers' market and amble over to the extra-wide ramparts for a brief stroll.

Others simply use this hostel as a launchpad for the next morning's ride over to England on the Chunnel train. As such, it's not bad.

How to get there:

By bus: From downtown, take DUO LINE bus to hostel.

By car: From Paris, take A1 and A26 to RN 42 to Boulogne. Or take A16.

By ferry: From England, take Seacat to Boulogne terminal, ½ mile away.

By train: Across street from Boulogne Ville train station.

RESIDENCE ROBERT REME

Grace de Dieu, 68, rue Eustache Restout, Caen, Calvados, 14300

Phone Number: 02–31–52–19–96

Fax Number: 02–31–84–29–49
Rates: 51 to 68 francs per HI member (about $9.00 to $11.00 US)
Credit cards: None
Beds: 58
Private/family rooms: Yes
Kitchen available: Yes
Season: June 1 to September 30
Office hours: 7:00 to 10:00 P.M.
Affiliation: HI-FUAJ
Extras: Laundry, breakfast ($), pool table, table tennis

The rooms here aren't bad at all, especially the family rooms, which include both their own bathroom facilities and, sometimes, kitchenettes. The English-speaking management is a plus, too. The game room includes a pool table and table tennis for fun.

Gestalt:
Caen and able

Party index:

William the Conqueror—not the guy who won the Ping-Pong game, but the one who won the Battle of Hastings and became king of England—makes another appearance as a must-see on your itinerary while here in Caen. He built a humongous castle nearby that offers tours. There's an absolutely stunning cathedral here, too.

How to get there:

By bus: Take 5 or 17 bus toward Grace de Dieu to Lycee Fresnel stop.

By car: Call hostel for directions.

By train: Caen station, 1 mile.

AUBERGE L'ÉTAPE

22, rue de Crevecour, Cambrai 59400

Phone Number: 03–27–74–98–03

Fax Number: 03–27–74–98–03
E-mail: aubergejeunesseetape@minitel.net
Rates: 51 to 68 francs per HI member (about $9.00 to $12.00 US)
Credit cards: None
Beds: 73
Private/family rooms: Yes
Kitchen available: Yes
Office hours: 8:00 A.M. to 7:00 P.M.
Affiliation: HI-FUAJ
Extras: Restaurant ($), TV

Be aware—this place gets a lot of schoolkids and other group bookings. Otherwise, it's okay as a stopping place in the north of France, with a television room and restaurant serving three meals for a fee.

Party index:

There's not much to do in Cambrai, but the Kermesse de la Bêtise festival does draw big crowds in early September. You Mainers out there reading this book might recognize the word "Kermesse," noting that a similarly titled end-of-the-summer festival occurs in towns where lots of French-Canadians wound up settling.

How to get there:

By bus: Call hostel for transit route.
By car: Call hostel for directions.
By train: Cambrai station nearby.

CHAUNY AUBERGE DE JEUNESSE

Boulevard Bad-Kostritz, Chauny, Aisne, 02300

Phone Number: 03–23–52–09–96

Fax Number: 03–23–39–90–92
Rates: 48 francs per HI member (about $8.00 US)
Credit cards: None
Beds: 40
Private/family rooms: Yes
Kitchen available: Yes
Office hours: 7:00 to 10:00 A.M.; 5:00 to 10:00 P.M.
Affiliation: HI-FUAJ
Extras: Laundry, catered meals for groups, pool table, table tennis, conference room, bike storage

A postmodern slab of architecture, this hostel is nonetheless fairly well equipped, with one double room, one quad, and six larger dormitories. The laundry's useful for single travelers, the conference room helpful to groups; nearby tennis courts, golf courses, and fishing make various outings possible.

Party index:

How to get there:

By bus: Lignieìes stop is close to hostel.
By car: Call hostel for directions.
By train: Chauny station, 1 mile.

CHERBOURG AUBERGE DE JEUNESSE

57, rue de l'Abbaye, Cherbourg, 50100

Phone Number: 02–33–78–15–15

Fax Number: 02–33–78–15–16
Rates: 51 francs per HI member (about $9.00 US)
Beds: 99
Private/family rooms: Yes
Kitchen available: Yes
Season: January 4 to December 23
Office hours: 8:00 A.M. to noon, 6:00 to 11:00 P.M.
Affiliation: HI-FUAJ
Extras: Meals (sometimes), TV, VCR, garden, bike storage, meeting rooms

A new hostel in a restored naval building, this place draws hostellers for its all-you-can-eat breakfast (which isn't free, by the way).

Rooms here consist of three doubles, one triple, eighteen quads, and four larger rooms of five to eight beds apiece; add in two wheelchair-accessible rooms with a total of five beds and that's the whole ball of wax. A garden, kitchen, television room with movies on tape, and meeting rooms fill out the amenities.

Gestalt:
Ferry tale
Party index:

Cherbourg, although filled with lots of gardens and festivals, is primarily known for its deep harbor—one of the biggest natural harbors in the world, in fact—which brings fishing boats and other commercial traffic here year-round. As a hosteller, though, you'll possibly pass through here while coming or going on a ferry to Ireland. It's not the most exciting place in this part of France to bunk up, not by

Cherbourg Auberge de Jeunesse
Cherbourg

(photo courtesy of FUAJ)

a long shot, but the hostel's certainly fine if you need to stay here.

How to get there:

By bus: Take 3 or 5 bus to Hotel de Ville stop; walk along rue de la Paix to rue de l'Abbaye.

By car: Take N13 to Cherbourg; hostel is near train station.

By ferry: From Cork, Ireland, or Rosslare, Ireland, take ferry to Cherbourg.

By train: From Cherbourg station, take 3 or 5 bus to Hotel de Ville stop; walk along rue de la Paix to rue de l'Abbaye.

DIEPPE AUBERGE DE JEUNESSE

48, rue Louis Fromager, Saint Aubin sur Scie (Dieppe), Seine-Maritime, 76550

Phone Number: 02–35–84–85–73

Fax Number: 02–35–84–89–62
E-mail: dieppe@fuaj.org
Rates: 65 francs per HI member (about $12 US)
Credit cards: None
Beds: 42
Private/family rooms: Yes

Kitchen available: Yes
Office hours: 8:00 to 10:00 A.M.; 5:00 to 10:00 P.M.
Lockout: 10:00 A.M. to 5:00 P.M.
Affiliation: HI-FUAJ
Extras: Breakfast, meals (sometimes), laundry, grill

Breakfast is included in this old house converted to a hostel, which is set in nicely peaceful surroundings near the sea.

Rooms include one double, a quad with en-suite bathroom, one big coed dorm room with bathroom, and one big one without. Everything's okay here; it's not central at all to downtown Dieppe, however. The grill is popular in summertime—a good place to grill that fresh fish or vegetables you bought at the six-day-a-week farmers' market. (Head there Saturday for the most entertainment and selection.)

Party index: 3 party hats

How to get there:

By bus: Take 2 bus to Chateau Michel.
By car: Take either the N27, D915, or D925 to the rondpoint des Canadiens, direction of Fécamp, then turn left at first traffic light.
By train: Dieppe station, 1½ miles.

DUNKERQUE AUBERGE DE JEUNESSE

Place Paul Asseman, Dunkerque, Nord, 59140

Phone Number: 03–28–63–36–34

Fax Number: 03–28–63–24–54
Rates: 48 francs per HI member (about $8.00 US)
Credit cards: None
Beds: Varies
Private/family rooms: Yes
Kitchen available: No
Season: January 2 to December 20
Office hours: Twenty-four hours (summer); 8:30 A.M. to 12:30 P.M.; 2:00 to 11:00 P.M. (rest of year)
Affiliation: HI-FUAJ
Extras: Meals ($), grill, TV

It's yet another hostel in a seaside resort town facing the English Channel (or the "Sleeve," as the French call it). Beds come in one double room, one quad room, and fifteen big dormitories. Amenities are limited, but they do serve meals here and make a barbecue available. For real couch potatoes, there's a television room.

Gestalt: Dunkerque to Enterprise

Party index: 2 party hats

Dunkerque is pretty blah, though, and is mostly associated as one of the beachheads the Allies used to liberate France during World War II.

How to get there:

By bus: Take 3 bus to Piscine stop.

By car: Take either the A25 or A16, then exit at Dunkerque centre. Go in direction of plage-casino and follow signs.

By train: Dunkerque station, 2 miles.

CENTRE DES FONTAINES

Rue des Fontaines, BP123, Eu, Seine-Maritime, 76260

Phone Number: 02–35–86–05–03

Fax Number: 02–35–86–45–12
Rates: 95 francs per HI member (about $17 US)
Credit cards: Yes
Beds: 55
Private/family rooms: Yes
Kitchen available: No
Season: January 5 to December 19
Office hours: 6:00 to 9:00 P.M.
Affiliation: HI-FUAJ
Extras: Meals ($), breakfast, bar, dance studio, TV

Eu isn't exactly on the tourist's beaten track, but this hostel—set in a really nice old home—fills the bill nicely as a budget bunk. Breakfast is included with your stay, a stellar little park surrounds the place, and there are unusual touches like a combination judo/dance studio right in the building. Definitely a little different.

Party index:

There is one quad room for families, plus eight dorm rooms for hostellers; a bar and meal service are available, as are a laundry and a television room.

Hikers and tree-huggers alike can ramble about the Fôret d'Eu, which sports three *massifs* (mountain peaks) called "le triage," plus two trees—an oak and a beech—that have grown so closely together for so many years that they appear to be one tree. Cool!

How to get there:

By bus: Take Courrier Automobiles Picard busline and stop at Place St-Laurent.

By car: Take the D925 in the direction of Dieppe then toward Eu. At Centre Ville go in direction of Camping.

By train: Station less than 1 mile.

CENTRE RÉGIONAL DE NAUTISME

Boulevard des Amiraux, Granville, Manche, 50400

Phone Number: 02–33–91–22–60

Fax Number: 02–33–50–51–99
E-mail: crng@dial.oleane.com
Rates: 72 to 101 francs per HI member (about $12 to $17 US); doubles 152 francs (about $26 US)
Credit cards: Yes
Beds: 165
Private/family rooms: Yes
Kitchen available: No
Season: January 3 to December 22
Office hours: Twenty-four hours
Affiliation: HI-FUAJ
Extras: Meals ($), game room, bar, bike storage

Socializing appears to be one of the chief activities here, but the beds are okay too—mostly in quad rooms that all have their own en-suite bathrooms. Among the amenities here are a game room, bar, and bike storage.

Gestalt:
Yard sail

Party index:

A sailing center occupies part of the building, as well, giving you an interesting recreational option with your free time. That's good, because Granville definitely isn't the most thrilling town to sightsee. At least it's rather close to stunning Mont-Saint-Michel, probably the main reason you're here paying for a bed.

How to get there:

By bus: Take #12 bus line to Cours Jonville.
By car: Call hostel for directions.
By train: Granville station, ⅓ mile.

AUBERGE DE JEUNESSE DE LILLE

12, rue Malpart, Lille, 59000

Phone Number: 03–20–57–08–94

Fax Number: 03–20–63–98–93
E-mail: lille@fuaj.org
Rates: 72 francs per HI member (about $12 US)
Credit cards: Yes
Beds: 168
Private/family rooms: Yes
Kitchen available: Yes

Season: February 1 to December 20
Office hours: 7:00 A.M. to noon; 2:00 P.M. to 1:00 A.M. (2:00 A.M in summer)
Affiliation: HI-FUAJ
Extras: Breakfast, meals (sometimes), projector, conference rooms, bar

Opened in July 1996 and right in downtown Lille's historic area, this brand-new hostel looks good and features more private and family rooms than you imagined possible.

How many? Well, this places offers twelve single rooms, ten doubles, twenty-two quads, and only two larger dorm rooms of five to eight beds each. There are four wheelchair-accessible rooms, as well. Breakfast is included with every bed. It's ideal for groups, so watch out for those occasional times when schools have booked the place rock-solid.

Party index:

Also make sure you book way in advance if you plan on visiting the first weekend in September, as a gigantic flea market, er, jumps into town. It's been reported that more than two million visitors come here to find deals, bargains, and white elephants. Take a break from the shopping frenzy and munch on the local specialty of mussels, fries, and beer.

How to get there:

By bus: Take 13 bus and stop at Hôtel de Ville.
By car: Take exit 2A (Lille centre) from autoroute.
By train: Lille-Flandres station ½ mile.
By metro: Take #1 line (direction CHR), then #2 line (direction Saint-Philibert); stop at Mairie de Lille.

KEY TO ICONS

- Attractive natural setting
- Ecologically aware hostel
- Superior kitchen facilities or cafe
- Offbeat or eccentric place
- Superior bathroom facilities
- Romantic private rooms
- Comfortable beds
- Editors Choice Among our very favorite hostels
- A particularly good value
- Wheelchair-accessible
- Good for business travelers
- Especially well suited for families
- Good for active travelers
- Visual arts at hostel or nearby
- Music at hostel or nearby
- Great hostel for skiers
- Bar or pub at hostel or nearby

AUBERGE LA HULOTTE

Citadette, rue Carnot, Montreuil-sur-Mer,

Pas de Calais, 62170

Phone Number: 03–21–06–10–83

Fax Number: 03–21–06–10–83
Rates: 45 francs per HI member (about $8.00 US)
Credit cards: None
Beds: 43
Private/family rooms: Yes
Kitchen available: Yes
Season: March 1 to October 30 (closed Tuesday)
Office hours: Call hostel for hours
Affiliation: HI-FUAJ
Extras: Laundry, camping

There's not much of a tale to tell here, just forty-five beds in bunkrooms and some room for families, too. A laundry is about the only extra special thing here, and the seaside location—while obviously desirable—can be beat in some other northern towns. Four covered campsites provide a supercheap option if you want to commune with nature for a night.

Party index:

If you've got some extra francs in your pocket (and we mean a *lot* of extra francs), you might want to get some of that great local seafood into your gullet by way of a pretty famous restaurant that's downtown. More likely, you'll be going the way of the budgetworthy farmers' market each Saturday.

How to get there:

By bus: Stop at Grande Place.

By car: Take A16 Calais/Paris to N39 Arras/Montreuil-sur-Mer, then N1 Boulogne-sur-Mer/Paris.

By train: From Montreuil station, walk ⅓ mile to hostel.

CENTRE DUGUESCLIN HOSTEL

Rue Patton, Pontorson, Manche, 50170

Phone Number: 02–33–60–18–65

Fax Number: 02–33–60–18–65
Rates: 48 francs per HI member (about $8.00 US)
Credit cards: None
Beds: 57
Private/family rooms: Yes

Kitchen available: Yes
Office hours: 8:00 to 11:00 A.M.; 5:00 to 10:00 P.M. (mid-September to mid-June) 8:00 A.M. to 9:00 P.M. (mid-June to mid-September)
Lockout: 10:00 A.M. to 6:00 P.M.
Affiliation: HI-FUAJ
Extras: Laundry, TV, table tennis, bike rental

This hostel's superuseful because it's so close—well, 8 miles—to the famous island monastery at Mont-Saint-Michel, where there obviously isn't a hostel. There are two quads in the stone three-story building, plus seven dorm rooms of five to eight beds each and one additional wheelchair-accessible room located on the ground floor.

Insiders' tip: Take day bus to Mont-Saint-Michel

Party index:

Everything's quiet and reasonably well appointed, including the bathrooms and showers. A game room and television room give you something to do at night, and they'll rent you a bike if you want to get some exercise on your way to that amazing island.

Too bad they kick you out all day long in the name of the dreaded lockout.

How to get there:

By bus: Call hostel for transit route.
By car: Take the RN175–176 autoroute.
By train: Pontorson station, ½ mile from hostel.

YVETOT AUBERGE DE JEUNESSE

4, rue de la Briqueterie, "Camping Municipal," Yvetot, Seine-Maritime, 76190

Phone Number: 02–35–95–37–01

Rates: 45 francs per HI member (about $8.00 US)
Credit cards: None
Beds: 8
Private/family rooms: Yes
Kitchen available: Yes
Season: April to October
Office hours: Call hostel for hours
Affiliation: HI-FUAJ

Voilá: one of smallest hostels in all France, just eight beds. That's all we're gonna tell you—that and the fact that there aren't many amenities at all, no laundry or meals or game rooms. At least there's a self-catering kitchen so that you can fix appropriately simple grub.

This former market town now draws tourists who come to see the stained-glass window panels in the Eglise-St-Pierre. Upon entering, you'll note that the colors of the windows are very soft, becoming increasingly brighter until you reach the depiction of Christ on the cross.

Party index:

How to get there:

By bus: Call hostel for transit route.
By car: Call hostel for directions.
By train: From Yvetot station, walk ½ mile to hostel.

ALSACE-LORRAINE AND EASTERN FRANCE

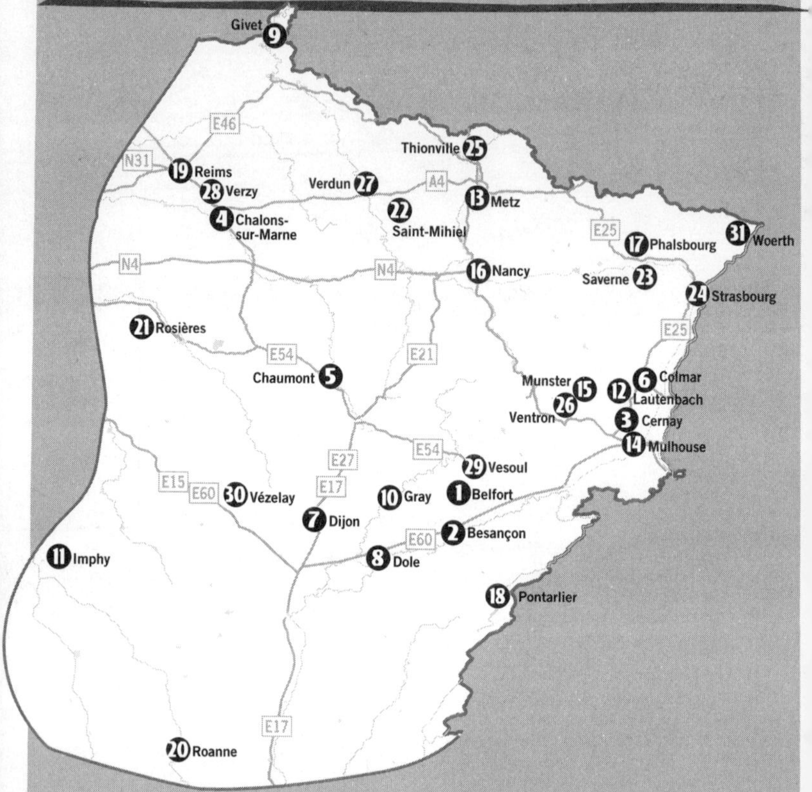

Page numbers follow town names.

ALSACE-LORRAINE AND EASTERN FRANCE

This chapter covers some pretty broad terrain, including at least six major French regional destinations.

The northern part of this area, Champagne-Ardennes, is for the most part dominated by rolling hills covered with vineyards. The graves of soldiers are also much in evidence here, grim reminders of the realities of war

Similarly rolling hills cover Burgundy, which is known of course for its robust red wines and flowers beautifully in springtime. Nice place to bike, Burgundy, and interesting larger towns like Macon and Beaune display distinctive red-and-yellow tile work that looks almost Spanish in character. Dijon's got one reason and one reason only to visit. Hint: It's yellow.

Traveling east toward Alsace-Lorraine, you'll notice a difference in culture. Alsace—right on the German border—is practically Germanic in its speech, customs, architecture, and food. Most people, when asked about places to see in France other than Paris, wholeheartedly recommend Strasbourg as a number-two destination, citing its great student ambience and cafe scene. Colmar is another incredibly scenic town.

Lorraine, just inland from Alsace, is known not only for the eponymous quiche but also for attractive and fairly hip cities like Nancy and Metz. Both regions have endured endless tugs-of-war between France and Germany, but they've maintained a cheery outlook in the face of this constant indecisiveness.

It's nature that directs people to the more underrated Franche Comté, dominated not by opposing governments but by rivers, mountains, and alpine cheeses. This is a good place to get away from the crowds.

Getting around these areas takes a lot of perseverance, though, or a budget that allows for extensive use of a rental car. If you're planning on visiting from the north, trains cruise from Paris to Metz and Strasbourg; from there, trains go some places, and buses (though slow and kind of expensive) go others. Buddy up with a few people and you'll increase the cost-effectiveness and your coolness quotient.

RÉSIDENCE MADRID

6, rue de Madrid, Belfort, 90000

Phone Number: 03–84–21–39–16

Fax Number: 03–84–28–58–95

Rates: 72 francs per HI member (about $13 US)
Credit cards: Yes
Beds: 20
Private/family rooms: Yes
Kitchen available: No
Office hours: 8:30 A.M. to 12:30 P.M.; 2:00 to 9:30 P.M.
Affiliation: HI-FUAJ, FJT
Extras: Breakfast ($), meals ($), laundry, bike storage

This joint is adequate, if not perfectly neat. Still, they have some singles and doubles, including some with showers, in addition to the dormitories. And the staff is pretty good. Breakfast costs extra; in fact, they serve three meals a day for a fee here. There's also a laundry.

Gestalt:
Bats in the Belfort

Cleanliness:

Party index:

Summer concert-goers will love the convenience of this hostel to the annual pop mayhem called the Eurokéenes festival. Yep, it's held in Belfort every year. You, too, can hear aging hipsters trying to milk their '60s hits for all they're worth or newer but also-aging wannabes whose fifteen minutes of fame are at fourteen and ticking . . . In any case, the hostel's sure to be a scene, no matter who you're listening to. For fun, count the Euro-poseurs thronging the stage and attempting to make eye contact with their idols.

More meaningfully, perhaps, at the beginning of September you can watch hot air make balloons rise during the International Montgolfiades. Anything to get us outside this not-so-clean hostel.

How to get there:

By bus: From Belfort, take 1 bus to rue de Madrid.
By car: Call hostel for directions.
By train: From Belfort station, walk ⅓ mile to hostel.

AUBERGE LES OISEAUX

48, rue des Cras, Besançon, 25000

Phone Number: 03–81–40–32–00

Fax Number: 03–81–40–32–01
Rates: 72 francs per HI member (about $12 US)
Credit cards: Yes
Beds: 20
Private/family rooms: None
Kitchen available: No
Office hours: Twenty-four hours

Affiliation: HI-FUAJ
Extras: Meals ($), laundry, bar

Not much to tell about the FUAJ-affiliated joint in Besançon, a nice little city of interesting stone in the Franche Comté. They've got both dorms and private rooms, plus meal service and a laundry.

Perhaps the most striking features of this university town are the four verdant hills that surround the downtown and the River Doubs's classic horseshoe bend that enfolds it. It all serves as the focal point for touristic adventuring. For starters, easily stroll to the Musée des Beaux-Arts or the Cathédrale St-Jean and Frenchify yourself.

Gestalt:
Besançon of Sam
Party index:

How to get there:

By bus: Take 1 bus and get off at Résidence Madrid stop.
By car: Call hostel for directions.
By train: Station less than 1 mile.

CERNAY AUBERGE DE JEUNESSE

16A, Faubourg de Colmar, Cernay, Haut-Rhin, 68700

Phone Number: 03–89–75–44–59

Fax Number: 03–89–75–87–48
Rates: 48 francs per HI member (about $8.00 US)
Credit cards: No
Beds: 55
Private/family rooms: Yes
Kitchen available: Yes
Season: January 2 to December 15
Office hours: 5:00 to 11:00 P.M. (summer); 5:00 to 10:00 P.M (winter)
Affiliation: HI-FUAJ
Extras: TV, bar, conference room, meals ($), bike storage

A two-story stone mansion with cute wooden shutters, this hostel is close to parks, horseback riding, and other Cernay-area distractions.

The hostel has two quad rooms (which are great for families) plus six larger bunkrooms and the usual French leisure combo: bar, television, and restaurant all in close proximity. A bike shed is available for velo enthusiasts or for those who are ahead of the pack during the Tour de France and want a chance to relax for a couple of days before hitting the road again.

Gestalt:
Weinerschnitzel
Party index:

You're in the decidedly Germanic region of Alsace, where "prosit!" is more likely to be heard than "santé!" as you're clinking your glasses of Riesling together. So go German: Order potatoes, eggy pastries, and stuff like that. You'll fit right in.

How to get there:

By bus: Take Voyages Chopin bus line to Cernay stop.
By car: Take the N83 and the 66.
By train: From Cernay station, walk 1 mile to hostel.

AUBERGE L'EMBELLIE

Rue Kellermann, Square Antral, Chalons-sur-Marne, Marne, 51000

Phone Number: 03–26–68–13–56

Rates: 41 francs per HI member (about $7.00 US)
Credit cards: None
Beds: 40
Private/family rooms: None
Kitchen available: Yes
Season: Year-round
Office hours: 5:00 to 10:30 P.M.
Affiliation: HI-FUAJ
Extras: Breakfast ($), laundry

This hostel's really inexpensive and not much used, except by French schoolkids, we'd guess. There are few amenities offered here, just breakfast—and it costs extra. Now there's a kitchen and a laundry for hosteller use. Chalons is in a pretty area on the way to Alsace. It's right on the express train line from Paris to Strasbourg, too.

Gestalt: Marne, all Marne

Party index:

How to get there:

By bus: Take bus toward Valée St. Pierre to Doulcet stop, then walk to hostel.
By car: Take either the A4 (Strasbourg–Paris) or the A26 (Lille/Dijon).
By train: From Chalons station, walk ½ mile to hostel.

AUBERGE DE JEUNESSE CHAUMONT

1, rue de Carcassonne, Chaumont, 52000

Phone Number: 03–25–03–22–77

Rates: 68 francs per HI member (about $12 US)
Credit cards: None
Beds: 34

Private/family rooms: Yes
Kitchen available: Yes
Office hours: Twenty-four hours
Affiliation: HI-FUAJ, FJT
Extras: Breakfast, meals ($), laundry, TV, table tennis, bar

Breakfast is included at this hostel, which also has decent-size kitchen, laundry, and game room. Unusually, there are three single rooms plus twelve doubles—so most bunks are pretty private. One triple and one quad are also available for family types.

William Tell wannabes who want to improve their archery skills might occasionally happen upon a class going on in the common room here. If you don't have a bow or a quiver of arrows, maybe you could volunteer your talents and be the one with the apple on his/her head? That should make for some exciting travel stories.

Party index:

Also on the grounds are a basketball court and a cool pool for swimming during the summer.

How to get there:

By bus: Take 1 bus to Cavalier.

By car: From Langres follow the arrows to Le Cavalier, then to auberge.

By train: Chaumont station, ½ mile.

AUBERGE DE JEUNESSE MITTELHARTH

2, rue Pasteur, Colmar, Haut-Rhin, 68000

Phone Number: 03–89–80–57–39

Fax Number: 03–89–80–76–16
Rates: 48 francs per HI member (about $8.00 US)
Credit cards: Yes
Beds: 110
Private/family rooms: Yes
Kitchen available: No
Season: January 15 to December 15
Office hours: 5:00 P.M. to midnight (summer); 5:00 to 11:00 P.M. (winter)
Affiliation: HI-FUAJ
Extras: Breakfast, meals ($), bike storage

Colmar's hostel features rooms in six-bed dorms, plus good showers and a free breakfast—the basics you need to explore a really neat town of half-timbered buildings, one of the finest in France. There's no curfew, either, and staff serves lunch and dinner for a fee after doling out your free continental breakfast. Beds come in a choice of eight double rooms, four quad rooms, or thirteen larger bunkrooms with five to eight beds each.

Insiders' tip:
Sauerkraut Days in September

Gestalt:
Stuck in the Mittleharth

Party index:

Oenophiles can travel the Alsatian Wine Road, exceptionally lovely—the stuff postcard dreams are made of—but heavily touristed, too. Along this route, you can stop at vineyards and sample the local product whenever there's a sign indicating DEGUSTATION. For free!

If you're planning on using the hostel kitchen, stock up on fresh vegetables and locally produced cheeses at the excellent farmers' market held Thursday and Saturday (Saturday being the more full-on of the two). August and September are good for catching food and wine festivals, too, in preparation for all those Oktoberfest-like things that happen in, well, yes, October.

How to get there:

By bus: Take 4 bus to Lycee Technique (Technical College).
By car: Call hostel for directions.
By train: Colmar station, 1 mile.

CENTRE DE RENCONTRES INTERNATIONALES

1, boulevard Champollion, Dijon, Côte d'Or, 21000

Phone Number: 03–80–72–95–20

Fax Number: 03–80–70–00–61
E-mail: crisd@planetb.fr
Rates: 72 francs per HI member (about $12 US)
Credit cards: Yes
Beds: 100
Private/family rooms: Yes
Kitchen available: No
Season: Closed Christmas
Office hours: Twenty-four hours
Affiliation: HI-FUAJ
Extras: Laundry, meals ($), breakfast, deck, TV, bar, game room

Insiders' tip:
Get your mustard elsewhere

Gestalt:
Hot dog

Flags greet the visitor to this hostel, a bland building outside downtown Dijon. The beds here come in quads (there are thirteen of 'em) or larger dorm rooms (of which there are seven). Breakfast is always included, and lunch and dinner are served for a charge. You can also visit a little booth where local food products are sold. Or check out the farmers' market, which sets up Tuesday, Friday, and Saturday, to get your fresh live chickens.

For recreation, the dreaded karaoke bar rears its ugly head here. Grab a beer and plug your ears. If you can't stand that, there's table tennis in the game room.

Dijon itself is alternately cute and blah, depending on what you like; culturally, it's pretty much a zero, but there are some mildly attractive buildings. And, of course, everybody's selling the ubiquitous mustard for an arm and a leg. Rather than endure tours of mustard factories—is this why you came to France??—make an excursion out into the pretty Burgundy countryside. Spring is especially beautiful.

How to get there:

By bus: Take #5 line and stop at Epirey.
By car: Take either A5, A31, A6, or A38.
By train: Station approximately 3 miles away.

AUBERGE LE ST. JEAN

Place Jean XXIII, B.P. 164, Dole Cedex, Jura, 39101

Phone Number: 03–84–82–36–74

Fax Number: 03–84–79–17–69
Rates: 68 francs per HI member (about $12 US)
Credit cards: None
Beds: 60
Private/family rooms: Yes
Kitchen available: Sometimes
Office hours: Twenty-four hours
Affiliation: HI-FUAJ
Extras: Laundry, restaurant ($), table tennis, TV, library

They serve meals in a restaurant at this hostel, which includes a library and laundry plus a table tennis set. Unusually, all fifty rooms here are either single rooms (forty) or doubles (ten); none have their own en-suite bathrooms, however.

Best bet for a bite: Farmers' markets

Gestalt: Green Pasteurs

The town sports the birthplace of Louis Pasteur (he of pasteurization fame), an old convent, and good farmers' markets on Tuesday, Thursday, and Saturday mornings as well as Friday afternoon. Spring and autumn are the best times of year to savor this mellow area bordering Alsace and the Franche-Comté.

How to get there:

By bus: Take bus to Place St-Jean.
By car: Take the A39, Route Nationale.
By train: From Dole station, walk ½ mile to hostel.

CHATEAU "MON BIJOU" HOSTEL

Route des Chaumieres, Givet, Ardennes, 08600

Phone Number: 03–24–42–09–60

Fax Number: 03–24–42–02–44
Rates: 45 francs per HI member (about $8.00 US)
Credit cards: None
Beds: 13
Private/family rooms: Yes
Kitchen available: Yes
Office hours: 5:00 to 8:00 P.M.
Affiliation: HI-FUAJ
Extras: Camping, laundry

We know little about this place, other than the fact that it's a ½ mile outside the village of Givet and has both family rooms and a hosteller kitchen available. It's open year-round, too. Givet sits right on the border of France and Belgium, so sneaking over to check out the Belgian way of life is definitely an option.

Gestalt:
Be-jeweled

Party index:

Fort Chaumont is the primary sight-seeing option of choice in this town, which sits on the Meuse River. If you want to see an atom split, go check out the nuclear power plant that's real close—maybe a little too close for comfort, actually. On second thought, skip it.

How to get there:

By bus: Stop at La Soie, less than 1 mile away.
By car: The RN51 will take you here.
By train: From Givet station, walk ½ mile toward Bon Secours.

LE FOYER HOSTEL

2, rue Andre Maginot, Gray, 70100

Phone Number: 03–84–64–99–20

Fax Number: 03–84–64–99–29
E-mail: le-foyer@wanadoo.fr
Rates: 51 francs per HI member (about $9.00 US)
Credit cards: Yes
Beds: 100
Private/family rooms: Yes
Kitchen available: Yes
Office hours: Twenty-four hours
Affiliation: HI-FUAJ
Extras: Laundry, meals ($), game room, bike storage

Located right in the midle of downtown Gray, this small, small hostel has something for everyone active: table tennis, volleyball, archery, and badminton, among other games. Or you could just sit lounging in the hostel yard on the banks of the river Saône.

Elsewhere in town, you can ride a horse, swat a tennis ball, hike, hire a boat, or check out the local Esperanto Museum (?!)—quite a choice, we'd say.

Gestalt: Shades of Gray

Party index:

How to get there:

By bus: Take bus to Gare Routière.

By car: Call hostel for directions.

By train: Besancon station is nearest. Call hostel for transit route.

FOYER LE VIGNOT

8, rue Jean Sounié, Imphy, 58160

Phone Number: 03–86–90–95–20

Fax Number: 03–86–38–31–87
Rates: 51 to 68 francs per HI member (about $9.00 to $12.00 US)
Credit cards: None
Beds: 20
Private/family rooms: Sometimes
Kitchen available: Yes
Office hours: Twenty-four hours
Affiliation: HI-FUAJ
Extras: Laundry, meals ($), bike storage

They serve meals and maintain a laundry at this hostel, which is conveniently open twenty-four hours a day. Private rooms are available in addition to the bunk beds.

Party index:

How to get there:

By bus: Take bus from Nevers toward Macon, getting off at Andre Dubois stop.

By car: Call hostel for directions.

By train: From Imphy station, walk ½ mile to hostel.

AUBERGE DYNAMO

La Schellimat, Lautenbach, Haut-Rhin, 68610

Phone Number: 03–89–74–26–81

Rates: 37 francs per HI member (about $6.00 US)
Credit cards: None

Beds: 30
Private/family rooms: None
Kitchen available: Yes
Office hours: Call hostel for hours
Season: Weekends and school holidays
Affiliation: HI-FUAJ
Extras: Grill, table tennis, camping

$

Okay, we're declaring this the cheapest hostel in France; skinflints, make a beeline directly here. For the equivalent of about six bucks American, you can sleep in a bunk—and get the use of a kitchen, something you often don't get in places that cost three times this much.

Gestalt: Dynamite

Party index:

It's even located in a handsome chalet-like building in a village at 3,300 feet, another welcome switch from the usual concrete slabs. You can play table tennis or use the grill.

However—this is a biggie—it's only open Saturday, Sunday, and French school holidays! Get the picture? It's seriously schoolkid oriented. Also, there's no electricity. (Okay, so you can't plug in your laptop or a hair dryer. Not that you had one with you anyway.) No private rooms here, either, just three bunkrooms.

And it's a bit inaccessible, via the Munster and Guebwiller valleys.

How to get there:

By bus: Take bus from Kunegek to Maison Forestiere; walk 1½ miles on path to hostel.

By car: From Col du Boenlesgrab, walk 1½ miles on path to hostel.

By train: Mulhouse station, 1½ miles away, is nearest stop.

AUBERGE DE JEUNESSE METZ-PLAGE

1, allée de Metz-Plage, Place de Pontiffroy, B.P. 573, Metz Cedex, 57010

Phone Number: 03–87–30–44–02
Fax Number: 03–87–33–19–80
E-mail: aubjeumetz@aol.com
Rates: 68 francs per HI member (about $12 US)
Credit cards: Yes
Beds: 62
Private/family rooms: Yes
Kitchen available: Yes
Office hours: Twenty-four hours

Affiliation: HI-FUAJ
Extras: Laundry, meals ($), breakfast, bikes, bureau de change, bar, patio, tours, grill, TV, conference room

What else could you want? Free breakfast, free bikes to crank around town on, free walking tours, access to a lake and a beach, friendly staff, a bureau de change, and terrific dinners. Basically this has everything we wanted in a French hostelling experience, and more.

There are two single rooms and one double, neither with its own bathroom, plus ten bunkrooms that average about six beds each. The bathroom line can get a bit long at times, but that's the single drawback here as far as we can tell.

To take advantage of the kitchen here, visit the local farmers' market, which sells fresh wares all days of the week with the best of the bunch held on Saturday.

Metz itself is an outstanding place to spend some quality time on one of its many lakes; you can either splash along the shores or venture out on a small sailboat. You can also rent bikes to toodle around the countryside from the hostel.

A great deal in a great location.

Gestalt: Amazing Metz

Hospitality:

Party index:

How to get there:

By bus: Take 3 or 11 bus to Place de Pontiffroy and walk to hostel.

By car: From downtown Metz, take rue des Benedictins to end and turn right; hostel is around bend.

By train: Metz station, ½ mile away.

FOYER CARREFOUR

6, rue Marchant, Metz, Moselle, 57000

Phone Number: 03–87–75–07–26

Fax Number: 03–87–36–71–44
E-mail: ascarrefour@wanadoo.fr
Rates: 68 to 91 francs per HI member (about $12 to $16 US)
Credit cards: Yes
Beds: 60
Private/family rooms: Yes
Kitchen available: Yes
Office hours: Twenty-four hours
Affiliation: HI-FUAJ
Extras: Breakfast, laundry, meals ($), bike storage

This is the other Hostelling International joint in the university town of Metz, the downtown location near the city cathedral and other central attractions. It's a little big, noisy, and sterile—but you're likely to get a single to yourself. Breakfast is included, and other meals are served for a charge.

Party index:

The aforementioned cathedral is a a real beaut: You can find only two cathedrals in France that are taller, and the painter Marc Chagall contributed some important works to it. Metz also leads France as a center of technology, by the way, which explains why the Ramblin' Wreck of Georgia Tech has a campus located here. You might see lots of computer programmer types and engineers strolling about. It's pretty exciting, we know, but try to keep your cool.

How to get there:

By bus: Take Circuit B bus to Ste. Segolene and walk 50 yards to hostel; or take 3, 4, 5, 7, 9, 11, 24, 25, or 29 bus to Place D'Armes.

By car: Call hostel for directions.

By train: Metz station, 1 mile away.

MULHOUSE HOSTEL

37, rue de l'Ilberg, Mulhouse, Haut-Rhin, 68200

Phone Number: 03–89–42–63–28

Fax Number: 03–89–59–74–95
Rates: 46 francs per HI member (about $8.00 US)
Credit cards: Yes
Beds: 74 (summer); 64 (winter)
Private/family rooms: Yes
Kitchen available: Yes
Office hours: 8:00 A.M. to noon; 5:00 to 11:00 P.M.
Affiliation: HI-FUAJ
Extras: Meals ($), camping, TV, table tennis, bike rental

This place emphasizes socializing through sports, what with its volleyball, basketball, and table tennis facilities and proximity to nearby fishing and miniature golf. The French have made even a humble game like minigolf into an opportunity for serious competition.

Gestalt:
Full house

Party index:

Hostellers choose from one single room, one double, two quads, and ten reasonably sized bunkrooms; there's also one handicapped-accessible room, and a campground. Meal service helps you get to know fellow hostellers, too.

Mulhouse itself is the second largest city in Alsace, and the most industrial. Its reputation is for textiles, so factories dominate the landscape. The city boasts of the town hall's trompe l'oeil facade, which could provide maybe ten minutes' worth of sight-seeing entertainment. For actual hours of enjoyment, check out the botanical park; some say it's pretty darned good.

How to get there:

By bus: Take 1 or 2 bus to Hericourt or Salles des Sports.
By car: Call hostel for directions.
By train: Mulhouse station, 2 miles.

AUBERGE LUTTENBACH

102, rue de la Gare, Munster, 68140

Phone Number: 03–89–77–34–20

Rates: 48 francs per HI member (about $8.00 US)
Credit cards: None
Beds: 30
Private/family rooms: Yes
Kitchen available: No
Office hours: Call hostel for hours
Affiliation: HI-FUAJ
Extras: Breakfast, catered meals for groups, bike storage

Gestalt: Munster mash

Party index:

All we know about this fairly obscure hostel (to foreigners, anyway) is that breakfast is included, they have private rooms in addition to the bunks, and they do catering when you're part of a large group.

The hostel serves as a good rest stop for those interested in scrambling up the Fecht Mountains, though. In addition, the town used to be a place to "take the waters," meaning that people flocked here from miles

KEY TO ICONS

- Attractive natural setting
- Ecologically aware hostel
- Superior kitchen facilities or cafe
- Offbeat or eccentric place
- Superior bathroom facilities
- Romantic private rooms
- Comfortable beds
- Editors Choice Among our very favorite hostels
- A particularly good value
- Wheelchair-accessible
- Good for business travelers
- Especially well suited for families
- Good for active travelers
- Visual arts at hostel or nearby
- Music at hostel or nearby
- Great hostel for skiers
- Bar or pub at hostel or nearby

around to seek rejuvenation in the area's many spas. Now, instead, rejuvenate your palate in early October when the burg throws its annual Tourte Festival. (Perhaps this savory pie is the antecedent for the famed tourtiere pie found throughout Québec.) Also stop by the Tuesday to Saturday farmers' market to pick up some of the famed mellow Munster cheese.

How to get there:

By bus: Take Transport Hautes Vosges bus line, which stops 1¾ miles before hostel.

By car: Take the A35 to Colmar, then the D414 to Munster.

By train: From Luttenbach station, walk 200 yards to hostel.

CHÂTEAU DE REMICOURT HOSTEL

149, rue de Vandoeuvre, Villers les Nancy, Nancy, 54600

Phone Number: 03–83–27–73–67

Fax Number: 03–83–41–41–35
Rates: 48 francs per HI member (about $8.00 US)
Credit cards: Yes
Beds: 60
Private/family rooms: Yes
Kitchen available: No
Office hours: 8:00 A.M. to 10:30 P.M.
Affiliation: HI-FUAJ
Extras: Meals ($), breakfast, bike rentals, TV, bike storage, bar

Calling this hostel a "castle" seems a bit of a stretch, but it's still nicely located in a green park and not too too far (okay, 2½ miles) from downtown Nancy. Imagine yourself as one of the Dukes of Lorraine as you stroll the grounds.

Party index:

People tend to stick around here all day, and those who love the nightlife don't return until the wee hours of the morning because of the lack of lockout or curfew, which isn't necessarily a good thing, but the digs here are okay. The beds break down this way: two single rooms, six doubles, three triple rooms, five quads, and three larger bunkrooms. Free breakfast is a bonus, and you get access to a television, too. They'll rent bikes if you want to explore Nancy on two wheels, and the park often hosts concerts and other activities.

Nancy is rather bland except for the remarkable Place Stanislas, named for good old Stanislas of Poland (apparently he married into the Hapsburg family), who was a rather self-indulgent ruler. His gourmet sensibility is seen throughout the region in the form of the memory-stirring Madeleine cookie, rum baba, and a plethora of restaurant stars in the *Michelin Guide*. The cafe scene here rivals that of Paris; the architecture is reminiscent of the School of Nancy founded by Emile Gallé, who introduced the tradition-breaking Art Nouveau style.

Swing by Les Soeurs Macarons for a cheap but yummy treat; this pastry shop has been running since after the French Revolution and was founded by nuns. Can't get much more French than THAT.

How to get there:

By bus: Take 4, 16, or 26 bus to St-Fiacre, Lycée Bio, or Basch stop.

By car: Take the A33 and exit at 2B, Nancy Barbois.

By train: Nancy station, 2 miles.

CENTRE DE EUROPÉEN DE RENCONTRES

6, rue du Général Rottembourg, Phalsbourg, 57370

Phone Number: 03–87–24–37–37

Fax Number: 03–87–24–13–56
Rates: 49 to 120 francs per HI member (about $9.00 to $20.00 US)
Credit cards: Yes
Beds: 70
Private/family rooms: No
Kitchen available: No
Office hours: 8:00 A.M. to 10:00 P.M.
Affiliation: HI-FUAJ
Extras: Meals ($), bar

Gestalt:
Over the Phalsbourg
Party index:

Meals are served at this surprisingly large hostel, bikes are rented, and it's wheelchair accessible. There are even some family rooms available.

Phalsbourg is actually a burg in the department of Lorraine, yet it sits right on the border of Alsace, putting it just 6 miles from the bigger city of Saverne with more restaurants and nightlife.

If you're sticking around, take your picnic to the fortified wall after you trip through the bellicose Military Museum. Later, balance all that war imagery with a peaceful walk through the Vosges; there are two national parks to help put you in a good mood as you scramble though peat bogs and up hills.

How to get there:

By bus: Take Rémy Bentz bus line, which stops at Gare de Phalsbourg.

By car: Take the A4 and exit at Phalsbourg/RN4.

By train: Lutzelbourg station, about 2 to 3 miles away, is closest stop.

PONTARLIER HOSTEL

2, rue Jouffroy, Pontarlier, Doubs, 25302

Phone Number: 03–81–39–06–57

Fax Number: 03–81–39–06–57
Rates: 48 francs per HI member (about $8.00 US)
Credit cards: None
Beds: 72
Private/family rooms: Yes
Kitchen available: Yes
Season: January 1 to November 15; December 26 to December 31
Office hours: 8:00 A.M. to noon; 5:30 to 10:00 P.M.
Affiliation: HI-FUAJ
Extras: TV, stereo, table tennis, bar

The hostel is located in the middle of Pontarlier village. The rooms here come in several different shapes and sizes. There are five private double rooms—three of which have their own bathrooms—plus two triples, two quads, and six dorm rooms.

Best bet for a bite:
Local cheese merchant (fromagerie)

Insiders' tip:
Distillery nearby

Party index:

For recreation of the indoor sort, they've got a television and stereo and sometime organize dances; a small game room area is also maintained for hostellers.

How to get there:

By bus: Take Mont Jura bus line from Besançon, and ask driver to stop at Auberge.

By car: Call hostel for directions.

By train: Hostel is very close to station.

CENTRE INTERNATIONAL DE SÉJOURS ET DE RENCONTRES

Parc Leo-Lagrange, Allee Polonceau, Reims, Marne, 51100

Phone Number: 03–26–40–52–60

Fax Number: 03–26–47–35–70
Rates: 65 to 82 francs per person (about $11 to $14 US); doubles 130 francs (about $22 US)
Credit cards: Yes
Beds: 150
Private/family rooms: Yes
Kitchen available: Yes
Season: January 2 to December 24

Office hours: Twenty-four hours
Affiliation: HI-FUAJ, UCRIF
Extras: Laundry, meals ($), TV, volleyball, conference room

This boring brick building, although a modern facility and in good condition, is very quiet and devoid of personality or excitement. The presence of a conference room gives you an idea right away that this place is not exactly party central.

About the closest they come is serving meals and throwing out a volleyball net. There's a television room, of course, but that's about it.

Party index:

Reims itself (say "remm") is of some interest, however, home to six museums and a nationally renowned art school. Also of note, all that bubbly stuff produced in France's Champagne region is shipped here to Reims first before it's distributed elsewhere in the world. Sniff the air and you may get a buzz. And, of course, you'd be remiss if you didn't sample some on your way to the famous Cathédrale Nôtre-Dame. Go see it as the sun goes down: The rose windows are magnificent.

How to get there:

By bus: Take B, E, M, or N bus to Colin stop. Or take H bus to Pont de Gaulle stop.

By car: Call hostel for directions.

By train: Reims station, 1 mile.

CENTRE JEUNESSE PIERRE BÉRÉGOVOY

4, rue Fontenille, Roanne, Loire, 42300

Phone Number: 04–77–72–52–11

Fax Number: 04–77–70–66–28
Rates: 69 francs per HI member (about $12.00 US)
Credit cards: None
Beds: 60
Private/family rooms: Yes
Kitchen available: Yes
Office hours: 8:00 A.M. to noon; 2:00 to 10:00 P.M.
Affiliation: HI-FUAJ
Extras: Laundry, meals ($), breakfast, TV, table tennis, bar, patio

Breakfast is now included—and required—here at the Roanne hostel, but they've also raised the price to compensate. Not everyone will be happy with the change, but there you go.

Oh, well. This institutional brick hostel seems well enough appointed and includes a bar, laundry, and meal service. The television room and table tennis present in so many French hostels are here as well. You'll sleep in either a single room (one of two—both with private baths), a double (two also, again with private baths), or a quad room (fourteen, although only two have private baths).

Party index:

Since you have a kitchen to play chef in, mosey over to the Roanne farmers' market Tuesday or Friday morning at the Hôtel-de-Ville (city hall) and, fittingly enough, Place du Marché (Market Place). Grab some fruit and cheese and bliss out.

How to get there:

By bus: From Roanne, take 1 or 10 bus to Clemenceau stop.

By car: From the N7, take avenue de Paris to Place St-Etienne and then to rue Fonteville.

By train: From Roanne station, walk ½ mile to hostel.

TROYÉS-ROSIÈRES AUBERGE DE JEUNESSE

Chemin Ste. Scholastique, Rosières, Aube, 10430

Phone Number: 03–25–82–00–65 or 03–25–49–07–38

Fax Number: 03–25–72–93–78
E-mail: troyes-rosieres@fuaj.org
Rates: 65 francs per HI member (about $11 US)
Credit cards: None
Beds: 104
Private/family rooms: Yes
Kitchen available: Yes
Office hours: 7:00 A.M. to 11:00 P.M.
Curfew: 11:00 P.M.
Affiliation: HI-FUAJ
Extras: Meals ($)

This homey-looking place packs in more than a hundred beds but manages to do it nicely. There are sixteen quad rooms, eight dorm rooms of five to eight beds apiece, and one larger dorm as well; they serve meals, let you use the kitchen, and have a nice lawn.

Gestalt:
Sweetheart Rosières

Party index:

One caveat: Staff tells us it's wildly popular with French school groups during certain times of the year, so beware.

How to get there:

By bus: Take 8 bus and stop at Liberté.
By car: Take the A25 or A5, then the RN71 or the RN77.
By train: Station is about 2½ miles away.

AUBERGE DE JEUNESSE SAINT-MIHIEL

12, rue sur Meuse, Saint-Mihiel, Meuse, 55300

Phone Number: 03–29–89–15–06

Rates: 41 francs per HI member (about $7.00 US)
Credit cards: None
Beds: 60
Private/family rooms: Yes
Kitchen available: Yes
Season: April to November 30
Office hours: 6:00 to 10:00 P.M.
Affiliation: HI-FUAJ
Extras: Meals ($)

We didn't hear much about this one, just that it serves breakfasts and dinners—both for a charge—and has some family room space among the sixty beds.

But we can brief you about the area. Located in the Meuse River district, Saint-Mihiel is a small village near the bigger town of Verdun. It's on the sacred church trail in Lorraine, with a couple of churches to take a look at if you're in the mood for quiet contemplation (or the mood to find a good rest room).

Party index:

The Saint-Mihiel Abbey Church was started way back in the twelfth century, with additions being completed by the late seventeenth century. The other church of interest here is the younger Saint-Etienne church, started and completed in the sixteenth century. French sculptor Ligier Richier worked for twenty years on *Entombment* during the Renaissance, and lucky you can view it here for just five minutes if you want; nobody'll care.

If you've seen enough holy art, go have a rip-roarin' time at the Domaine de Marsoupe fun park nearby. You should be able to kill lots of time on rides created solely for the purpose of making you lose your expensive French lunch.

How to get there:

By bus: Take Nancy–Verdun bus line and stop at Auberge de Jeunesse.
By car: Call hostel for directions.
By train: Commercy station, 11 miles, is nearest stop.

CHATEAU DES ROHANS

Saverne, Bas-Rhin, 67700

Phone Number: 03–88–91–14–84

Fax Number: 03–88–71–15–97
E-mail: saverne@fuaj.org
Rates: 65 to 83 francs per HI member (about $11 to $14 US); doubles 166 francs (about $28 US)
Credit cards: None
Beds: 86
Private/family rooms: Yes
Kitchen available: No
Season: January 15 to December 19
Office hours: 8:00 to 10:00 A.M.; 5:00 to 10:00 P.M.
Lockout: 10:00 A.M. to 5:00 P.M.
Curfew: 10:00 P.M.
Affiliation: HI-FUAJ
Extras: Meals ($), TV, breakfast

This really is a château! An eighteenth-century castle, one that stands right on Saverne's town square and includes a museum within its walls, but part hostel nonetheless. Cool.

Insiders' tip:
Thursday flea market

Gestalt:
Saverne and surely

Party index:

Inside, it's pretty good bunking. You climb a bunch of stairs until you arrive on the third floor, which is quiet for sleeping but still has great views of the area. Rooms range from two single rooms to one double, one triple, three quads, and ten bunkrooms; they're simpler (obviously) than the palace part of the building but still decent accommodations.

Breakfast comes free, and they'll serve you another meal for a fee. There's a television room, though we can't imagine why anyone would hang out there in this part of France. After all, you're near the Parc Regional des Vosges du Nord—if you like fresh air—or Saverne's lively little restaurant scene, if you're just hungry for local chow and human company. Hang by the fountain in the square afterward and watch the world going by.

Toward the end of June you might happen upon the Festival de la Rose; it's usually the third or fourth Sunday of this typically floral month. If you're really intent on showing up specifically for this event, contact the local tourist bureau or Maison de la France (French tourist office) for this year's specific date.

How to get there:

By bus: Call hostel for transit route.

By car: Call hostel for directions.

By train: From Saverne station, turn right and walk ⅓ mile to town square. Hostel is on square.

STRASBOURG

Some think Strasbourg is the berries, and others find it unutterably boring. We fall somewhere in between: leaning toward liking it for the lively student life and cafe scene, while admitting that it isn't the most exciting place on Earth. (Zip across the border to Germany for more authentic and interesting towns.)

Anyway, the top hostel in town is also its most central. All three are quite good, for a change, but you won't save much: For some reason, Strasbourg's hostels cost a lot. Oh, well. It's nice to see several great hostels in a city, for a change.

STRASBOURG HOSTELS at a glance

	RATING	PRICE	IN A WORD	PAGE
CIARUS hostel		86 to 177 francs	superb	p.128
Parc du Rhin		72 francs	sylvan	p.129
Auberge René Cassin		72 francs	social	p.127

AUBERGE RENÉ CASSIN

Montagne Verte, 9, rue de L'Auberge de Jeunesse, Strasbourg, Bas-Rhin, 67200

Phone Number: 03–88–30–26–46

Fax Number: 03–88–30–35–16
Rates: 72 francs per HI member (about $12 US)
Credit cards: None
Beds: 280
Private/family rooms: Yes
Kitchen available: Yes
Season: February to December 31
Office hours: Twenty-four hours
Affiliation: HI-FUAJ
Extras: Breakfast, restaurant ($), laundry, TV, jukebox, camping, bike storage

This place, located in an island of greenery 2 miles southwest of central Strasbourg, isn't exactly central. Nevertheless, this is a pretty hoppin' place—the meal service, jukebox, and very large campground on site all see to that—and free breakfast is included.

Of course you can't leave Strasbourg without gobbling some of its famous choucroute (sauerkraut). The Alsatians have taken the humble cabbage to exquisite heights with this savory dish that usually includes locally made sausage and bacon: Vegetarians beware!

Gestalt:
101 Alsatians

Party index:

How to get there:

By bus: Take bus 3 or 23 to Auberge de Jeunesse stop.

By car: From Paris take N4 to Strasbourg; just west of downtown, turn right onto rue de Schnokeloc and go to end; turn left on Route de Schirmeck and make immediate left to hostel.

By train: Strasbourg station, 1 mile.

CENTRE INTERNATIONAL D'ACCUEIL ET DE RENCONTRE UNIONISTE DE STRASBOURG (CIARUS)

7, rue Finkmatt 6700, Strasbourg, Bas-Rhin, 67000

Phone Number: 03–88–15–27–88

Fax Number: 03–88–15–27–89
Rates: 86 to 117 francs per person (about $15 to $30 US); doubles 232 francs (about $39 US)
Credit cards: Yes
Beds: 199
Private/family rooms: Yes
Kitchen available: No
Curfew: 1:00 A.M.
Affiliation: UCRIF
Extras: Breakfast, bar, video games, cafeteria ($)

A UCRIF hostel, this place is easily the closest to town of the three hostels in Strasbourg—and it's just wonderful, possibly one of the best hostels in France. Just remember that you can't reserve by phone on the weekends, a small minus in an otherwise good place.

Party index:

They've got singles, doubles, and dorm rooms with anywhere from three to twelve beds—each with its own kind of pricing; we won't even try to explain the structure.

There's a bar here, and it's fun even if the bars downtown are as good or better, plus they serve you free breakfast. (Other meals can be had for a charge.) As another good bonus, all rooms have their own en-suite shower and bathroom facilities. This place is a dream come true.

How to get there:

By bus: Call hostel for transit route.
By car: Call hostel for directions.
By train: Call hostel for transit route.

CENTRE INTERNATIONAL DE RENCONTRES DU PARC DU RHIN

Rue des Cavaliers, B.P. 58, Strasbourg Cedex, Bas-Rhin, 67017

Phone Number: 03–88–45–54–20

Fax Number: 03–88–45–54–21
E-mail: strasbourg-parc-du-rhin@fuaj.org
Rates: 72 francs per HI member (about $12 US)
Credit cards: Yes
Beds: 221
Private/family rooms: Yes
Kitchen available: Yes
Season: January 1 to November 4; November 30 to December 22
Office hours: Twenty-four hours
Affiliation: HI-FUAJ
Extras: Breakfast, meals ($), bar, disco, TV, table tennis, bike storage

Gestalt: Rhin and dine
Party index:

This hostel, one of two Hostelling International–affiliated joints in Strasbourg, occupies a handsome structure on the banks of the Rhine. (That's Germany over yonder.) Rooms have just three to four beds, and all have their own showers; four wheelchair-accessible quad rooms are also available. Free light breakfast is included with a night's stay and more substantial meals are served.

Get to know your fellow hostellers while swatting a table tennis ball or shooting some hoops—or don some really bad clothing and make like John Travolta in the hostel disco/bar. This place, like the other HI hostel, is pretty social, and for that we applaud it.

It's still a bit pricey, though, considering that Strasbourg is fun but not exactly Paris. Also, it's fully 3 miles from the city's active restaurant and bar scene—and public transit doesn't exactly beat a path out here. Something to consider.

How to get there:

By bus: From downtown, take 2 or 21 bus to Parc du Rhin stop.

By car: From downtown Strasbourg, take Route du Rhin to just before the German border; at Office du Tourisme, turn right (south) onto rues des Cavaliers and follow to end.

By train: Strasbourg station, 2½ miles away.

AUBERGE SALVADOR ALLENDE

3, Place de la Gare, Thionville 57100

Phone Number: 03–82–56–32–14

Fax Number: 03–82–56–16–06
Rates: 51 francs per HI member (about $9.00 US)
Credit cards: None
Beds: 60
Private/family rooms: Yes
Kitchen available: Yes
Office hours: 8:00 to 11:00 A.M.; 5:00 to 9:00 P.M.
Affiliation: HI-FUAJ
Extras: Meals (sometimes), TV, bike storage

Once a military hospital, this fairly spare hostel is nevertheless just a two-minute walk from downtown Thionville (sounds like—and feels like—Yawnville), so if that's where you're headed, you're in good shape here. Public transportation is right around the corner, too.

Services here are pretty limited, though: There's a television room, meals are catered for groups, and breakfast is a possibility if you reserve in advance. There are two double rooms for couples

KEY TO ICONS

- Attractive natural setting
- Ecologically aware hostel
- Superior kitchen facilities or cafe
- Offbeat or eccentric place
- Superior bathroom facilities
- Romantic private rooms
- Comfortable beds
- Editors Choice Among our very favorite hostels
- A particularly good value
- Wheelchair-accessible
- Good for business travelers
- Especially well suited for families
- Good for active travelers
- Visual arts at hostel or nearby
- Music at hostel or nearby
- Great hostel for skiers
- Bar or pub at hostel or nearby

or families, plus ten bunkrooms with an average six beds apiece.

Thionville was an important strategic point during several wars, culminating in construction of a fort that became part of the Maginot Line defense system during the end of the nineteenth century: Yes, history buffs, just in time for the first Big One. So you're standing amid history, even if you don't realize it.

Gestalt:
General hospital

Party index:

For sight-seeing, it's basically potluck; you can probably explore most of what Thionville has to offer in a day. St-Maximin Church has a groovy organ that someone might be playing during the daytime. Or try not to break anything at the Musée de la Tour aux Puces, which sounds like a flea market but is actually the ceramics museum.

How to get there:

By bus: Hostel is near bus station.
By car: Call hostel for directions.
By train: Hostel is near Thionville station.

AUBERGE LES ROCHES

Lieudit Fondronfaing, Ventron, Vosges, 88310

Phone Number: 03–29–24–19–56

Rates: 41 francs per HI member (about $7.00 US)
Credit cards: Yes
Beds: 36
Private/family rooms: Yes
Kitchen available: Yes
Office hours: Twenty-four hours
Affiliation: HI-FUAJ
Extras: Grill, camping, volleyball, laundry

A renovated old farmhouse in a peaceful natural setting, this place features a good kitchen and a few private rooms in addition to the usual bunks. Facilities are pretty spare, but at least they've thought to set up a grill for barbecuing. This place seems good as a rusticating getaway from the city life.

Party index:

How to get there:

By bus: Take bus to Cornimont, 4½ miles away.
By car: Coming from Ventron, go in direction of Ermitage Frère Joseph, then follow the signs.
By train: Kruth station, 6 miles away.

AUBERGE DE JEUNESSE CENTRE MONDIAL DE LA PAIX

Place Monseigneur Ginisty, Verdun 55100

Phone Number: 03–29–86–28–28

Fax Number: 03–29–86–28–82
Rates: 68 francs per HI member (about $13 US)
Credit cards: None
Beds: 69
Private/family rooms: Yes
Kitchen available: Yes
Season: February 1 to December 31
Office hours: 8:00 A.M. to noon; 5:00 to 11:00 P.M.
Affiliation: HI-FUAJ
Extras: Breakfast, cafeteria ($), bar, TV, video games, conference room, laundry

Verdun's hostel, not terribly far from Paris proper, is mostly made up of big dorms, although five of the sixteen bunkrooms are at least reasonably small enough to sometime be converted to private rooms. There are also ten wheelchair-accessible rooms, a thoughtful touch.

Gestalt: Verdun deal

Party index:

This is a handsome structure with great views of the town of Verdun, and breakfast is included with the price of a bed. The TV room, video games, and hostel bar serve as mixers.

Verdun's generally associated with a famous battle that took place during World War I. If you're a history enthusiast, you'll probably ignore the lack of good, frequent transportation here and relive the past at the eerie ossuary, which contains the bones of unknown soldiers.

How to get there:

By bus: Take bus to Centre Mondial de la Paix stop.
By car: Take A4 or N3 to Verdun.
By train: From Verdun station, walk ½ mile to hostel.

AUBERGE DE JEUNESSE VERZY

16, rue du Bassin, Verzy, Marne, 51380

Phone Number: 03–26–97–90–10

Rates: 41 francs per HI member (about $7.00 US)
Credit cards: None
Beds: 48
Private/family rooms: Yes

Kitchen available: Yes
Season: March 1 to November 30
Office hours: 7:30 to 10:00 A.M.; 5:00 to 10:00 P.M.
Affiliation: HI-FUAJ
Extras: Meals ($), store

This hostel's decent, although you'll want to call ahead if you're coming on a weekend: It closes down altogether on certain Sundays. The staff serves three meals a day for a fee, but a kitchen is available, too.

The village produces lots of wine for a small place, and it also is home to an odd-looking grove of beech trees known as the Faux de Verzy, which, for you speakers of French, doesn't mean "false" but rather "faou"—a Latin word for beech. These trees rival California's ancient redwoods: Some of them are known to be well past 1,000 years of age!

Party index:

How to get there:

By bus: Take bus to Beaumont-sur-Vesle stop.
By car: Call hostel for directions.
By train: Reims station, 10 miles.

AUBERGE ZONE DE LOISIRS

Vesoul, Vaivre-Montoille, Haute-Saône, 70000

Phone Number: 03–84–76–48–55 or 03–84–76–22–86

Fax Number: 03–84–75–74–93
Rates: 48 francs per HI member (about $8.00 US)
Credit cards: None
Beds: 72
Private/family rooms: Yes
Kitchen available: No
Office hours: Call hostel for hours
Affiliation: HI-FUAJ
Extras: Restaurant ($), laundry, bar, karaoke, conference room

Quite unusually, this hostel consists of eighteen little wooden cabins with four beds apiece, all located by the shore of an artificial lake (with what one can guess is an artificial beach, too). There's also a karaoke bar; this place must be a vacation getaway for slaphappy French families.

Gestalt:
Vesoul while you work

Party index:

How to get there:

By bus: Take 1 bus to Camping stop.

By car: Drive in direction of Vesoul ouest, then follow direction of Camping Lac.

By train: From Vesoul station, 1 mile to hostel.

AUBERGE CROIX SAINTE-MARTHE

Route de l'Etang, Vézelay, Yonne, 89450

Phone Number: 03–86–33–24–18

Fax Number: 03–86–33–24–18
Rates: 45 francs per HI member (about $8.00 US)
Credit cards: None
Beds: 42 (summer); 10 (winter)
Private/family rooms: Yes
Kitchen available: Yes
Office hours: 5:30 to 10:00 P.M.
Affiliation: HI-FUAJ
Extras: Camping, bike storage

A nice location, half a mile in the hills outside Vézelay, matches the nice hostel here—it's actually, as hostels go, fairly upmarket. Besides the three bunkrooms, there are four quad rooms and a large campground. There's a hostel kitchen, as well. Recreational opportunities are plentiful in the area and include kayaking, walking, sightseeing, and other stuff.

Party index:

The striking Eglise Abbatiale de la Madeleine is a nonsecular reason to visit; you'll be amazed at the frescoes and sculptures inside. The town of Vézelay is a little more decadent, though definitely worth a look for its medieval visage.

How to get there:

By bus: Call hostel for transit route.

By car: Call hostel for directions.

By train: Sermizelles station, 5 miles away.

LA MAISON DES SOEURS

10, rue du Moulin, Woerth, Bas-Rhin, 67360

Phone Number: 03–88–54–03–30

Fax Number: 03–88–09–58–32
E-mail: woerth@fuaj.org

Rates: 48 francs per HI member (about $8.00 US)
Credit cards: None
Beds: 60
Private/family rooms: Yes
Kitchen available: Yes
Season: March 1 to November
Office hours: 8:00 to 10:00 A.M.; 5:00 to 11:00 P.M.
Affiliation: HI-FUAJ
Extras: Meals ($), camping, laundry, catered meals for groups, grill

A very handsome hostel, this one, in typical Alsatian style and standing among green trees. But it's geared toward groups—witness the catered meals for groups only and the badminton and volleyball facilities. Lone hostellers can take comfort in the grill and free breakfast.

Gestalt:
Woerth it

Party index:

Repeat: it's ONLY OPEN WEEKENDS. There, considered yourself warned.

There are four quad rooms here and five bunkrooms, most of which share bathrooms; a few, however, do have their own facilities.

How to get there:

By bus: Take bus company CTE lines #15 and #17.
By car: Call hostel for directions.
By train: Hagenau station, 9 miles away.

THE FRENCH ALPS

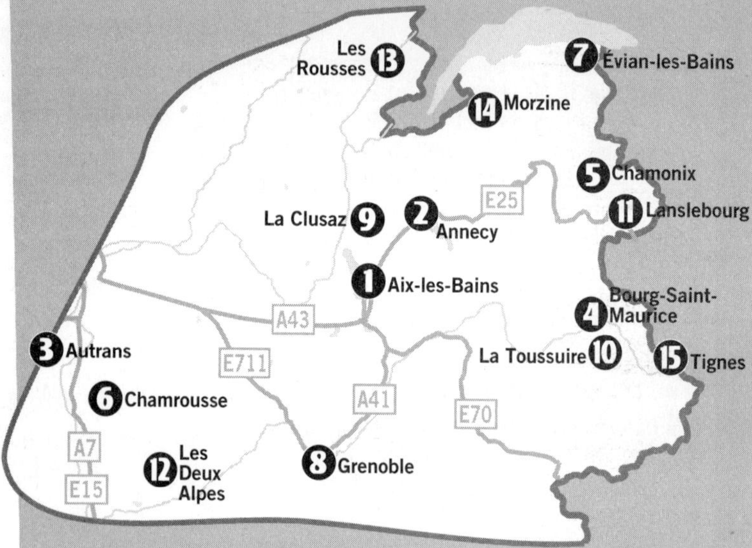

Page numbers follow town names.

THE FRENCH ALPS

France's Alps are spectacular, all right, and the hostels here are usually good enough to meet the challenge of the scenery. Be aware, though: At a few of these places, you need to become a "member" of the hostel and then stay at least one week. Great if you want a protracted outdoors experience, not so great if you're just passing through.

But if you're here, it's pretty lively. Almost every one of these places has a bar, a restaurant, ski or bike rental, volleyball, or table tennis. Why? Because the French demand it, that's why. And *you'll* benefit.

AIX-LES-BAINS AUBERGE DE JEUNESSE

Promenade du Sierroz, Aix-les-Bains, Savoie, 73100

Phone Number: 04–79–88–32–88

Fax Number: 04–79–61–14–05
E-mail: aix-les-bains@fuaj.org
Rates: 49 francs per HI member (about $9.00 US)
Credit cards: Yes
Beds: 90
Private/family rooms: Yes
Kitchen available: Yes
Season: February 5 to November 5; December 23 to January 3
Office hours: 7:00 to 10:00 A.M.; 5:00 to 11:00 P.M.
Affiliation: HI-FUAJ
Extras: Laundry, meals ($)

Gestalt:
Aix marks the spot

Party index:

A red, chalet-style building in a field, this wheelchair-accessible hostel is located in prime ski and mountain biking country. They serve meals for a charge and maintain a laundry; private rooms are also available.

How to get there:

By bus: Call hostel for transit route.
By car: Call hostel for directions.
By train: Call hostel for transit route.

Annecy Auberge de Jeunesse
Annecy

(photo courtesy of FUAJ)

ANNECY AUBERGE DE JEUNESSE

4, route du Semnoz, Annecy, Haute-Savoie, 74000

Phone Number: 04–50–45–33–19

Fax Number: 04–50–52–77–52
Rates: 72 francs per HI member (about $12 US)
Credit cards: Yes
Beds: 117
Private/family rooms: Yes
Kitchen available: Yes
Office hours: Twenty-four hours
Affiliation: HI-FUAJ
Extras: Laundry, breakfast, bar, game room, bike storage

This place is well run and brand-new, located near Annecy's (sounds like "antsy") lake, old town, and walking trails. Entry is with key cards, breakfast is included in the dorm price, and everything's kept orderly. Kill two birds with one stone: Hang out in the game room or at the hostel bar while doing your laundry.

Annecy is a pretty little town blessed with a lake and interlaced by canals and brightly painted houses. Cafe life is strong here, though eats are definitely not for the lactose intolerant—fondue and raclette are mainstays. Pick some up at the farmers' market, which hops highest Tuesday and Saturday along rue Sainte-Claire; pick out a Beaufort d'alpage (made high in the mountains and aged for a couple years) or a peppery Tomme de Savoie. Wash 'em down with a well-chosen Jurassic/Rhône-ish wine if your budget allows it.

Who said hostellers didn't know how to eat?

Gestalt: Annecy-schmancy

Cleanliness:

Party index:

How to get there:

By bus: Annecy bus station, 2 miles; take 91 bus to hostel.
By car: Call hostel for directions.
By train: Annecy station, 2 miles; take 91 bus to hostel.

AUBERGE LES HIRONDELLES

Les Gaillards, Autrans, 38880

Phone Number: 04–76–94–77–15

Fax Number: 04–76–94–77–89
E-mail: autrans@fuaj.org
Rates: 48 francs per HI member (about $8.00 US)
Credit cards: None
Beds: 55
Private/family rooms: Sometimes
Kitchen available: No
Office hours: 8:00 A.M. to 12:30 P.M.; 5:00 to 8:00 P.M.
Affiliation: HI-FUAJ
Extras: Pool, tennis, meals ($)

Located within the boundaries of Vercors Park, this one's best for hikers and skiers and is just a teensy walk from the village of Autrans.

Dorms have four to six beds each and are standard issue. They've gone out of their way to make provisions for sporty types—note the nearby presence of a swimming pool and a tennis court. They serve meals for a charge, too.

Gestalt: Autransition

Cleanliness:

Party index:

How to get there:

By bus: Contact hostel for transit route
By car: Take A41 or 43 highway to Villard de Lans exit and continue to Autrans.
By train: Nearest train station is in Grenoble, 25 miles away; contact hostel for transit route.

AUBERGE DE JEUNESSE LA VERDACHE

Seez, Bourg-Saint-Maurice, Savoie, 73700

Phone Number: **04–79–41–01–93**
Fax Number: 04–79–41–03–36
E-mail: seez-les-arcs@fuaj.org
Rates: 51 francs per HI member (about $9.00 US)
Credit cards: Yes
Beds: 80
Private/family rooms: Yes
Kitchen available: No
Season: December 19 to September 30 (individuals); year-round for groups
Office Hours: 8:00 A.M. to 10:00 P.M.
Affiliation: HI-FUAJ
Extras: Meals ($), grill, camping (groups only), pool table, TV, meeting rooms, bar

Gestalt:
Seez the day
Party index:

Not actually in Bourg-Saint-Maurice, but rather 3 miles outside town in the village of Seez, this is a very social hostel despite its oh-so-green location. It features a bar, game room, television, grill, and neat riverside deck—all the stuff you need to make friends fast. They reportedly have nightly grilling parties in summertime.

The building was renovated about five years ago, so it still looks pretty decent. Dorms mostly come six beds to a room; there are also three doubles and three quad rooms. Breakfast is included with your bed, and other meals can be had for a charge.

The staff runs lots of outings, taking groups for rafting and hiking trips in the mountains. If you're really into the Alps in all their

KEY TO ICONS

- Attractive natural setting
- Ecologically aware hostel
- Superior kitchen facilities or cafe
- Offbeat or eccentric place
- Superior bathroom facilities
- Romantic private rooms
- Comfortable beds
- Editors Choice Among our very favorite hostels
- A particularly good value
- Wheelchair-accessible
- Good for business travelers
- Especially well suited for families
- Good for active travelers
- Visual arts at hostel or nearby
- Music at hostel or nearby
- Great hostel for skiers
- Bar or pub at hostel or nearby

Chamonix Auberge de Jeunesse
Chamonix

(photo courtesy of FUAJ)

outdoor splendor, sack out in one of the sixteen covered campsites.

How to get there:

By bus: From Bourg-Saint-Maurice, take Martin bus toward Longefoy to Seez.

Or take bus to Tignes or Val d'Isere, getting off at hostel.

By car: Call hostel for directions.

By train: Bourg-Saint-Maurice station, 2½ miles away.

CHAMONIX AUBERGE DE JEUNESSE

127, Montée J. Balmat, Les Pélerins d'en Haut, Chamonix (Haute-Savoie), 74400

Phone Number: 04–50–53–14–52

Fax Number: 04–50–55–92–34
E-mail: chamonix@fuaj.org
Rates: 65 francs per HI member (about $11 US)
Credit cards: None
Beds: 118
Private/family rooms: Yes
Kitchen available: No
Season: January 1 to October 1; December 10 to 31

Office hours: Twenty-four hours
Affiliation: HI-FUAJ
Extras: Laundry, pool table, table tennis, darts, breakfast

This modern hostel, set in woodland just outside the resort of Chamonix and at the foot of the local Bossons glacier, has great facilities. The views here—of Mont Blanc and other big mountains—are about as outstanding as you're going to get from a French hostel. Even walking up here alongside a river from the chic town gave us goosebumps.

Insiders' tip:
Local chairlift rides

Gestalt:
Chamonix-high

Party index:

Beds come in quad rooms, a welcome change. Angle for the chalet-like building if you can, as it's the best of the bunch, although you really can't go wrong. A delicious breakfast is included with your night's stay, and for once, even the showers were great.

Take note of the activities program offered by the FUAJ organization, basically package deals designed to orient you to the Alps. They include room and board, any equipment you might need, instruction in activities, and transportation. Activities might include skiing or hang gliding—certainly something a novice wouldn't want to undertake alone in this intense terrain.

How to get there:

By bus: From Les Pelerins bus stop, walk 300 yards to hostel; call hostel for transit route.
By car: Take the RN205.
By train: From Les Pelerins station, walk ½ mile to hostel.

CHAMROUSSE AUBERGE DE JEUNESSE

Le Recoin, Chamrousse, Isere, 38410

Phone Number: 04–76–89–91–31

Fax Number: 04–76–89–96–66
E-mail: chamrousse@fuaj.org
Rates: 61 francs per HI member (about $11 US)
Credit cards: Yes
Beds: 85
Private/family rooms: Yes
Kitchen available: No
Season: December 1 to May 1; June 1 to September 15
Office hours: 8:00 to 10:00 A.M.; 5:00 to 10:00 P.M.
Affiliation: HI-FUAJ

Extras: Restaurant ($), bar, game room

This one definitely falls under the category of "ski hostel," though it's also got facilities for warm-weather fun. Set on a shallow, sloping hill, the hostel features ten nice double and triple rooms with en-suite bathrooms, eleven quads—again, each with its own facilities—plus three dorms with five to eight beds apiece.

Party index:

You can store skis here, they include breakfast with your night's stay, and there's a volleyball net for summertime. Raining? No problem. Hit the Euro-style bar or work on your table tennis game. But let's face it, you're here to telemark or watch the annual competitions in Chamrousse.

How to get there:

By bus: Take VFD bus which stops near hostel.

By car: Call hostel for directions.

By train: Grenoble station, 20 miles away, is closest stop; call hostel for transit route.

CENTRE INTERNATIONAL DE SÉJOUR

Avenue de Neuvecelle, B.P. 31, Évian-les-Bains Cedex, Haute Savoie, 74501

Phone Number: 04–50–75–35–87

Fax Number: 04–50–75–45–67
E-mail: jptreil@cur-archamps.fr
Rates: 100 francs per HI member (about $18 US)
Credit cards: Yes
Beds: 50
Private/family rooms: Yes
Kitchen available: Yes
Office hours: Monday to Friday only, 8:00 A.M. to 8:00 P.M.
Affiliation: HI-FUAJ, UCRIF
Extras: Restaurant ($), bar, laundry, TV, pool table, table tennis, volleyball

Évian-les-Bains is located in spectacular countryside, and this hostel is just 1 mile from the town. There's a laundry here, breakfast is included, meals are served, and you're deep in ski and bike country. They've done a nice job of setting up social situations, too—a bar, game room with pool table, volleyball net, and the like give you plenty of opportunities to mix, mingle, imbibe, and perspire (not necessarily in that order).

There are an unusally high number of single rooms here: fifteen, and twelve of them even have some form of private bathroom facilities. Ten double rooms and five triple rooms make up the remainder of the digs—again, all with their very own en-suite bathrooms.

We can't emphasize enough the excellent *stages* (pronounced "stah-zh") programs you can try while staying at France's hostels in the Alps. If you want to try something strenuous and challenging in a low-pressure situation, this is an excellent opportunity: You get room and board plus a gentle ski lesson at a fraction of what instruction in Aspen or Lake Tahoe would cost you.

Gestalt:
Alp-eau

Party index:

Of course, while in town you're going to want to sample the pricey *l'eau de source* (spring water) from right here in Evian that's found on supermarket shelves around the globe. Yep, that's right, you might be able to taste this crystal-clear H_2O right near *la source.*

You'd also be remiss to miss the jumpin' farmers' market that really hits its stride on Tuesday but is also held on Friday.

How to get there:

By bus: Call hostel for transit route.
By car: Call hostel for directions.
By train: From Évian-les-Bains station, walk 1 mile to hostel.

LA QUINZAINE HOSTEL

10, avenue du Gresivaudan, Echirolles (Grenoble), Isere, 38130

Phone Number: 04–76–09–33–52

Fax Number: 04–76–09–38–99
E-mail: grenoble-echirolles@fuaj.org
Rates: 68 francs per HI member (about $13 US)
Credit cards: Yes
Beds: 120
Private/family rooms: Yes
Kitchen available: Yes
Office hours: 7:30 A.M. to 11:00 P.M. (Monday to Saturday); 7:30 to 10:00 A.M.; 5:30 to 11:00 P.M. (Sunday only)
Curfew: 11:00 P.M.
Affiliation: HI-FUAJ
Extras: Laundry, breakfast, meals ($), TV, bar, table tennis, soccer, bikes, meeting room, pool table

Opened in 1968 to coincide with the then-occurring Olympics, this plain two-story building is situated right in Jean Jaurès park about 3 miles outside downtown Grenoble. It's at the foot of rugged mountains, of course.

Facilities are okay, geared toward convenience, although rooms can get a bit tight on space. A couple of single rooms here are equipped with their own bathrooms, but they're generally reserved for wheelchair users. Breakfast comes free with your night's stay; there's an active game room with pool table, bar, and table tennis; a grassy field allows soccer nuts to do their Zidane impressions; and so forth.

Gestalt:
Wall nuts

Party index:

On the downside, there's a curfew—and that's tricky because it's hard to get back here by bus late at night from Grenoble. All in all, this place is pretty well done and therefore overly popular.

Anyone who's nuts about walnuts, by the way, will be thrilled to learn that Grenoble's menus feature them. You can sample walnuts in pastries, wines, and even in a local salad that features greens alongside walnuts, chèvre (goat cheese), croutons, and bacon. Go see 'em growing in the groves surrounding the city. You also might get some discounts in town at a place like the new Musée de Grenoble, which features paintings by some heavy hitters like Matisse and Picasso. Not too shabby.

How to get there:

By bus: From Grenoble, walk 3 miles to hostel or take 8 bus.

By car: Call hostel for directions.

By train: Grenoble station, walk 3 miles to hostel or take 8 bus.

KEY TO ICONS

- Attractive natural setting
- Ecologically aware hostel
- Superior kitchen facilities or cafe
- Offbeat or eccentric place
- Superior bathroom facilities
- Romantic private rooms
- Comfortable beds
- Editors Choice Among our very favorite hostels
- A particularly good value
- Wheelchair-accessible
- Good for business travelers
- Especially well suited for families
- Good for active travelers
- Visual arts at hostel or nearby
- Music at hostel or nearby
- Great hostel for skiers
- Bar or pub at hostel or nearby

CHALET LE MARCORET HOSTEL

Route du Col de la Croix Fry, B.P. 47, La Clusaz, Haute-Savoie, 74220

Phone Number: 04–50–02–41–73

Fax Number: 04–50–02–65–85
E-mail: la-clusaz@fuaj.org
Rates: 51 francs per HI member (about $9.00 US)
Credit cards: Yes
Beds: 85
Private/family rooms: Yes
Kitchen available: No
Season: December 17 to September 26
Affiliation: HI-FUAJ
Extras: Bar, patio, game room, restaurant ($), outings

Two buildings, an old one and a brand-new one, make up this hostel plunked down in a good old Alpine resort town. It's notable mostly for its prime location—amid pastures—and its good on-premises restaurant. Can't splurge? Breakfast costs extra, but it's an all-you-can-eat affair, so hit that at least. There's no curfew here at night, either; you can always get in the door with the pass code after a night out on the village.

The staff organizes an amazing variety of outdoor activites here, including (but not limited to, take a breath) rock-climbing, mountain biking, canyon walking, skiing, snowboarding, cross-country skiing, and—our personal favorite—snowshoeing. Nice to see *les racquettes* being used for once instead of some noisy snowmobile.

In summer try swimming in Lake d'Annecy, known for its warmer-than-normal water temperatures. But remember that this area is superpopular in the summer, and so it brings a whole other breed of tourist who might dampen your visit by their sheer numbers and cluelessness. Better to stop by in the shoulder season, when there's nothing but you and *les montagnes.*

Party index:

If you're around, make sure to get to the Reblochon Cheese Festival, held during the first half of August in La Clusaz. This fest—the French have a fest for just about everything, don't they?—celebrates the nutty succulent cheese, created by locals since around the fourteenth century. Man, that's old!

How to get there:

By bus: From downtown La Clusaz, take bus to hostel.

By car: From Annecy, take A41 approximately 20 miles (32 kilometers) toward Thones to La Clusaz; from Bonneville, drive A40 toward Station des Aravis approximately 15 miles (25 kilometers) to La Clusaz.

By train: From Annecy station, take bus to La Clusaz.

AUBERGE LA TOUSSUIRE

Fontcouverte, La Toussuire, Saint-Jean-de-Maurienne, Savoie, 73300

Phone Number: 04–79–56–72–04

Fax Number: 04–79–83–00–93
Rates: 48 francs per HI member (about $8.00 US)
Beds: 72
Private/family rooms: Yes
Kitchen available: No
Season: November 30 to April 30; July 1 to September 15; November 30 to December 31
Office hours: Call hostel for hours
Affiliation: HI-FUAJ
Extras: Meals ($), movies, TV, table tennis, karaoke, bar, bike storage

All twelve dorm rooms have six beds apiece in this fun hostel, located in the Alpine foothills.

Facilities at the hostel include a bar (open from 6:00 to 11:00 P.M.) with karaoke, meal service, a television room, and a game room. The common space faces south, looking out over the impressive Aiguilles d'Arves range, so you've certainly got scenery galore to gape at between *bieres.* It's an especially good place to bunk up for groups coming on ski outings.

Party index:

How to get there:

By bus: Take RDTS bus to La Toussuire.

By car: From Paris, take the A6 (Paris–Lyon), then A43 (Lyon–Chambery)/RN6.

By train: Saint-Jean-de-Maurienne station, 11 miles away; call hostel for transit route.

LANSLEBOURG/VAL-CENIS HOSTEL

Les Champs, Lanslebourg, Savoie, 73480

Phone Number: 04–79–05–90–96

Fax Number: 04–79–05–82–52
E-mail: valcenis@fuaj.org
Rates: 48 francs per HI member (about $8.00 US)

Credit cards: None
Beds: 75
Private/family rooms: None
Kitchen available: No
Season: December 12 to April 30; June 15 to September 20
Affiliation: HI-FUAJ
Extras: Meals ($), movies, slide shows, parties

A couple of simple buildings built in Savoyard design and tucked beneath impressive scenery, this place is deceptively quiet from the outside. But this isn't a broom closet or hiker's hut; nope, rooms have just two to five beds each and all have their own en-suite bathrooms.

Gestalt: Savoie special

Party index:

Furthermore, the staff is nothing short of amazing when it comes to brokering social activities, hosting crepe and fondue parties, dances, slide shows, and films to get everyone together. A little tame, okay, but you gotta applaud the effort. (Don't wear bobby sox, though.)

Once you actually get outside the building, you're quite close to Vanoise National Park and at the foot of Mount Cenis—so options for sight-seeing, skiing, and hiking abound.

How to get there:

By bus: From Lans le Villard, take bus to Hameau-des-Champs.

By car: Take the N6 (Chambéry/St Jean de Maurienne) to Modane/Lanslebourg.

By train: Modane station, 15 miles away.

LES BRULEURS DE LOUPS HOSTEL

Les Deux Alpes, Isere, 38860

Phone Number: 04–76–79–22–80

Fax Number: 04–76–79–24–15
E-mail: les-deux-alpes@fuaj.org
Rates: 48 francs per HI member (about $8.00 US)
Credit cards: Yes
Beds: 57
Private/family rooms: Yes
Kitchen available: No
Season: December 4 to April 20; June 17 to September 30
Office hours: 8:00 A.M. to 12:30 P.M.; 2:00 to 7:30 P.M.
Affiliation: HI-FUAJ
Extras: Meals ($), bike storage, bar, TV, pool table, grill

Yet another Alpine ski hostel here, decked out with the usual (for France, anyway!) bar, television, pool table, grill, and ski-heads. Rooms come in these configurations: one double, one triple, ten quads, and two dorms with five to eight beds each.

In town, you can do anything from play squash to enjoy a Jacuzzi to ride in a helicopter. Not simultaneously, however.

Gestalt:
Loup the loup

Party index:

How to get there:

By bus: From Grenoble, take VFD bus to Les Deux Alpes.

By car: From Grenoble, take RN 91 to Briancon, then take D213.

By train: Grenoble station, 45 miles away, is closest station; call hostel for transit route.

LES ROUSSES AUBERGE DE JEUNESSE

Le Bief de la Chaille, Les Rousses, Jura, 39220

Phone Number: 03–84–60–02–80

Fax Number: 03–84–60–09–67
Rates: 48 francs per HI member (about $8.00 US)
Credit cards: None
Beds: 50
Private/family rooms: Yes
Kitchen available: Yes
Season: December 20 to April 24; May 11 to September 25
Affiliation: HI-FUAJ
Extras: Meals ($), TV, bar, game room, snowshoes, camping

About 2 miles outside the already speckish hamlet of Les Rousses, this hostel is notable for its very unusual—and this is France we're talking about—no-smoking policy. Right away, they get a little thumb up from us for that; hostellers shouldn't be forced to inhale the unfiltered tar of European cigarettes in the bedroom, in the lounge, or in the kitchen for cripes' sake.

Gestalt:
Rolls Rousses

Party index:

Rooms consist of one double, two quads, and seven dorm rooms of five to eight beds each. You can also camp here for less dough than a bunk. There's a bar, game room, and—yes!—snowshoes (ah, how we love *les racquettes*)—for your enjoyment.

Be sure to stop by the Cooperative Fromagere Les Rousse early in the A.M. to watch local *fermiers* (farmers) churn butter in a wooden barrel twice a week and make dairy products like raclette, crème fraîche, and the unique Morbier cheese with a line of ash going right up the middle. Kinda like the dotted line on the Maine Turnpike.

How to get there:

By bus: From Morez, take bus to Les Rousses.

By car: Call hostel for directions.

By train: From Morez station, 6 miles away, take bus to Les Rousses.

HOLIDAY CAMPUS HOSTEL

La Coutettaz, B.P. 74, Morzine, Haute-Savoie, 74110

Phone Number: 04–50–79–14–86

Rates: 62 francs per HI member (about $11 US)
Credit cards: Yes
Beds: 76
Private/family rooms: Yes
Kitchen available: In summer
Season: December 24 to April 22; June 14 to September 12
Affiliation: HI-FUAJ
Extras: Breakfast, meals ($), game room, bar, TV, grill

Breakfast is included at this dreamy little chalet in an Alpine village. Rooms here come in an assortment of situations: several doubles that come equipped with bathroom facilities, eleven family rooms, and six bunkrooms.

Gestalt:
Morzine scene

Party index:

The bar, television, grill, and game room that you've come to expect here in the Alps are all present and accounted for. Don't forget the meal service, either, although you can use the kitchen during the summer. Take a dip in the pool in balmy July and August.

Go see the Gorges of the Devil's Bridge while you're here, or (if that seems too scary) learn about local fish at the Ecomuseum instead.

How to get there:

By bus: Bus stops close to hostel at the Office du Tourisme.

By car: Take the Bonneville or Cluses exit off the Autoroute Blanche.

By train: Cluses station (18 miles away) and Thonon station (20 miles away) are closest stops. Call hostel for transit route.

AUBERGE LES CLARINES

Les Boisses, Tignes, 73320

Phone Number: 04–79–06–35–07 or 04–79–41–01–93 (reservations)

Fax Number: 04–79–41–03–36
E-mail: tignes@fuaj.org
Rates: 68 francs per HI member (about $12 US)
Credit cards: Yes
Beds: 66
Private/family rooms: Yes
Kitchen available: No
Season: January 1 to January 5; June 29 to December 31
Affiliation: HI-FUAJ
Extras: Meals ($)

This former hotel is a cool place to stay, poised amid high mountains close to the Italian border (the town has more Italy in it than France, we say). The hostel staff is chipper and cheery, they serve a dee-licious dinner, and bedrooms have en-suite bathrooms.

In short, this hostel offers everything you need for a mountain getaway—with or without the family.

Gestalt: Tignes beat

Hospitality:

Party index:

How to get there:

By bus: Get off bus at Tignes les Boisses.

By car: Coming from Albertville, take the RN90 until Moutiers–Bourg-St-Maurice, then take the D902 in the direction of Val d'Isère. The hostel is on the right just after the *barrage* facing the church.

By train: Call hostel for transit route.

CENTRAL FRANCE

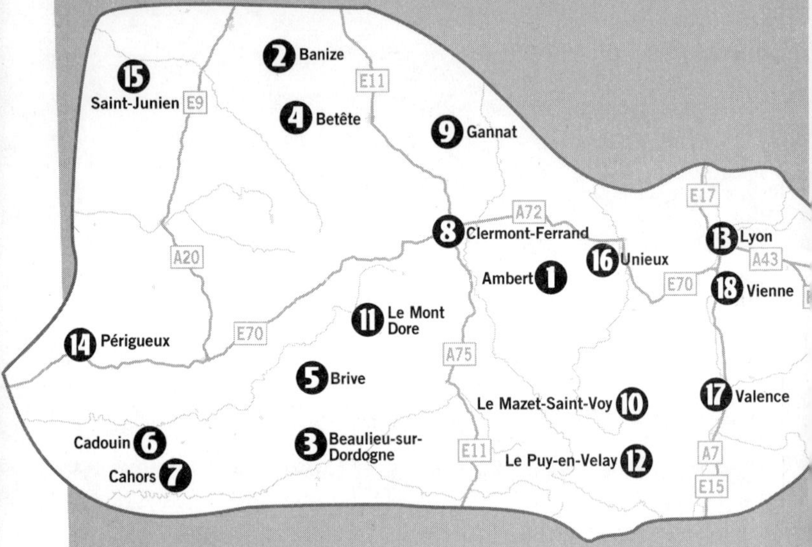

Page numbers follow town names.

CENTRAL FRANCE

France's center: brooding, rocky, rarely visited by tourists. At least you won't be inundated like you would on the coast; most towns are just going about their business like they do every day.

Clermont-Ferrand, the main town here, is hardly worth visiting. Lyon, France's second-biggest city, is better—great eating, for one thing—but still not worth making a major detour. Hostels here are unfortunately pretty blah, used mostly by French schoolkids.

L'AUBERGE DE SAINT MARTIN

Saint-Martin-des-Olmes, Ambert, Puy de Dome, 63600

Phone Number: 04–73–82–01–38

Fax Number: 04–73–82–01–38
Rates: 48 francs per HI member (about $8.00 US)
Credit cards: None
Beds: 48
Private/family rooms: Yes
Kitchen available: Yes
Season: Mid-February to mid-November
Office hours: Call hostel for hours
Affiliation: HI-FUAJ
Extras: Laundry, meals ($), game room, volleyball, bike storage

This hostel's situated in an old convent in the mountains of central France. There are three triple rooms, six quads, and three bunkrooms with five to eight beds apiece. Recreation at the hostel includes table tennis inside and a volleyball court outside. They've got family rooms and a guest laundry, too.

If you're fixin' to fix a picnic, haul your hard-earned francs to the local boulangerie for whole-wheat loaves and then amble on to Abonnec's cheese shop, where you can splurge on some tasty local Saint-Nectaire. Fresh produce can be had each Thursday in the village at the farmers' market, but remember to let them pick it out for you; don't even think of squeezing those melons yourself!

Insiders' tip: Cheese museum in town

Party index:

How to get there:

By bus: Call hostel for transit route.

By car: From Ambert, take the D996 in the direction of St-Etienne for about 3 miles.

By train: Ambert station, 4½ miles away.

CENTRE D'HÉBERGEMENT LOU PÉLÉLÉ (BANIZE HOSTEL)

Centre d'Hébergement et d'Animation Puy Joint, Banize, 23120

Phone Number: 05–55–66–00–63

Fax Number: 05–55–66–02–07
Rates: 48 francs per HI person (about $8.00 US)
Credit cards: None
Beds: 29
Private/family rooms: None
Kitchen available: Yes
Office hours: Twenty-four hours
Affiliation: HI-FUAJ
Extras: Garden, campground, meals ($)

Rooms break out this way: There's one dorm with five beds, another with eight, and then one more with sixteen. And that's it—a tiny place to be sure. But the amenities do include a kitchen, garden, and meal service.

Gestalt:
Banizey does it

Hospitality:

Cleanliness:

Party index:

How to get there:

By bus: From Aubusson station, 10 miles away, take bus toward hostel and then walk 2 miles to hostel.

By car: Take N141, D16, and D10 highways to Aubusson.

By train: From Aubusson station, 10 miles away, take bus toward hostel and then walk 2 miles to hostel.

LA RIVIERA LIMOUSINE HOSTEL

Place du Monturu, Beaulieu-sur-Dordogne, Corrèze, 19120

Phone Number: 05–55–91–13–82

Fax Number: 05–55–91–26–06
E-mail: beaulieu@fuaj.org
Rates: 41 francs per HI member (about $8.00 US)
Credit cards: Yes
Beds: 28
Private/family rooms: None
Kitchen available: Yes
Season: April 1 to September 30
Office hours: 7:00 to 11:00 A.M.; 6:00 to 10:00 P.M.
Affiliation: HI-FUAJ
Extras: Breakfast, laundry, meals ($), bike storage

A cute three-story Swiss-style house built in the fourteenth century, this hostel has great position smack in the middle of a little village on the Dordogne River. The Dordogne is a mere 50 yards away, and while the obvious draw here is the prehistoric caves at Lascaux or Lacave, you can also swim, fish, or canoe the river.

There's one double, one triple, one quad, and three bunkrooms; breakfast is included with every bunk, and all the rooms have en-suite bathrooms no matter what size they are.

Party index:

How to get there:

By bus: Call hostel for transit route.
By car: Take D940 25 miles to the south of Tulle et de Brive.
By train: Bretenouz-Biars station, 4½ miles away.

AUBERGE DE JEUNESSE VERTE (COUNTRY HOSTEL)

Centre d'Animation de l'Abbaye de Prébenoit, Prébenoit, Betête, Creuse, 23270

Phone Number: 05–55–80–78–91

Fax Number: 05–55–80–86–80
Rates: 45 francs per HI member (about $8.00 US)
Credit cards: None
Beds: 51
Private/family rooms: Yes
Kitchen available: Yes
Season: April 1 to November 1
Office hours: 8:00 A.M. to 10:00 P.M.
Affiliation: HI-FUAJ
Extras: Laundry, meals ($), camping

This hostel has fifty-one beds, a laundry, private rooms, and a fairly sizable campground—twenty covered sites and forty more out in the open.

If you've got wheels—four wheels or two—you could do no better than go for a scenic cruise around the Creuse valley (sorry), a place where time has not moved since the eighteenth or nineteenth centuries. Since it's mostly farms around here, be sure to slow down that bike or car for any animals that may take their own sweet time crossing the two-laner.

Party index:

How to get there:

By bus: Call hostel for transit route.
By car: The hostel is on the N940, between Guéret and la Châtre.
By train: La Châtre station, 20 miles away, is nearest stop.

BRIVE AUBERGE DE JEUNESSE

Parc Monjauze, 56, avenue Marechal Bugeaud, Brive, Corrèze, 19100

Phone Number: 05–55–24–34–00

Fax Number: 05–55–84–82–80
E-mail: brive@fuaj.org
Rates: 48 francs per HI member (about $8.00 US)
Credit cards: Yes
Beds: 100
Private/family rooms: Yes
Kitchen available: Yes
Office hours: 8:00 A.M. to 11:00 P.M.
Affiliation: HI-FUAJ
Extras: Meals ($), bike storage, bike rental

This joint's pretty big—more than a hundred beds—so it's no surprise that groups can rent it out. They serve three meals and let you use the kitchen for fixing your own chow.

There's nothing particularly special about Brive, except for maybe the midweek farmers' markets, which bring in great produce from around the Auvergne region. (Skip the liver pâtés, though, unless you like participating in goose torture.) Also, the town is a good stopover point if you begin to tire of quaint French villages and yearn for the big-city splendor of London—the train will deliver you to Calais the next day, and then it's on to England.

Party index:

How to get there:

By bus: From bus station, walk 1 mile to hostel.
By car: Call hostel for directions.
By train: Brive station, 1 mile.

CADOUIN AUBERGE DE JEUNESSE

Place de l'Abbaye, Cadouin, 24480

Phone Number: 05–53–73–28–78

Fax Number: 05–53–73–28–79
Rates: 68 francs per HI member (about $12 US)
Credit cards: None
Beds: 73
Private/family rooms: Yes
Kitchen available: Yes
Season: February 1 to December 15
Office hours: 8:00 A.M. to 1:00 P.M.; 5:00 to 11:00 P.M.; 8:00 A.M. to 11:00 P.M (June 1 to August 31)

Cadouin Auberge de Jeunesse
Cadouin

(photo courtesy of FUAJ)

Affiliation: HI-FUAJ
Extras: Laundry, meals ($), breakfast, bike rentals, TV, VCR, garden, bar

Now this is interesting: a twelfth-century monastery with its own church and cloister . . . and, now, a bar! (It used to be the abbey baker's oven.) Disco dances even take place sometimes. Wild!

Accommodations consist of six doubles, one triple, ten quads, and one larger bunkroom—so you're virtually guaranteed a private room or small room. There's even a seven-bed wheelchair-accessible room with its own bathroom. Breakfast is always included, and each floor has a handy lounge for socializing. The requisite television lounge with VCR is here, as is a game room, playground, and garden.

There's lots to do in the area: everything from exploring ancient caves to canoeing the Dordogne's gentle course or checking out a museum. Plenty of events also hit the area, especially in summertime.

Insiders' tip:
Bicycle museum in town

Gestalt:
Holy spirits

Party index:

How to get there:

By bus: Call hostel for transit route.

By car: Take the D936 (Bordeaux–Bergerac), then the D710 (Périgueux–Le Buisson)/Agen, Villeneuve, then toward Cadouin by the D71.

By train: Le Buisson de Cadouin station, 3 miles.

CAHORS AUBERGE DE JEUNESSE

20, rue Frédéric Suisse, Cahors, 46000

Phone Number: 05–65–35–64–71 or 05–65–53–97–02

Fax Number: 05–65–35–95–92
Rates: 49 francs per HI member (about $9.00 US)
Credit cards: None
Beds: 30
Private/family rooms: Yes
Kitchen available: Yes
Office hours: 9:00 A.M. to 11:00 P.M.
Affiliation: HI-FUAJ
Extras: Laundry, store, meals ($), bike storage

A pretty small hostel, this one—just thirty beds. It used to be a convent. They've got some amenities, though, such as a laundry, small food store, and some family rooms. You can use the kitchen, too.

Gestalt:
Cahors cents

Party index:

Despite its tiny size, the hostel has a lot going for it in terms of location: The river Lot, on which Cahors sits, is particularly lovely. Also check out the interesting Divona spring that abuts the Valentre Bridge.

How to get there:

By bus: Call hostel for transit route.
By car: Call hostel for directions.
By train: From Cahors station, walk ⅓ mile to hostel.

AUBERGE CHEVAL BLANC

55, avenue del'URSS, Clermont-Ferrand, Puy-de-Dome, 63000

Phone Number: 04–73–92–26–39

Fax Number: 04–73–92–99–96
Rates: 48 francs per HI member (about $8.00 US)
Credit cards: None
Beds: 60
Private/family rooms: Yes
Kitchen available: Yes
Season: March 1 to October 31
Office hours: 7:00 to 10:00 A.M.; 5:00 to 11:00 P.M.
Curfew: 11:00 P.M.
Affiliation: HI-FUAJ
Extras: Catered meals for groups, bike storage

This place didn't grade out too well with our hostel-watchers, who whispered to us that it isn't hospitable and has been worn out by the years. If you're still staying, they don't offer much in the way of amenities, either—no breakfast, no meals, no nothin' unless you're coming as part of a group. Phooey to that, we say!

However, if you're looking for volcanoes and massifs, this is your place; just don't expect to head for the Parc Naturel Regional des Volcans via any public transport. There is none. If you're doomed to explore this fairly bleak, uninteresting city—so boring it's got two names—check out the Michelin store where you can absorb more info on tires than you may ever need again.

Gestalt: Massif disappointment

Hospitality:

Party index:

How to get there:

By bus: Bus stops at train station.
By car: Call hostel for directions.
By train: Hostel close to train station.

MAISON DU FOLKLORE HOSTEL

Route de St. Priest, Gannat, 03800

Phone Number: 04–70–90–28–29

Fax Number: 04–70–90–19–22
E-mail: maison.du.folklore@wanadoo.fr
or jeanroche@compuserve.com
Rates: 51 to 68 francs per HI member (about $9.00 to $12.00 US)
Credit cards: No
Beds: 66
Private/family rooms: Yes
Kitchen available: No
Office hours: 8:00 A.M. to 7:00 P.M.
Affiliation: HI-FUAJ
Extras: Meals ($), bar

A medium-sized hostel, this place serves three meals a day and has private rooms in addition to its dorms. Come during July for the World Cultures Festival.

Party index:

How to get there:

By bus: Call hostel for transit route.
By car: Take exit 13 from autoroute and go in direction of Ebreuil (after tollbooth), then follow signs to Gannat.
By train: Gannat station, 1¾ miles from hostel.

AUBERGE FERME DU BESSET

Foyer de Ski de fond de Lisieux, La Bataille, Le Mazet-Saint-Voy, Haute Loire, 43520

Phone Number: 04–71–65–00–35

Fax Number: 04–71–65–00–54
Rates: 48 francs per HI member (about $8.00 US)
Credit cards: None
Beds: 30
Private/family rooms: Yes
Kitchen available: Yes
Office hours: Twenty-four hours
Affiliation: HI-FUAJ
Extras: Laundry, bike storage, TV, game room, classroom

This low-lying stone farmhouse seems tailor made for school groups: It features a really big kitchen, two huge bunkrooms, and areas to play tennis, basketball, or volleyball. Solitary hostellers can store bikes here, use the laundry, and hang out by the tube.

Area attractions include golf, fishing, and especially the local ski trails; winter is definitely busier for this hostel.

Party index:

How to get there:

By bus: Bus stops at Chazot, 6 miles away.

By car: Take the RN88 toward Yssingeaux centre-ville, then to Araules, then to Mazet Saint Voy. Follow signs to Ferme du Besset.

By train: Call hostel for transit route.

AUBERGE LE GRAND VOLCAN

Le Sancy, Le Mont Dore, Puy-de-Dome, 63240

Phone Number: 04–73–65–03–53

Fax Number: 04–73–65–26–39
E-mail: le-mont-dore@fuaj.org
Rates: 51 francs per HI member (about $9.00 US)
Credit cards: Yes
Beds: 90
Private/family rooms: Yes
Kitchen available: In summer
Office hours: 7:30 A.M. to 10:00 P.M.
Affiliation: HI-FUAJ
Extras: Meals ($), laundry, TV, library, game room, camping, bike storage

Built of wood, set in woods, this hostel is useful for rusticating. Room configurations here include eight singles, twelve doubles, two triples, five quad rooms, and six dormitories. You can chill in the game room, library, or television area when you're not poking around the ski and hiking trails in the area.

Gestalt:
Joe versus the volcano

Party index:

This region of France is best known for its distinctive rocks, lakes, and other geological formations created by ancient volcanoes. You can put on your best pair of expensive European walking shoes and set off on many of the trails emanating from town. Load up on trail food Fridays at the farmers' market in Le Mont Dore.

How to get there:

By bus: Get off bus at Sancy stop. Navette Mont Dore runs only in winter and stops at 6:00 P.M.

By car: Call hostel for directions.

By train: Call hostel for transit route.

LE PUY-EN-VELAY HOSTEL

Centre Pierre Cardinal, 9, rue Jules Valles, Le Puy-en-Velay, 43000

Phone Number: 04–71–05–52–40

Fax Number: 04–71–05–61–24
E-mail: cpc@es-conseil.fr
Rates: 41 francs per HI member (about $7.00 US)
Credit cards: None
Beds: 70
Private/family rooms: Yes
Kitchen available: Sometimes
Season: October 1 to March 31 (weekends and school vacations); April 1 to September 30
Office hours: 2:00 to 11:00 P.M.; 8:00 to 10:00 P.M (Sunday only)
Curfew: 11:00 P.M.
Affiliation: HI-FUAJ
Extras: Breakfast ($), TV, conference room

On a big hill, this seventeenth-century building is close to the village's local attractions—a cathedral, a rock, a chapel—and provides the basic comfort requirements for a hostel. They serve breakfast for a fee, have a TV and conference room, and will point you to a nearby laundry. The rooms here consist of thirteen quads plus one big bunkroom, so privacy is possible although not guaranteed.

Be a smart tourist: Avoid the crowds and high prices during the summer months and go in September, especially in this region, where there are some interesting festivals that offer real local color. For starters, the Festival of the Bird King is an all-night affair with everybody done up a la the Renaissance. Beats the heck out of those lame-o Renaissance Fairs back home where the entrance fee is, like, $23 to get in. Also remember that Catholic pilgrims begin a famous walking route to Spain from here (the town, not the hostel), so you're sure to get into some interesting religious conversations.

Gestalt:
Pilgrims' progress

Party index:

How to get there:

By bus: Call hostel for transit route.
By car: Call hostel for directions.
By train: Short distance to hostel from station.

AUBERGE DE JEUNESSE DU VIEUX LYON

41-45 Montée du Chemin Neuf, Lyon, Rhone, 69005

Phone Number: 04–78–15–05–50

Fax Number: 04–78–15–05–51
E-mail: lyon@fuaj.org
Rates: 69 francs per HI member (about $12 US)
Credit cards: Yes
Beds: 180
Private/family rooms: Yes
Kitchen available: Yes
Office hours: Twenty-four hours
Affiliation: HI-FUAJ
Extras: Garden, patio, bar, e-mail, tourist information, bike storage, laundry, breakfast

Lyon's second, more central Hostelling International hostel is every bit as good as the other one! Amazing, especially since this city really isn't a big destination; visitors are usually rushing through on their way to somewhere else.

Breakfast is included (although lunch and dinner aren't served), and you can send or receive e-mail. There's a laundry, patio, extremely popular bar, and garden. No meals are served, but you get use of a kitchen. Views of downtown Lyon from the upper floors are absolutely awesome, and the building has been completely renovated in recent years, so it's in pretty good shape.

The beds consist of two doubles, three quads, and twenty bunkrooms with an average nine beds each—definitely a little too big, the only drawback here. There are also four wheelchair-accessible rooms and a wing of family rooms that can be delightfully cool or dreadfully chilly depending on time of year.

Social life is the real draw here, though. The happy-go-lucky staff keeps the fun (and booze) flowing and serves a free and popular breakfast of juice, cereal, bread, and coffee. Lyon as a town is also surprisingly fun, packed with eateries and clubs and other fun stuff, plus a gorgeous church right beneath your window. Come on, check it out—it's only two hours by fast train from Paris, after all.

Insiders' tip:
Metro is great

Gestalt:
Lyon sleeps tonight

Hospitality:

Cleanliness:

Party index:

How to get there:

By bus: From Part Dieu station, take 28 bus to hostel; from Perrache station, take 31 bus to hostel.

By car: From Paris, take A6 to Lyon; from Marseille, take A7 to Lyon; call hostel for directions.

By subway: From downtown, take D subway line to St-Jean stop.

By train: From Part Dieu station, take 28 bus to hostel; from Perrache station, take 31 bus to hostel.

LYON-VÉNISSIEUX AUBERGE DE JEUNESSE INTERNATIONALE

51, rue Roger Salengro, Vénissieux (Lyon), Rhone, 69200

Phone Number: 04–78–76–39–23

Fax Number: 04–78–77–51–11
E-mail: lyon-venissieux@fuaj.org
Rates: 68 francs per HI member (about $12 US)
Credit cards: None
Beds: 118
Private/family rooms: Yes
Kitchen available: Yes
Office hours: 7:00 A.M to noon; 2:00 to 11:00 P.M.
Lockout: 10:00 A.M. to 5:30 P.M.
Curfew: 11:00 P.M.
Affiliation: HI-FUAJ
Extras: Laundry, meals ($), TV, patio, bar, breakfast, Internet access, snack bar, pool table

This fairly new joint is really nice, reason enough to stop in Lyon for the night even when you're bound for Paris or Nice. The location, however, stinks; it reminds us of some forlorn East Coast expressway burb back home. Oh, well.

Free breakfast is just the start of the experience. The rooms consist of two doubles, sixteen quads, and ten bunkrooms with average of six beds apiece. They're fine. The real star here is the common facilities: There's a bar, Internet access, a cool patio and deck, meal service, and more. It all adds up to superior socializing with the other folks who've landed in Lyon for the night.

The city, by the way, has some of France's biggest outdoor produce markets; hit the one on the banks of the Saone Tuesday through Sunday. The city also possesses a wide array on excellent (though somewhat snobbish) restaurants.

Best bet for a bite: Markets galore

Gestalt: Lyon's share

Hospitality:

Cleanliness:

Party index:

How to get there:

By bus: From Part Dieu station, take 36 bus to highway underpass and walk beneath underpass; hostel is on right. From Perrache station, take 53 bus to hostel.

By car: Take Laurent Bonneway ring road to Lyon Etats-Unis exit, turning toward Vénissieux.

By subway: Take D subway line to Vénissieux.

By train: From Part Dieu station, take 36 bus to hostel. From Perrache station, take 53 bus to hostel.

PÉRIGUEUX HOSTEL

Rue des Thermes Prolongés, Périgueux, Dordogne, 24000

Phone Number: 05–53–06–81–40

Fax Number: 05–53–06–81–49
E-mail: fjtdordogne@wanadoo.fr
Rates: 96 francs per HI member (about $16 US)
Credit cards: None
Beds: 16
Private/family rooms: No
Kitchen available: No
Office hours: 4:00 to 9:00 P.M.
Affiliation: HI-FUAJ
Extras: Meals ($), laundry, breakfast

You've gotta pay for breakfast and lunch here when you check in, so the price is a little steeper, but it still works out to be a decent deal—just don't forget to eat. Beds are mostly quads, which is good, and the rules are laid-back.

However—and it's a big however—this neighborhood's a bit sketchy, so be aware of your surroundings at night and try not to travel alone. Singles are sometimes available.

The town is mostly a base for exploring ruins and local caves. The Musée de Périgord is a good local anthropological lesson, and there's a farmers' market daily.

Gestalt: Captain Caveman

Party index:

How to get there:

By bus: From downtown Périgueux, take 5 bus to Gare Routière-Place Francheville.

By car: Take the RN89 or the RN21.

By train: From Périgueux station, walk ½ mile to hostel.

AUBERGE DE JEUNESSE SAINT-JUNIEN

13, rue de St-Amand, Saint-Junien, Haute-Vienne, 87200

Phone Number: 05–55–02–22–79

Fax Number: 05–55–02–22–79
Rates: 46 francs per HI member (about $8.00 US)
Credit cards: None
Beds: 50
Private/family rooms: Yes
Kitchen available: No
Office hours: 8:00 A.M. to 10:00 P.M.
Affiliation: HI-FUAJ
Extras: Laundry

We haven't heard much about this place at all, so we'll pass on the bare statistics, which don't lie: fifty beds, a few private rooms, an office that stays open all day long, and that's it. There's also a laundry and a kitchen for hostellers' use, but it's definitely not a party joint.

Party index:

How to get there:

By bus: Take Saint-Junien-Limoges bus line; stops 1 mile before hostel.

By car: Take the RN141.

By train: Saint-Junien station; walk 1 mile to hostel.

AUBERGE LE PERTUISET

Les Echandes, Unieux, Loire, 42240

Phone Number: 04–77–35–72–94

Fax Number: 04–77–35–72–94
Rates: 45 francs per HI member (about $8.00 US)
Credit cards: None
Beds: 49

Private/family rooms: Yes
Kitchen available: Yes
Season: May 1 to November 1
Office hours: Call hostel for hours
Affiliation: HI-FUAJ
Extras: Camping, bike storage

Party index:

This summer and fall–only hostel includeds a medium-size campground (twenty-five open-air spots) in its basic facility, which doesn't have a laundry, meal service, or much else other than bunk beds. Family rooms can be arranged.

How to get there:

By bus: Take 2 bus, which stops less than 1 mile before hostel.

By car: From Unieux, after Le Pertuiset follow the peninsula Echandes.

By train: Firminy station, 3 miles away.

L'EPERVIERE AUBERGE DE JEUNESSE

Vacanciel l'Eperviere, Chemin de l'Eperviere, Valence, Drôme, 26000

Phone Number: 04–75–42–32–00
Fax Number: 04–75–56–20–67
Rates: 51 francs per HI member (about $9.00 US)
Credit cards: Yes
Beds: 48
Private/family rooms: Yes
Kitchen available: No
Office hours: Twenty-four hours
Affiliation: HI-FUAJ
Extras: Laundry, meals ($), bike storage, pool, minigolf, bowling

This place looks fun, although a bit tacky—like a little town in fact with its minigolf course access, cafeteria, and pool. Reminded us of a KOA—not that we've ever stayed in one.

Gestalt: Off Valence

Party index:

How to get there:

By bus: From bus station, take 1 bus to Valensolles.

By car: Take the A7 and the A49.

By train: Near Valence station.

VIENNE HOSTEL

Isere, 11, Quai Riondet, Vienne, 38200

Phone Number: 04–74–53–21–97

Fax Number: 04–74–31–98–93
Rates: 48 to 86 francs per person (about $8.00 to $15.00 US)
Credit cards: None
Beds: 56
Private/family rooms: Yes
Kitchen available: Yes
Season: Year-round (closed weekends September 16 to May 15)
Office hours: 9:00 A.M. to 8:00 P.M.
Affiliation: HI-FUAJ, UCRIF
Extras: Catered meals for groups

This hostel's not very big, though it's well located next to the tourist office. Most of the fifty beds come in bunkrooms of three to eight beds apiece, plus there are a few private rooms. It's pretty simple and standard, offering very few of the amenities that most French hostels include.

Party index:

How to get there:

By bus: Take 1, 2, 3, 4, or 5 bus; all stop at tourist office.

By car: Take the RN7, then follow direction toward centre-ville to Vienne.

By train: Vienne station, ⅓ mile.

PROVENCE, CÔTE D'AZUR AND CORSICA

Page numbers follow town names.

PROVENCE, CÔTE D'AZUR, AND CORSICA

The Côte d'Azur is everything you want it to be, but more, too: glitz, glitter, sun, more sun—and miles of god-awful condominiums stretching to the horizon. There are also tons of hostels here, most near public transit; but a few are really hard to get to, making them a frustrating journey unless you want to stick around awhile. Sadly, a couple great hostels in beautiful areas restrict entry to hostellers under age thirty, so we've left them out of this book. Otherwise, hostels along the coast are okay; but the area's wild popularity makes getting a bed in summer almost impossible unless you call months ahead. Do not drop into Nice in July expecting a bunk.

Inland Provence is a whole different story: tempered by the sun and harder to get to without public transit, it's absolutely stunning. Not many hostels here—and you'll probably need a car to reach them—but they give you a taste of the Southern France that the bikinis and sand cover up.

AUBERGE LE JAS DE BOUFFAN

3, avenue Marcel-Pagnol, Aix-en-Provence, Bouches-du-Rhône, 13090

Phone Number: 04–42–20–15–99

Fax Number: 04–42–59–36–12
Rates: 68 francs per HI member (about $12 US)
Credit cards: Yes
Beds: 100
Private/family rooms: Yes
Kitchen available: No
Season: February 1 to December 20
Office hours: Twenty-four hours (summer); 7:00 A.M. to midnight, Monday through Saturday; 7:00 A.M. to noon, 5:00 P.M. to midnight (winter, Sunday and holidays)
Lockout: 10:00 A.M. to 5:00 P.M.
Curfew: Midnight
Affiliation: HI-FUAJ
Extras: Breakfast, laundry, meals ($), volleyball, tennis, bar, bike rentals, foosball, table tennis, basketball court, meeting room

This was a definite mixed-bag experience. First of all, we had to work our way out to the edge of town. Then we dealt with extremely unfriendly staff—and learned about a killer lockout *and* curfew with no exceptions. Man.

The biggest plus, if you wanna call it that: Breakfast is included here. You also can use the local tennis courts, if you've got the energy, or play volleyball on the hostel grounds. The television room seems superfluous with so much culture around. The hostel restaurant is okay, but you might as well dive into the actual restaurants here instead unless you're seriously cramped for cash.

Insiders' tip:
Cybercafe on edge of Aix' Old Town

Gestalt:
Aix marks the spot

Hospitality:

Party index:

What makes this all the more painful is that Aix, of course, is a very cool place to hang out. Not cheap, not at all, but the cafe scene is France's best (well, not counting Paris). Sipping a coffee, eating a leisurely (and expensive) meal, roaming the city's markets . . . you can't get a better slice of Southern French life anywhere. Problem is, that curfew and the tremendous distance you've got to traverse make it tough to enjoy a night out on the town.

Anyone wanna start an indie hostel up here??

How to get there:

By bus: Take 12 bus to Jas de Bouffan Vasarely stop.

By car: From either the A8, A51, or RN7, exit at Aix ouest or Jas de Bouffan, then drive in direction of AJ/Vasarely.

By train: Aix-en-Provence station, 1 mile.

ALLOS AUBERGE DE JEUNESSE

La Foux d'Allos, Allos, 04260

Phone Number: 04–92–83–81–08

Fax Number: 04–92–83–83–70
Rates: 48 francs per HI member (about $8.00 US)
Beds: 72
Private/family rooms: Yes
Kitchen available: No
Season: December 10 to April 25; June 10 to September 15
Office hours: 8:00 A.M. to 11:00 P.M.
Affiliation: HI-FUAJ
Extras: Camping, bike storage, meals ($), bar

Party index:

This joint is definitely a ski bum's hostel, first and foremost; the kind of place that some dude or dudette from Colorado was born to love. Facilities are pretty slim, though at press time there was talk of serving some meals. You basically come here for access to the 5,400-foot Alpine foothills nearby.

How to get there:

By bus: Call hostel for transit route.
By car: Call hostel for directions.
By train: Call hostel for transit route.

ARLES AUBERGE DE JEUNESSE

20, avenue Maréchal Foch, Arles, Bouches-du-Rhône, 13200

Phone Number: 04–90–96–18–25

Fax Number: 04–90–96–31–26
Rates: 77 francs per HI member (about $13 US)
Credit cards: Yes
Beds: 108
Private/family rooms: None
Kitchen available: No
Season: February 5 to December 20
Office hours: 7:00 to 10:00 A.M.; 5:00 P.M. to midnight (summer); 7:00 to 10:00 A.M.; 5:00 to 11:00 P.M. (winter)
Lockout: 10:00 A.M. to 5:00 P.M.
Curfew: Midnight
Affiliation: HI-FUAJ
Extras: Breakfast, cafeteria ($), lockers, bike storage, TV, bike rental

This hostel is a very nice, if a bit expensive, place to begin: It supplies you with a convenient close-to-downtown base to begin your appreciation of Southern France.

The place is well outfitted with a grill, free lockers, free breakfast, and outstanding dinners—one of the best we tasted in a French hostel, and that's saying something! There are twelve bunkrooms, all pretty big. There are no private or couples' rooms.

The only real drawback here is a problem we found in lots of other hostels in Southern France: Surly (or at least unhelpful) staffing sometimes marred the experience a bit.

But we quickly recovered, escaping before the school groups poured in and took over the place. One suggestion to the proprietors: Lose the 'tudes and add some private rooms.

Oops, that's two suggestions.

Insiders' tip: Take 1 bus to Van Gogh's bridge

Gestalt: Sn'Arles

Hospitality:

Party index:

How to get there:

By bus: From downtown, take 3 or 8 bus (Fourchon) toward Fournier to hostel.

By car: Take Nîmes–Marseille expressway to exit 6.

By train: Arles station, 1 mile; from station, take 4 bus to Boulevard des Lices; change to 3 bus and continue to hostel.

AVIGNON SQUASH CLUB HOSTEL

32, boulevard Limbert, Avignon

Phone Number: 04–90–85–27–78

Rates: 58 francs per person (about $10 US)
Credit cards: None
Beds: 40
Private/family rooms: None
Season: February 1 to September 31
Office hours: 8:00 to 11:00 A.M.; 5:00 to 11:00 P.M. (summer, Monday to Saturday only); 9:00 A.M. to 10:00 P.M. rest of year
Affiliation: None
Extras: Bar, squash racquets

This is weird, a hostel located inside a squash club. It's not very clean or good or safe, but at least it's convivial: They'll sell you a drink or rent you a squash racquet. We'd take a cheap hotel instead anytime.

Gestalt: Squashed

Hospitality:

Cleanliness:

Party index:

At least the old city of Avignon makes a good base for the area. If you're like a lot of other smart travelers, you'll start exploring Provence from right here in Avignon: It's a few hours on the superfast TGV train from Paris and makes a less frenetic first-night jumping-off point than Nice or, God forbid, Marseille. Grab a bike in town, or suss out the local buses and trains, and head for the hill towns that Peter Mayle made infamous.

How to get there:

By bus: From Avignon station, take 7 bus to Université stop.

By car: Call hostel for directions.

By train: From Avignon station, call hostel for directions.

CANNES AUBERGE DE JEUNESSE

35, avenue de Vallauris, Cannes

Phone Number: 04–93–99–26–79

Rates: 70 to 80 francs per person (about $12 to $14 US)
Beds: 64
Private/family rooms: Yes
Kitchen available: Yes (2)
Office hours: 8:00 to 10:00 A.M.; 3:00 to 10:00 P.M.
Curfew: Midnight
Affiliation: HI-FUAJ
Extras: TV, laundry

Cannes is located in one of the worst stretches of the Riviera—developmentwise, we mean—so we'd avoid it most days.

Still coming? Well, this hostel seems okay to us. In fact, it's very contemporary. Rooms are small, with four to six beds each, which is good, but they kind of nickel-and-dime you (franc-and-centime you, actually) here by charging extra for everything: breakfast, blankets, sheets, and towels.

Gestalt: Cannes do

Party index: 🎉🎉

How to get there:

By bus: Call hostel for transit route.
By car: Call hostel for directions.
By train: From Cannes station, walk ¼ mile to hostel.

LE CHÂLIT

27, avenue Maréchal Galliéni, Cannes

Phone Number: 04–93–99–22–11

Fax Number: 04–93–39–00–28
Rates: 90 francs per person (about $15 US)
Credit cards: None
Beds: 30
Private/family rooms: None
Kitchen available: Yes
Office hours: 8:30 A.M. to 12:30 P.M.; 5:00 to 10:00 P.M.
Lockout: 10:30 A.M. to 5:00 P.M.
Affiliation: None
Extras: Sheets ($)

Not far from Cannes's train station, this second new hostel in town sounds, from early reports, a little friendlier and better than the other one. But you must reserve in advance to get a bed; you can't just walk in. Dorms are the usual, not segregated by sex; the feel is laid-back, there are fewer rules than in HI hostels, and the facilities appeared nice.

Gestalt: Cannes can

Hospitality: 👍

Cleanliness: 👍

Party index: 🎉

How to get there:

By bus: Call hostel for transit route.
By car: Call hostel for directions.
By train: From Cannes station, call hostel for transit route

AUBERGE LES CALANQUES 👍

La Fontasse, Cassis, Bouches-du-Rhone, 13260

Phone Number: 04–42–01–02–72

Rates: 48 francs per HI member (about $8.00 US)
Credit cards: None
Beds: 65
Private/family rooms: None
Kitchen available: Yes
Office hours: 7:30 to 10:00 A.M.; 5:00 to 10:00 P.M.
Affiliation: HI-FUAJ
Extras: Laundry

This is a supersimple experience, an ecohostel where you trade some creature comforts for stunning scenery and the knowledge that, yes, you're sparing the Earth a little bit of impact.

Location? Natch. We're talking a clifftop spot overlooking the azure Mediterranean that's so nice you'll pee your shorts. And granola types will love the setup: showers without hot water, compost toilets, everything powered by solar energy and built of recycled materials. A simple kitchen and laundry have been added, though they're also in tune with the ecovibes permeating the place.

Bliss out, dude.

Insiders' tip: Nude beaches nearby

Party index:

How to get there:

By bus: Car de Cassis stops 2½ miles away.

By car: Coming from Marseille, take the D559; about 7 miles after, take a right onto a short road. From Cassis, go about 3 miles and take a road leading to hostel on the right.

By train: Cassis station, 4½ miles away.

CORSICA HOSTELS at a glance

	RATING	PRICE	IN A WORD	PAGE
U Tavignanu	👍	80 to 160 francs	orderly	p.175
U Carabellu	👍	75 francs	groovy	p.174
Auberge L'Avillanella	—	68 francs	good	p.176

RELAIS INTERNATIONAL DE LA JEUNESSE U CARABELLU

Route de Pietramaggiore, Calvi, Corse

Phone Number: 04–95–65–14–16

Fax Number: 04–93–80–65–33
Rates: 75 francs per person (about $13 US)
Credit cards: None
Office hours: 9:00 A.M. to noon; 5:00 to 11:00 P.M.
Season: June 1 to September 30
Affiliation: None
Extras: Breakfast, meals ($), sheets ($)

A lively place on the great island of Corsica (La Corse to the French), this hostel comes with good water views, which you'll pay for with a back-breaking uphill hike. Calvi isn't all that interesting—well, actually it's the only thing resembling a metropolis in these parts, so you can find the most diverse food in town—but you could use it as a base for striking out into the (also-striking) Corsican countryside.

Party index: 4

How to get there:

By bus: Call hostel for transit route.
By car/ferry: Call hostel for directions.
By train: Call hostel for transit route.

U TAVIGNANU HOSTEL

Corte, Corse

Phone Number: 04–95–46–16–85

Fax Number: 04–95–61–14–01
Rates: 80 to 160 francs per person (about $14 to $27 US)
Beds: 16
Private/family rooms: No
Office hours: Twenty-four hours
Affiliation: None
Extras: Breakfast ($), meals ($), camping

Small but good describes this place in the city of Corte. It's run by folks who are kindly, not wild partiers. They offer two meals a day for a price, keep the sixteen bunk beds clean, and just generally make it a good experience.

Best bet for a bite:
Casino Supermarket

Gestalt:
Of Corse

Party index: 2

How to get there:

By bus: Call hostel for transit route.
By car/ferry: Call hostel for directions.
By train: Call hostel for transit route.

AUBERGE L' AVILLANELLA

Poggio Mezzana, Corse, 20230

Phone Number: 04–95–38–50–10

Fax Number: 04–95–38–50–11
Rates: 68 francs per HI member (about $12 US)
Credit cards: None
Beds: 100
Private/family rooms: Yes
Kitchen available: Yes
Season: May 1 to October 30
Office hours: 7:30 A.M. to 11:00 P.M.
Affiliation: HI-FUAJ
Extras: Bike rentals, laundry, meals ($), breakfast, library, camping, bike storage

This place looks pretty well equipped, and although the town of Poggio Mezzana's not exactly on the usual quickie hosteller itinerary of Corsica, it does seems worth consideration if you're backroading around the big island.

Gestalt:
On Corse

Party index:

Situated in a park near ocean and mountain, the hostel serves free breakfast with all beds and has added en-suite bathrooms to all the bunkrooms. Family rooms are possible, too. Among the amenities: a small library, meal service, camping, and bikes for rent.

There are tons of outdoor possibilities here—from hill walking to horseback trips to more aquamarine pursuits.

How to get there:

By bus: From Bastia, take to Poggio Mezzana.
By car: Call hostel for directions.
By ferry: Take ferry from Marseille to Bastia, then bus from Bastia to Poggio Mezzana.
By train: Call hostel for transit route.

FONTAINE-DE-VAUCLUSE AUBERGE DE JEUNESSE

Chemin de la Vignasse, Fontaine-de-Vaucluse, Vaucluse, 84800

Phone Number: 04–90–20–31–65

Fax Number: 04–90–20–26–20
Rates: 65 francs per HI member (about $11 US)

Fontaine-de-Vaucluse Auberge de Jeunesse

Fontaine-de-Vaucluse

(photo by Martha Coombs)

Credit cards: None
Beds: 50
Private/family rooms: Yes
Kitchen available: Yes
Season: February 15 to November 15
Office hours: 7:30 to 10:00 A.M.; 5:00 to 11:00 P.M.
Lockout: 10:00 A.M. to 5:00 P.M.
Affiliation: HI-FUAJ
Extras: Laundry, bike rentals, camping, breakfast, catered meals for groups, grill

Located in a quiet, simple two-story stone house, this hostel's superbly positioned—it's located in a marvelous cycling area, France's best in our opinion, an area rich with history, food, and scenery.

Flowery fields and old olive trees surround the complex, which is overlooked by huge rugged peaks; in short, this is rural France, baby. The hostel itself is kinda standard but extremely well run; rooms come in four quads, four dormitories with five to eight beds apiece and one larger dorm room. The services here include meals, bicycle rentals, free breakfast, and a laundry, plus access to a communal grill. There's also a campground.

The outdoor kitchen is cool (literally so in summer), the family rooms nice, and the common room a great place to meet others. In short, this place has everything you'd want in a small rural hostel.

It's an experience. It's also quite popular with piles of schoolkids—and not just French ones—so be sure to book ahead.

Best bet for a bite: Super U

Insiders' tip: Great weekend market in l'Isle-sur-la-Sorgue

Gestalt: Fontaine of youth

Party index:

Downtown Fontaine is one of the cuter French towns you'll find. Hang out by the placid green river, which trickles off those craggy peaks, or sit on a *terrasse* in town drinking *pastis.* Cyclists will feel they've died and gone to heaven, as we mentioned; head for other hyphenated towns in the area like l'Isle-sur-la-Sorgue.

How to get there:

By bike: From village, ride across bridge along route de Cavaillon to junction with route Touristique de Gordes. Turn left and follow signs to hostel.

By bus: From Avignon, take bus to Fontaine-de-Vaucluse.

By car: From Paris, take A7 to Avignon exit; continue on D22 to D24, then follow D24 to Fontaine-de-Vaucluse. From South of France, take A7 to Cavaillon exit, and take D24 to Fontaine-de-Vaucluse.

By train: Isle-sur-la-Sorgue station, 5 miles away; call hostel for transit route. From Avignon station, take bus to Fontaine-de-Vaucluse.

AUBERGE ST. RAPHAEL-FRÉJUS

Chemin du Counillier, Fréjus, Var, 83600

Phone Number: 04–94–53–18–75

Fax Number: 04–94–53–25–86
Rates: 65 to 80 francs per HI member (about $11 to $14 US)
Credit cards: None
Beds: 120
Private/family rooms: Yes
Kitchen available: Yes
Office hours: 7:00 to 10:00 A.M.; 6:00 P.M. to midnight (summer); 7:30 to 10:00 A.M.; 5:30 to 11:00 P.M. (winter)
Lockout: 10:00 A.M. to 6:00 P.M.
Curfew: 11:00 P.M.
Affiliation: HI-FUAJ
Extras: Camping, breakfast, meals ($), grill, table tennis, conference rooms

You couldn't possibly beat the green, beachside setting of this gorgeously located hostel on the French Riviera—even better, it's so well run that we'll go ahead and call it one of the better hostels in

France. You won't break your piggybank to stay here, either, and management (by a husband-and-wife team) is incredibly friendly and helpful, despite limited English.

Rooms—two singles, four quads, four medium dorms, and five bigger ones—are all okay and all thankfully come with en-suite bathrooms; some even have stunning views of the cliffs and fields nearby. Unfortunately the kitchen's only available in winter; it converts to a basic restaurant in high season. Your compatriots will be a cool mix of Euros, Americanos, and French folks—fun but not raucous, so you'll get to sleep at night. Must be that Mediterranean air.

There's plenty to do in the morning, too. Walk a mile to town and check out the heavily French crowd in Fréjus and Saint-Raphaël, who are here to soak up sun and wine in laid-back Provence. Or take a shuttle to the beach. Or speed over to Ventimiglia, Italy, by train for a different experience and even better food.

Another very popular option is to day-trip over to Saint-Tropez and/or Cannes, where the scenery is gorgeous and the air is thick with cell phones, gold cards, and topless bathers. You can get there several ways—hydrofoil ferry is quickest, or you can take a longer bus trip right from the hostel.

Best bet for a bite:
Monoprix in town

Insiders' tip:
Funky Internet place in town

Hospitality:

Cleanliness:

Party index:

One added bonus at this place is the huge campground (try 450 campsites!), one of the best hostel campgrounds in all of Europe—if your goal is making friends and seeing great sights while saving a buck, check it out for sure.

Do take note, though, that it's quite some distance from the local bus/train station to the hostel, at least an hour's walk—and that can be a hot walk in summertime, down a long driveway that seems never to end. The hostel runs a shuttle once a day at 6:00 P.M.; it returns first thing in the morning. For fun you might try taking the boat to ritzy Saint-Tropez (ignore the snobby looks) or a bus to Les Calanques, the reddish cliffs that overlook the Mediterranean and make for some primo hiking.

What, breakfast is included with every bunk? Okay, okay, we'll even forgive them for locking us out all day and locking the door at 11:00 P.M. sharp.

You heard it here first. Be there or be square.

How to get there:

By bus: Hostel bus runs once per night from station. Call hostel for details.

By car: Call hostel for directions.

By ferry: Fréjus ferry dock, 1 mile.

By train: Saint-Raphaël station, 3 miles; hostel bus runs once per night. Call hostel for details.

AUBERGE LA ROCHETTE

Les Quatres Vents, Route de la Gare, Guillestre, Hautes Alpes, 05600

Phone Number: 04–92–45–04–32

Fax Number: 04–92–45–04–32
Rates: 48 francs per HI member (about $8.00 US)
Credit cards: None
Beds: 65
Private/family rooms: Yes
Kitchen available: Yes
Season: December 1 to September 30
Office hours: Call hostel for hours
Affiliation: HI-FUAJ
Extras: Meals ($), laundry, camping, bike storage

Not much to report about this place, other than its position in the high country of Provence—in the Alps, really—and the availability of both a laundry and meal service. Family rooms and a self-catering kitchen are also available. Camping is also available should you want to commune with *la nature.*

Party index:

How to get there:

By bus: Call hostel for transit route.
By car: Call hostel for directions.
By train: Guillestre-Mont Dauphin station.

AUBERGE IMMENSE BOTTE DE PAILLE

Route de la Maline, La Palud-sur-Verdon, Alpes de Haute Provence, 04120

Phone Number: 04–92–77–38–72

Fax Number: 04–92–77–38–72
Rates: 66 francs per HI member (about $11 US)
Credit cards: None
Beds: 67
Private/family rooms: Yes
Kitchen available: Yes
Season: March 1 to October 31
Office hours: 5:00 P.M. to 10:00 A.M.
Affiliation: HI-FUAJ
Extras: Laundry, breakfast, catered meals for groups, camping, bike storage

This medium-size hostel is pretty inaccessible unless you've got a car, but if you make it this far, you're rewarded with fewer crowds than more popular Alps stops and plenty of nature to go around. Free breakfasts are included with your bunk, family rooms can be arranged, and they've got a laundry and campground, too.

Gestalt: Alpenglow

Party index:

How to get there:

By bus: From Marseille, take bus to Castellang (Monday, Wednesday, Saturday only); or call hostel for transit route.

By car: From Nice or Grenoble, take route Napoléon highway to Castellane, then take D952 to La Palud.

By train: Manosque station, 45 miles away, is closest stop; call hostel for transit route. From Marseille station, take bus to Castellang (Monday, Wednesday, Saturday only).

AUBERGE SERRE-CHEVALIER

Serre Chevalier-Les Bez, B.P. 2, La Salle-les-Alpes, Hautes-Alpes, 05240

Phone Number: 04–92–24–74–54

Fax Number: 04–92–24–83–39
E-mail: serre-chevalier@fuaj.org
Rates: 48 francs per HI member (about $8.00 US)
Credit cards: Yes
Beds: 147 (summer), 127 (winter)
Private/family rooms: Yes
Kitchen available: Sometimes
Office hours: 8:00 A.M. to midnight; 8:00 A.M. to 10:00 P.M. (low season)
Affiliation: HI-FUAJ
Extras: Meals ($), camping, bar, disco, bike storage

We were surprised to learn how large this place is, but the big building at the foot of mountains is ideal for skiers and hardcore hikers and mountain bikers, so perhaps we shouldn't have been. This place is simple, but social—a couple of the vaulted-ceiling rooms conceal a bar and disco! They serve meals, but that means you can't use the kitchen except on Sundays, when the hostel restaurant is closed.

Gestalt: Mountain momma

Party index:

Walking, skiing, and cycling trails leave right from the hostel. They don't rent bikes or skis here, however.

How to get there:

By bus: Take bus toward Rignon to Villeneuve la Salle stop.
By car: Call hostel for directions.
By train: Briançon station, 5 miles away.

AUBERGE LE TRAYAS

9, avenue de la Véronese, Le Trayas, Theoule-sur-Mer, Alpes-Maritimes, 06590

Phone Number: 04–93–75–40–23

Fax Number: 04–93–75–43–45
Rates: 48 francs per HI member (about $8.00 US)
Credit cards: None
Beds: 110
Private/family rooms: Yes
Kitchen available: Yes
Season: February 15 to January 2
Office hours: 8:00 to 10:00 A.M.; 6:30 to 9:30 P.M.
Lockout: 10:00 A.M. to 5:00 P.M.
Affiliation: HI-FUAJ
Extras: Meals ($), laundry, camping, bike storage

Lesser known than the wonderful hostel in nearby Fréjus, this one's an option when that joint happens to be booked full—and don't be surprised if that happens should you come without an advance booking in midsummer. But be forewarned that the hostel doesn't take advance reservations by phone.

Party index:

One problem here—probably the reason there's usually room at the auberge—is that it's isolated and a bit of an uphill hike from the train station. Things are fairly plain here, but meals are served, and there's a laundry and very small campground.

The advantageous location is pretty close to Cannes, which looks like a set for *Lifestyles of the Rich and Famous* and hosts that annual film festival. The beaches around can be really good, but development blights the hillsides. This isn't a destination in and of itself, but you might find it relaxing after Nice or Marseille.

How to get there:

By bus: From Saint-Raphaël, take bus to Auberge Blanche stop.
By car: Take the RN98 in the direction of Le Trayas.
By train: Le Trayas station; take bus to hostel stop and walk 1 mile to hostel.

MANOSQUE HOSTEL

Parc de la Rochette, Manosque, Alpes de Haute-Provence, 04100

Phone Number: 04–92–87–57–44

Fax Number: 04–92–72–43–91
Rates: 48 francs per HI member (about $8.00 US)
Credit cards: None
Beds: 60
Private/family rooms: Yes
Kitchen available: Yes
Office hours: Call hostel for hours
Affiliation: HI-FUAJ
Extras: TV, camping, meals ($), volleyball, grill

This joint, located in a sports park, obviously is ideal if you want a weekend getaway from Paris; as such, most of the guests tend to be French folks on holiday. You can play tennis, fish, spike volleyballs, even try that distinctively Provençal sport of *petanque* (known as boules or bocce in other places).

Party index:

If you're lucky, you'll score one of the two doubles; otherwise, it's one of the nine dormitories, none of which are so big that you'll get lost. A small campground, grill, television room, and meal service keep things rolling along here.

The Luberon region made famous by British author Peter Mayle isn't too too far away from this hostel by car (forget trying to get around by public transit, though), and the gorges of Verdon are another popular stop for natural-wonder gawkers.

How to get there:

By bus: Take 35 bus to Centre-Ville stop.
By car: Call hostel for directions.
By train: Manosque station, 2½ miles away.

AUBERGE BONNEVEINE

47, avenue Joseph-Vidal (Impasse du Dr. Bonfils), Marseille, Bouches-du-Rhône, 13008

Phone Number: 04–91–73–21–81

Fax Number: 04–91–73–97–23
E-mail: marseille@fuaj.org
Rates: 49 to 72 francs per HI member (about $9.00 to $12.00 US)
Credit cards: Yes
Beds: 150

Private/family rooms: Yes
Kitchen available: No
Season: February 1 to December 31
Office hours: Twenty-four hours
Curfew: 1:00 A.M.
Affiliation: HI-FUAJ
Extras: Meals ($), breakfast, laundry, lockers, bar, bike rentals

As it's almost on the beach, this hostel is the first pick in town of the Euro-beach bums—you know the type: wraparound shades, Jetsons-era rave clothes, cigarettes perpetually dangling out of their mouths, and attitudes out to here. So if you, too, want to hang with a young, partying crowd, by all means come.

Gestalt: Marseille what?

Safety:

Party index:

Breakfast is included with your bed here, they serve meals, and there's a laundry for washing your bathing suit afterward.

Be warned, though, that crime is a problem in the area—and at the hostel. Use the lockers they offer, but also take other precautions; even lockers aren't crook-proof. In fact, since you're in the heart of the Marseille waterfront, some extra caution is definitely in order. This workabout area is about as diverse as any you'll find in France—a sweltering melting pot of cultures and economic classes all scrabbling to wheel and deal themselves into a better (if not exactly straight-arrow) life.

This might be the town where the expression "thick as thieves" was invented, so be very, very careful at night. Heck, even during the daytime, try to travel with a group.

How to get there:

By bus: Take 44 bus to Place Bonnefons stop.

By car: Call hostel for directions.

By subway: Take #2 Metro (subway) line to Prado stop.

By train: Marseille/St-Charles station, 3 miles; from station, take #2 Metro (subway) line to Rond Point du Prado stop.

CHATEAU DE BOIS-LUZY

Allée des Primeveres, Marseille, Bouches-du-Rhône, 13012

Phone Number: 04–91–49–06–18

Fax Number: 04–91–49–06–18
Rates: 48 francs per HI member (about $8.00 US)
Credit cards: None
Beds: 90 (summer), 80 (winter)
Private/family rooms: Yes

Kitchen available: Yes
Office hours: 7:30 A.M. to noon; 5:00 to 10:30 P.M.
Lockout: Noon to 5:00 P.M.
Curfew: 10:30 P.M.
Affiliation: HI-FUAJ
Extras: Meals ($), laundry, TV, bike storage

This nineteenth-century mansion is much superior to the beachside hostel in town. Know why? It's pretty darned far out of town, that's why! Try almost 5 miles from the smoggy city center. But if you can negotiate public transit and strap on your walking shoes—or somehow have brought a car to the coast (are you nuts??)—then this is hostel heaven: simple, clean, attractive, and above all peaceful.

Rooms come in a variety of shapes, sizes, and colors. You've got your four double rooms, your four triple rooms, and your five quad rooms. Finally, there are eight dorm rooms—but none has more than eight beds, and most have about six.

The facility is surrounded by green fields, some of which are used for sports contests. Plenty of shops and restaurants are nearby, too, though they won't be anywhere as cheap or gritty as the stuff you can get right in the heart of Marseille. Ah, well, what price paradise?

Gestalt: Marseille hey!

Cleanliness:

Party index:

How to get there:

By bus: Take 6 or 8 bus to J. Thierry or Marius-Richard stop.
By car: Call hostel for directions.
By train: Marseilles/St-Charles station, 3 miles; call hostel for transit route.

MENTON AUBERGE DE JEUNESSE

Plateau St-Michel, Menton, Alpes-Maritimes, 06500

Phone Number: 04–93–35–93–14

Fax Number: 04–93–35–93–07
Rates: 68 francs per HI member (about $12 US)
Credit cards: None
Beds: 80
Private/family rooms: None
Kitchen available: No
Season: February 1 to November 30
Office hours: 7:00 A.M. to noon; 5:00 P.M. to midnight; 7:00 to 10:00 A.M.; 5:00 to 11:00 P.M. (winter)
Lockout: 10:00 A.M. to 5:00 P.M.
Curfew: Midnight

Affiliation: HI-FUAJ
Extras: Laundry, breakfast, meals ($)

Set high enough that it commands splendid views of the Riviera coast, this hostel's a real sleeper—"Menton? Where's that??"—but a winner. It's close enough to the action that you'll get a relaxing shot of coastal scenery and sea breeze without the requisite crowds, hassle, and tourist crush of Nice, Cannes, et al.

But bring those walking shoes: To get here, you hike a mile from the train station, and then UP hundreds of steps to get to the front door. We had heard in advance it was a nice climb. Well, it is! Take your time making the ascent: As you rise, each new step will bring you another slice of color from the trees, roofs, leaves, and water. Truly beautiful.

Cleanliness:

Party index:

Breakfast is included with your bunk, which will certainly be in one of the dorm rooms—there are no couple or private accommodations here. They serve other meals for a charge, offer a laundry, and maintain a television room—but we don't know why anyone would hang out there.

There are two or three things to do in fairly sleepy Menton: One, hightail it to Cannes, Nice, etc., for a day trip. We didn't do this. Two, walk to the beach—yeah, we did, and it was really nice and uncrowded. Three, best of all, grab that wallet (don't waste a Eurail pass day) and make a short day excursion across the border into Italy, which is only minutes away. The food gets better, people and buildings look different, but the coast is still as wonderful as it was back in France.

KEY TO ICONS

- Attractive natural setting
- Ecologically aware hostel
- Superior kitchen facilities or cafe
- Offbeat or eccentric place
- Superior bathroom facilities
- Romantic private rooms
- Comfortable beds
- Editors Choice Among our very favorite hostels
- A particularly good value
- Wheelchair-accessible
- Good for business travelers
- Especially well suited for families
- Good for active travelers
- Visual arts at hostel or nearby
- Music at hostel or nearby
- Great hostel for skiers
- Bar or pub at hostel or nearby

How to get there:

By bus: Take bus to Camping St-Michel stop.
By car: Call hostel for directions.
By train: Menton station, 1 mile.

MONTPELLIER AUBERGE DE JEUNESSE

Rue des Ecoles Laiques, Montpellier, Hérault, 34000

Phone Number: 04–67–60–32–22

Fax Number: 04–67–60–32–30
Rates: 68 francs per HI member (about $12 US)
Credit cards: Yes
Beds: 89
Private/family rooms: Yes
Kitchen available: No
Season: January 9 to December 15
Office hours: 7:30 A.M. to 2:00 A.M.
Lockout: 10:00 A.M. to 1:00 P.M.
Curfew: 2:00 A.M.
Affiliation: HI-FUAJ
Extras: Breakfast, meals ($), bar, TV, grill, pool table, bike storage

The young, studenty crowd that frequents this joint is somehow appropriate in a town famous around France for its big university. As a hostel, though, it's only so-so.

That's partly because of the bar, so common in bigger French hostels, and here a rowdy center of social life. We liked that—but sleeping later was tough, as the bar rages until at 2:00 A.M., and the noise carries. Dorms and bathrooms aren't too great, either, probably because this place is so popular that they've become worn out. We counted three double rooms, five triples, five quad rooms, three medium-size dorms, and three much bigger dorms.

At least breakfast is included with your bed. A lot of thought has gone into socializing here—there's a grill, television room, and pool table in addition to the bar—so you're sure to meet some Europeans. Just deal with the noise, occasional chaos, and sometimes stubborn management and you'll survive.

Hospitality:

Party index:

How to get there:

By bus: Take 2, 3, 5, 6, 7, 9, or 16 bus to Usulines stop.
By car: Call hostel for directions.
By train: From Montpellier station, walk ½ mile to hostel, or take 2, 3, 5, 6, 7, 9, or 16 bus to Usulines stop.

NICE-AREA HOSTELS at a glance

	RATING	PRICE	IN A WORD	PAGE
Auberge de Nice		68 francs	Anglo	p.188
Clairvallon Relais		72 francs	nice	p.190
Backpackers' Hostel		70 francs	uncomplicated	p.189
Hôtel Belle Meunière Hostel		76 to 100 francs	groovy	p.191
Hôtel Les Orangiers Hostel		75 to 100 francs	handy	p.192
Espace Magnan		50 francs	horrific	p.190

AUBERGE DE NICE

Route Forestiere du Mont-Alban, Nice, Alpes-Maritimes, 06300

Phone Number: 04–93–89–23–64

Fax Number: 04–92–04–03–10
Rates: 68 francs per HI member (about $12 US)
Credit cards: None
Beds: 56
Private/family rooms: None
Kitchen available: Yes
Office hours: 7:00 A.M. to noon; 5:00 P.M. to midnight
Lockout: noon to 5:00 P.M.
Curfew: 12:30 A.M.
Affiliation: HI-FUAJ
Extras: Laundry, TV, bike storage, breakfast

Superpopular and packed with North Americans, this isn't the place to meet French people. It's miles above the city, in fact, in a beautiful but distant setting on the edge of the mountains that frame the coast below and shield it from bad weather. You'll get to know those mountains personally.

It's pretty nice, if simple. All beds here come as bunks, most of them pretty reasonable size; there's only one monster dorm here. Breakfast is included, too, plus we used a kitchen for fixing lunch and dinner. (The all-day lockout ensured that we didn't eat lunch on the premises, however.)

Don't forget that the latest bus from downtown Nice leaves at something like 8:00 P.M., so figure this into any evening plans; it's one hell of an expensive cab ride if you miss the bus. At least you're a reasonable walk (downhill) to the beach. Just remember: When you walk back, it's gonna be very steeply uphill.

Best bet for a bite: Along rue de la Préfecture

Gestalt: Nice try

Party index: 2

How to get there:

By bus: From downtown, take 14 or 17 bus toward Mont Boran to auberge (hostel) stop.

By car: Call hostel for directions.

By train: Nice station, 2½ miles away; take 14 or 17 bus toward Mont Boran to auberge (hostel) stop.

BACKPACKERS' HOSTEL

32, rue Pertinax, Nice

Phone Number: 04–93–80–30–72

Rates: 70 francs per person (about $12 US)
Beds: 20
Private/family rooms: None
Affiliation: None

This laid-back place, right on top of a restaurant that serves good fish stew, is okay. The chief amenity is its closeness to Nice's train station (but, then again, so are a couple of other hostels). Everything is just okay here, nothing special.

Gestalt: Back on track

Party index: 3

How to get there:

By bus: From bus station, take any bus to train station. Exit train station and turn left on avenue Theirs. At avenue

KEY TO ICONS

- Attractive natural setting
- Ecologically aware hostel
- Superior kitchen facilities or cafe
- Offbeat or eccentric place
- Superior bathroom facilities
- Romantic private rooms
- Comfortable beds
- Editors Choice Among our very favorite hostels
- A particularly good value
- Wheelchair-accessible
- Good for business travelers
- Especially well suited for families
- Good for active travelers
- Visual arts at hostel or nearby
- Music at hostel or nearby
- Great hostel for skiers
- Bar or pub at hostel or nearby

Malaussena, cross street and take a right. Continue to hostel on left.

By car: Contact hostel for directions.

By train: Exit train station and turn left on avenue Theirs. At avenue Malaussena, cross street and take a right. Continue to hostel on left.

CLAIRVALLON RELAIS INTERNATIONAL DE LA JEUNESSE

26, avenue Scuderi, Cimiez (Nice), Alpes-Maritimes, 06000

Phone Number: 04–93–81–27–63

Rates: 72 francs per person (about $12 US)
Credit cards: None
Beds: 220
Office hours: Call hostel for hours
Lockout: 9:30 A.M. to 5:00 P.M.
Curfew: 11:00 P.M.
Affiliation: None
Extras: Garden, pool, breakfast, tennis and basketball courts, TV

Gestalt: Far and away

Cleanliness:

Party index:

This big, fancy-looking place seemed good to us, outfitted with such nice extras as a decent pool, a garden, and tennis and basketball courts. We're talking champagne taste on a beer budget. Breakfast is included with all beds, too, which all looked clean. We've heard mixed reviews about the staff, but we didn't have any problem with them.

The only drawback here is the location, almost 3 miles outside the central city/beach area.

How to get there:

By bus: From downtown, take 15 bus to hostel.
By car: Call hostel for directions.
By train: Call hostel for transit route.

ESPACE MAGNAN HOSTEL

31, rue Louis-de-Coppet, Nice, Alpes-Maritimes, 06000

Phone Number: 04–93–86–28–75

Fax Number: 04–93–44–93–22
Rates: 50 francs per person (about $9.00 US)
Season: June 15 to September 15
Lockout: 10:00 A.M. to 6:00 P.M.
Curfew: Midnight
Affiliation: None

We can't imagine things getting much worse than this. Yeah, it might be the most central hostel of the four in Nice. But geeeez! It's, like, the worst hostel in France. So don't bother.

Things are abysmal here. Dorms are way too big, staff shouts down hostellers, facilities are poorly maintained and not clean. Yes, it's a bed, but we'd rather stay in a hotel than bunk here. And Magnan is the most boring part of Nice—just a bunch of blocky buildings, nothing at all of interest to keep you here. Give it up. Try somewhere else. Get a hotel. Anything.

Gestalt: Nice and desist

Hospitality:

Party index:

How to get there:

By bus: Take 3, 9, 10, 12, 22, or 24 bus to hostel.
By car: Call hostel for directions.
By train: Call hostel for transit route.

HÔTEL BELLE MEUNIÈRE HOSTEL

21 avenue Durante, Nice

Phone Number: 04–93–88–66–15

Rates: 76 to 100 francs per person (about $13 to $17 US)
Credit cards: Yes
Affiliation: None
Extras: Garden, breakfast, patio

Hostellers seem to like this unaffiliated hotel-and-hostel so far, which has some dorms with en-suite bathrooms and some without. The garden and the patio are extremely popular, and breakfast is included with your night's stay.

Gestalt: Belle du jour

Party index:

How to get there:

By bus: From bus station, take any bus to train station. Walk straight out front of train station down avenue Durante; hostel is on right.
By car: Contact hostel for directions.
By train: Walk straight out front of train station down Durante; hostel is on right.

HÔTEL LES ORANGIERS HOSTEL

10b, avenue Durante, Nice

Phone Number: 04–93–87–51–41

Fax Number: 04–93–82–57–82
Rates: 75 to 100 francs per person (about $13 to $17 US); doubles 200 to 210 francs (about $34 to $35 US)
Credit cards: Yes
Beds: Number varies
Private/family rooms: Yes
Season: January 1 to October 1; December 1 to 31
Affiliation: None
Extras: Breakfast ($)

This is another independent hostel in Nice, located just steps from the train station; in fact, it's practically across the street from the Belle Meunière (see page 191).

Gestalt: Orangier Crush

Party index:

The dorms are four- to six-bedded, and—get this—the rooms have refrigerators (yes) and shower rooms (yes). It's getting popular with backpackers as the word spreads, though, so book ahead if you really wanna come.

How to get there:

By bus: From bus station, take any bus to train station. Walk straight out front of train station down avenue Durante; hostel is on left.

By car: Contact hostel for directions.

By train: Walk straight out front of train station down avenue Durante; hostel is on left.

NÎMES AUBERGE DE JEUNESSE

Chemin de la Cigale, Nîmes, Gard, 30900

Phone Number: 04–66–23–25–04

Fax Number: 04–66–23–84–27
E-mail: nimes@fuaj.org
Rates: 68 francs per HI member (about $12 US)
Credit cards: Yes
Beds: 76
Private/family rooms: Yes
Kitchen available: Yes
Season: April 1 to September 30
Office hours: Twenty-four hours (summer); 7:30 A.M. to 11:30 P.M. (winter)
Affiliation: HI-FUAJ

Extras: Breakfast, meals ($), bar, garden, table tennis, shuttle, camping, bike rentals, laundry

French hostelling strikes again! Supersocial and well run, this hostel revolves around its bar—filled with Euros—but also enjoys good staffing, a nice location up on a big-g-g-g hill, and a fun outdoor garden and grove of olive trees.

It's not so big that you'll lose yourself. Dorms are coed and quite clean, arranged usually in rooms of three to eight bunks apiece; there are also two singles and two doubles up for grabs, plus a campground. Free breakfast is included with every bed, and things stay lively; the experienced staff controls things without putting a damper on all this fun. They serve meals, maintain a small game room, rent bikes, and will point you to such places as the close-by botanical park or the famous Roman ruins a little farther distant. You can also rent a kayak around here.

Alternative-transportation types will enjoy checking out the nonvehicular and Roman Pont du Gard, which you can hike or bike across or canoe under for a memorable snapshot.

You're some distance from the town, to be sure, but a hostel shuttle does help whisk you to the bars and back, too. Definitely a thumbs-up.

Best bet for a bite: Marché U

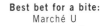

Hospitality:

Cleanliness:

Party index:

How to get there:

By bus: Take 2 bus toward Ales-Villeverte to Stade stop; walk uphill to hostel.

By car: From the auto route, take Nîmes Ouest (west) exit and drive in direction of Arles. Enter city via the Periphique (perimeter) and follow arrows to hostel.

By train: Nîmes station, 2 miles away; from station, take 2 bus to Stade stop; walk uphill to hostel.

KEY TO ICONS

- Attractive natural setting
- Ecologically aware hostel
- Superior kitchen facilities or cafe
- Offbeat or eccentric place
- Superior bathroom facilities
- Romantic private rooms
- Comfortable beds
- Editors Choice Among our very favorite hostels
- A particularly good value
- Wheelchair-accessible
- Good for business travelers
- Especially well suited for families
- Good for active travelers
- Visual arts at hostel or nearby
- Music at hostel or nearby
- Great hostel for skiers
- Bar or pub at hostel or nearby

AUBERGE LES CHAUMETTES

Savines-le-Lac, Hautes-Alpes, 05160

Phone Number: 04–92–44–20–16

Fax Number: 04–92–44–24–54
Rates: 48 francs per HI member (about $8.00 US)
Credit cards: None
Beds: 80
Private/family rooms: Yes
Kitchen available: Yes
Season: April 1 to November 30
Office hours: Call hostel for hours
Affiliation: HI-FUAJ
Extras: Meals ($), camping, bar

Not many hostellers get to this place, tucked in the high corner of Provence, but we did find that it serves three meals a day at a reasonable cost and maintains a pretty big campsite in addition to its dorms and family rooms. A rustic, outdoorsy kinda place from the look of things—not the place to find friends or social action, but rather Mother Nature.

Party index:

How to get there:

By bus: Call hostel for transit route.
By car: Call hostel for directions.
By train: Embrun station, 6 miles.

AUBERGE TARASCON

31, boulevard Gambetta, Tarascon, Bouches-du-Rhône, 13150

Phone Number: 04–90–91–04–08

Fax Number: 04–90–91–54–17
E-mail: tarascon@fuaj.org
Rates: 48 francs per HI member (about $8.00 US)
Credit cards: None
Beds: 65
Private/family rooms: Yes
Kitchen available: Yes
Season: March 1 to December 15
Office hours: 7:30 to 10:00 A.M.; 5:30 to 11:00 P.M.
Affiliation: HI-FUAJ
Extras: Breakfast, bike rentals, bike storage, store

Up in a forgotten corner of Provence that owes more to Italy than France, this hostel features a good location near the Rhone.

Party index:

It's so nice inside that it's almost like a family home—a home with tons of bunk beds and a few family rooms, that is. There's a laundry near the hostel, they serve meals on premises (mostly to groups), and they'll rent you a bike for exploring the countryside. Fishing is popular, and we noted an area for playing *petanque*—the Provençal regional sport, we dare say, and one that almost any shape or size hosteller could try.

How to get there:

By bus: Call hostel for transit route.

By car: Take the N570 and then the D9–A7 exit for Avignon or the A9 exit for Remoulins.

By train: From Tarascon station, walk ⅓ mile to hostel.

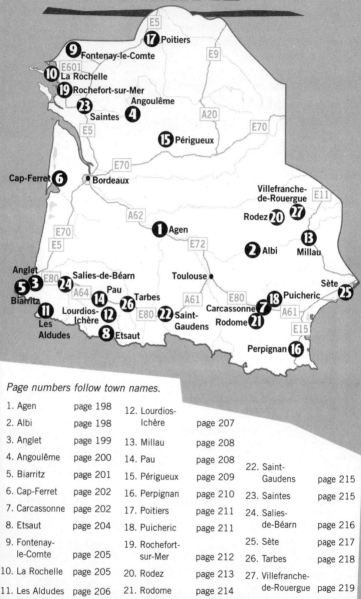

SOUTHWESTERN FRANCE

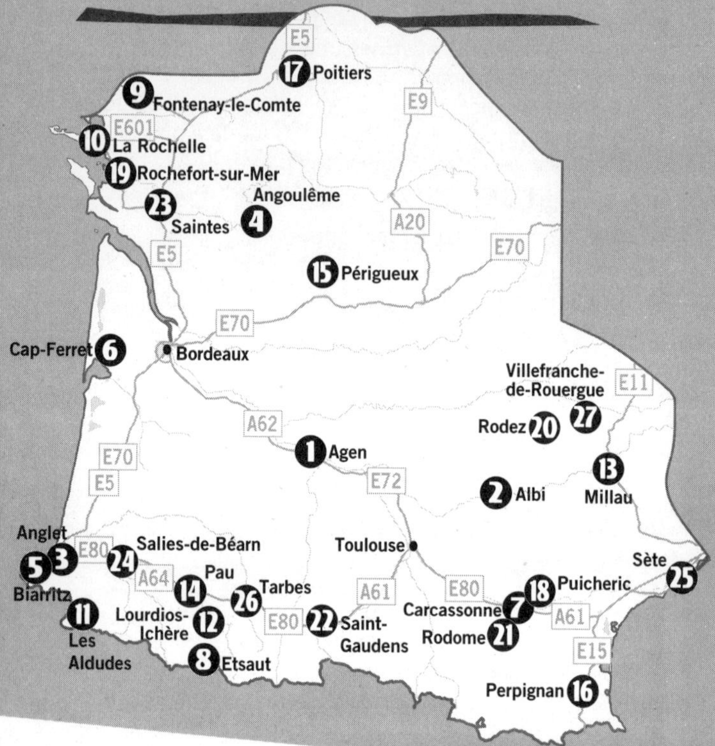

Page numbers follow town names.

SOUTHWESTERN FRANCE

Southwestern France—as defined in this book, anyhow—is a big region. We have included quite a broad swath of cultures and places with this region, so bear with us.

The Languedoc-Roussillon region is quickly becoming an antidote to the high-profile Côte-d'Azur, offering the same sunny, warm climate; inviting beaches; and intriguing cuisine. But the crowds are almost nonexistent, the people possibly even friendlier, and the costs not nearly as exorbitant.

The Midi-Pyrénées and Pyrénées Atlantique are rugged, mountainous regions inhabited by the Basques, who give the region a decidedly Spanish tinge—although the spoken language borrows nothing from French or Spanish and is as incomprehensible to outsiders as Gaelic or Bretonese would be. Here you'll find great hiking trails, and your companions will most likely be sheepherders and their flocks.

Poitou-Charentes is a strip of western coastline bordering the Loire. Culturally it has nothing in common with its southern neighbors, but it has a lot going for it in terms of history. La Rochelle, for example, was an English town for many years after the territory was reclaimed by France and therefore a haven for Protestants.

Exploring this area takes patience and commitment. From the north, a natural extension of your jaunt around the Loire can take you in various directions. Hostels are in no particular order or line, so you'll have to pick and choose. You'd do best to hit the ones in Poitiers, La Rochelle, Saintes, Angoulême, and Perigueux.

The "poor man's Riviera" at Biarritz and Anglet is a great surfing and sunning destination with good hostels, warm sand—and a complex local tongue called Euskalduna spoken only by the Basque residents. Language scholars find it a real mystery and are still trying to figure out its origins.

Coming from the south (as in Provence), Montpellier, Perpignan, Toulouse, and the great hostel in the fascinating city of Carcassonne are all not to be missed.

If you've got time and love riding buses, there are also some small, basic hostels in the dry mountains of the southwest—villages like Tarbes and Salies-de-Bearn, where few tourists are found. Harder to reach are Cahors, Rodez, Pau Millau, and Albi, though they are all no less interesting than their big-city counterparts and are rich in a blend of Spanish and French cultures.

AGEN AUBERGE DE JEUNESSE

17, rue Léo Lagrange, Agen, Lot-et-Garonne, 47000

Phone Number: 05–53–66–18–98

Fax Number: 05–53–47–78–81
Rates: 45 francs per HI member (about $8.00 US)
Credit cards: None
Beds: 60
Private/family rooms: None
Kitchen available: Yes
Office hours: 6:00 to 11:00 P.M.
Affiliation: HI-FUAJ
Extras: Breakfast ($), laundry

This place is simple—sixty beds, all bunks, plus a kitchen and laundry. They serve breakfast, but it costs a little extra cash to get it.

The town of Agen is a nice off-the-beaten track introduction to the southwest of France, on the train line. The town is located on the pretty Garonne River, which pushes its way out of the mountains of central France and heads to the dunes and beaches of the Atlantic. Agen's about halfway along, and it's mighty attractive. Hit a local cafe.

Gestalt:
Ragin' Agen
Party index:

How to get there:

By bus: Take bus toward Lalande to Léon Blum stop.
By car: Call hostel for directions.
By train: Agen station, 1 mile away.

MAISON DES JEUNES ET DE LA CULTURE

13, rue de la République, Albi, Tarn, 81000

Phone Number: 05–63–54–53–65

Fax Number: 05–63–54–61–55
Rates: 48 francs per HI member (about $8.00 US)
Credit cards: None
Beds: 36
Private/family rooms: Sometimes
Kitchen available: Yes
Office hours: Twenty-four hours
Affiliation: HI-FUAJ
Extras: Laundry, meals ($)

This place is a mixed-bag deal, for sure. Cleanliness suffers, and the big dorms ain't much fun, either. However, the staff cooks pretty decent meals. Even though you'll probably partake in these meals, there is a great little market that sets up only two Tuesdays a month.

One potential drawback: The place is also used as temporary housing for local workers, creating the possibility of "us versus them" interactions. Also, office hours shorten on the weekends. All in all, it's not the most convenient place in the world, though the laundry is handy.

Gestalt: Albi seein' ya

Cleanliness:

Party index:

Albi made its historical mark by being the center for a religious dissenters known as the Cahars, who believed in giving up material things. They received the same mistreatment as other religious nonconformists during that violent period at the hands of a suspicious Catholic church. Some were tossed off the local cliffs as punishment, and you might feel punished, too, after a few nights at this place.

How to get there:

By bus: Take 2 or 5 bus top Rascol stop.

By car: Near Lignes; call hostel for directions.

By train: Albi Ville station, 1½ miles away; call hostel for transit route.

AUBERGE GAZTÉ ETXEA

19, route des Vignes, Quartier Chiberta, Anglet, Pyrénées-Atlantiques, 64600

Phone Number: 05–59–58–70–00

Fax Number: 05–59–58–70–04
E-mail: biarritz@fuaj.org
Rates: 49 to 74 francs per HI member (about $9.00 to $13.00 US)
Credit cards: Yes
Beds: 96
Private/family rooms: Sometimes
Kitchen available: Yes
Season: February 15 to November 15
Office hours: Twenty-four hours
Affiliation: HI-FUAJ
Extras: Cafeteria ($), bar, surfboard rentals, outings, game room, bike rentals, bike storage

Just a third of a mile from the beach, this place is superpopular. Hmm. Wonder why. Could it be the famous surfing waves?

Yep. That's the ticket. Sure enough, they'll rent you a board here, too, or lead you on a kayak outing.

Otherwise, it's a standard French joint—geared more toward fun and distraction than actual comfort. Dorms contain four to seven beds apiece, which is certainly tolerable. There are also two quad rooms better for families, and there's neither a lockout nor a nighttime curfew. During fall, winter, and spring, you can cook in the hostel kitchen. Come summer, though, a cafeteria and hip Euro-bar take over the premises, scrapping kitchen use as an option.

Gestalt:
Acute Anglet
Party index:

Most hostellers here want to catch some waves or visit the nearby Basque country of Spain. Participate in local culture by trying out the popular game of *pelota,* something like squash but with a Spanish accent.

How to get there:

By bus: Take 4 or 72 bus (which stops at Sables) to hostel.

By car: Go in direction of Cinqcantons, then follow arrows to hostel.

By train: Hostel is 2 miles from Biarritz station, 4½ miles from Bayonne station; call hostel for transit route.

ANGOULÊME AUBERGE

Ile de Bourgines, Angoulême, Charente, 16000

Phone Number: 05–45–92–45–80

Fax Number: 05–45–95–90–71
E-mail: angouleme@fuaj.org
Rates: 51 to 68 francs per HI member (about $9.00 to $12.00 US)
Credit cards: Yes
Beds: 84
Private/family rooms: None
Kitchen available: No
Season: January 4 to December 18
Office hours: 7:30 A.M. to 10:30 P.M. (May 1 to October 15); 8:00 A.M. to 10:00 P.M. (October 16 to April 30)
Curfew: 11:00 P.M.
Affiliation: HI-FUAJ
Extras: Meals ($), bike rentals, laundry, bar, boats, kayaks, TV, pool table, conference rooms, grill, karaoke

In truth a couple miles outside Angoulême, this joint occupies some choice digs on an island in the smoothly flowing Charente River. The place is really geared toward outdoor and social pursuits, too: You can get a kayak or boat here, shoot some hoops, fish, sit at the great big bar singing along to the karaoke machine, and so forth.

Other comforts are also provided, like family rooms and a laundry. For eats, it's a restaurant on premises or the good kitchen; take your pick.

This town's singularly interesting feature appears to be the CNBDI, the national comics museum—an extraordinary orgy of worship for the art. Most of the museum concerns French comics, but American and other work is also represented here in a big, big building. This love for the comic strip culminates in a big comic strip festival in January.

Summertime hostellers can avail themselves of fresh veggies and fruits at the covered markets Tuesday through Sunday. On Saturday the market changes location and becomes open-air.

Gestalt: Comics relief

Party index:

How to get there:

By bus: Take 7 bus to Pont St. Antoine stop.
By car: Call hostel for directions.
By train: Angoulême station, 1 mile.

BIARRITZ AUBERGE DE JEUNESSE

8, rue Chiquito de Cambo, Biarritz, 64200

Phone Number: 05–59–41–76–00 or 05–59–58–70–00

Fax Number: 05–59–41–76–07 or 05–59–58–70–07
E-mail: biarritz@fuaj.org
Rates: 72 francs per HI member (about $12 US)
Credit cards: Yes
Beds: 96
Private/family rooms: Yes
Kitchen available: No
Office hours: 8:00 A.M. to 1:00 P.M., 5:00 TO 11:00 P.M. (winter); 8:00 A.M. to 11:00 P.M. (June 1 to August 31)
Season: January 20 to December 20
Affiliation: HI-FUAJ
Extras: Breakfast, lockers, conference rooms, computers, surf shop, bike rentals, bike storage, meals (sometimes)

This new lakeside hostel is obviously pretty modern; it features such amenities as three conference rooms with space for one hundred—watch out for school groups—a key-card system that allows you to enter the hostel and your room anytime you like, and a surf shop. This area is surf central, a mecca for lots of Aussies and Euros, and the hostel crowd sometimes reflects that fact; they're thrilled to be just a mile from some good surfing and sunbathing.

Dorms are pretty small, in a good way: There are eight double rooms and four triples—and all seventeen remaining rooms are quads. So every place in the joint is a potential private room, and each has an en-suite bathroom. Neat. A kitchen's available here sometimes, but in spring and fall it converts to a restaurant serving meals to groups, so come prepared for that possibility.

Gestalt:
Biarritz cracker
Party index:

Biarritz, once a posh resort area, is now pretty much known as the "poor man's Riviera." Summer is packed with Basque families trying to take a break. You can take part in the culture through corridas, bandas processions, and in bodegas, where you can sample local wine.

How to get there:

By bus: Take 2 bus from train station.
By car: Take A63 to Biarritz exit; continue 1 mile to hostel.
By train: Biarritz station, ⅓ mile from hostel.

CAP-FERRET AUBERGE

87, avenue de Bordeaux, Cap-Ferret, Gironde, 33970

Phone Number: 05–56–60–64–62

Rates: 45 francs per HI member (about $8.00 US)
Credit cards: None
Beds: 60
Private/family rooms: None
Kitchen available: No
Season: July 1 to August 31
Office hours: 7:30 A.M. to 1:00 P.M.; 6:00 to 9:00 P.M.
Affiliation: HI-FUAJ
Extras: Camping, bike storage

Gestalt:
Cap crusader
Party index:

Quite simple, this hostel sports a camping area with fifty-six campsites in addition to the bunkrooms. There are no family rooms, kitchen, meals, or laundry.

How to get there:

By bus: Call hostel for transit route.
By car: Call hostel for directions.
By train: Arcachon station nearby; call hostel for transit route.

AUBERGE DE LA CITÉ MÉDIEVALE

Rue du Vicomte Trencavel, Carcassonne, Aude, 11000

Phone Number: 04–68–25–23–16

Fax Number: 04–68–71–14–84

E-mail: carcassone@fuaj.org
Rates: 72 francs per HI member (about $12 US)
Credit cards: Yes
Beds: 120
Private/family rooms: Yes
Kitchen available: Yes
Season: February 1 to December 15
Office hours: Twenty-four hours
Affiliation: HI-FUAJ
Extras: Breakfast, cafe ($), laundry, bike storage, TV, bar, patio, garden, Internet access, luggage storage

Gestalt: EuroDisney

Hospitality:

Cleanliness:

Party index:

It's not often you can lodge yourself in the walls of an old, old city like this, but Carcassonne's hostel scores big, in our opinion—delivering a one-two punch of history and good accommodations.

For starts, you're sleeping right inside some of the oldest structures in the city—the fortress walls known as the "Cité." Talk about history! The walls were first constructed by those pesky Romans back in the B.C. years. Later—well, relatively speaking, in the 1200s—King Louis IX made the Cité uniquely French and uniquely medieval. That's where the hostel is.

The star rooms here are the two doubles with en-suite bathrooms and the eight quad rooms (not all of which have their own bathrooms). There are also fourteen larger dorm rooms; none has more than eight beds, and lots have four to six apiece. Either way, though, a yummilicious breakfast is included with your bed.

KEY TO ICONS

- Attractive natural setting
- Ecologically aware hostel
- Superior kitchen facilities or cafe
- Offbeat or eccentric place
- Superior bathroom facilities
- Romantic private rooms
- Comfortable beds
- Editors Choice Among our very favorite hostels
- A particularly good value
- Wheelchair-accessible
- Good for business travelers
- Especially well suited for families
- Good for active travelers
- Visual arts at hostel or nearby
- Music at hostel or nearby
- Great hostel for skiers
- Bar or pub at hostel or nearby

This city is a joy to check out on foot, despite an overdependence on tourist tack. A path set between the two sets of walls allows you to make a circuit of the place; at the same time you can glimpse both the town and the landscape beyond the walls. Later, the tourist crush eases and you've got the old streets largely to yourself. Tons of festivals also come through town: July brings dance and theater to the town, August a medieval feel.

Despite the stream of hostellers, staff does a good job keeping things relatively neat.

How to get there:

By bus: Take 4 then 2 bus.

By car: Call hostel for directions.

By train: From Carcassonne station, take 4 then 2 bus to hostel.

CENTRE INTERNATIONAL DE SÉJOUR

Vallée d'Aspe, Etsaut, Pyrénées Atlantiques, 64490

Phone Number: 05–59–34–88–98

Fax Number: 05–59–34–86–91
Rates: 48 francs per person (about $8.00 US)
Credit cards: None
Beds: 70
Private/family rooms: Yes
Kitchen available: Yes
Office hours: Twenty-four hours
Affiliation: HI-FUAJ, UCRIF
Extras: Meals ($), laundry, garden, store, TV

Just 10 or so miles from the Spanish border, this place is located in bona fide wilderness territory—one of the last in France. Bears are still seen in this region of the Pyrénées. There's even a museum located in the town dedicated to the bear. Get our drift? Lots of walks are possible in the hills, too, but most hostellers find this simple stone hostel for the nearby skiing possibilities.

Gestalt:
Runnin' for the border

Party index:

Meals are offered, there's a laundry on premises, and they've got a garden.

How to get there:

By bus: Take Etsaut bus to Eglise (church) stop, walk to hostel.

By car: Call hostel for directions.

By train: Oloron station, 25 miles away, is closest stop; call hostel for transit route.

FOYER LES TROIS PORTES (THREE DOORS HOSTEL)

16, rue des Gravauts, B.P. 347, Fontenay-le-Comte, 85206

Phone Number: 02–51–69–13–44

Fax Number: 02–51–69–04–23
Rates: 114 francs per HI member (about $19 US)
Credit cards: Yes
Beds: 72
Private/family rooms: Yes
Kitchen available: Yes
Season: June 15 to September 15
Office hours: Twenty-four hours
Affiliation: HI-FUAJ
Extras: Laundry, meals ($), store, bike storage, TV, conference room, game room, bar, grill, garden

You can't help but get privacy at this hostel—the entire rooming arrangements at the joint consist of ten single rooms plus ten doubles. Among the other fun perks: grilling supplies in the gardenside terrace, a television room, and a "hall d'accueil" 200 yards away complete with a bar and game room. This area gets very social, lots of mixing and friend-making.

The price is steep, but only because your breakfast and dinner are included with the price of a bed. Is it worth then equivalent of an extra ten bucks? Yeah, probably, especially if you want to cruise the countryside during the day instead of counting centimes looking for the cheapest cheese.

Too bad this is a summer-only hostel, and not really close to anything of note besides the French countryside, because it's pretty good.

Gestalt:
Three doors down

Party index:

How to get there:

By bus: Call hostel for transit route.
By car: Call hostel for directions.
By train: From Fontenay-le-Comte station, walk ½ mile to hostel.

CENTRE INTERNATIONAL DE SÉJOUR

Avenue des Minimes, B.P. 305, La Rochelle Cedex, Charente-Maritime, 17013

Phone Number: 05–46–44–43–11

Fax Number: 05–46–45–41–48
Rates: 72 francs per HI member (about $12 US)

Credit cards: None
Beds: 244 (summer), 224 (winter)
Private/family rooms: Yes
Kitchen available: No
Season: January 1 to December 20
Office hours: 6:30 A.M. to midnight
Lockout: 10:00 A.M. to 12:30 P.M.
Curfew: 1:30 A.M.
Affiliation: HI-FUAJ
Extras: Meals ($), laundry, breakfast, bike rentals, store, camping, bar

An institutional building with all the character of a block of cheese, this place manages to wedge in more than 200 beds in the popular and pleasant seaside resort of La Rochelle. (Actually, the hostel is just outside of town. But we digress.)

Our hosteller snoops seemed to like it, though. Among the things they cited: the laid-back atmosphere of this beach town, the local bird life (hey, who said hostellers were an insensitive bunch?), proximity to good beaches, and good nightlife potential in town. The foosball table gets a workout, they reported, and the hostel is frequented by interesting young men and women from all corners of Europe.

Gestalt:
La Rochelle,
La Rochelle

Party index:

You can pay extra for breakfast, lunch, or dinner here; camp in one of ten campsites; or rent a bike and tool around the beaches and backroads. The lockout here's mercifully short, too.

You might get a sense that things here aren't quite as "French" as in other areas you've visited. That's because the English occupied the town until fairly recently (well, recent in a historical sense), when they lost the 100 Years War.

How to get there:

By bus: Take 4 bus to Auberge de Jeunesse (hostel) stop.
By car: Call hostel for directions.
By train: La Rochelle station, 1 mile from hostel.

ASSOCIATION ECOLE DES BUISSONS (LES ALDUDES HOSTEL)

Urtxintxenea Route d'Urepel, Les Aldudes, 64430

Phone Number: 05–59–37–56–58

Fax Number: 05–59–37–56–58
E-mail: urtxintx@aol.com

Rates: 48 francs per HI member (about $8.00 US)
Credit cards: None
Beds: 80
Private/family rooms: No
Kitchen available: No
Season: February 15 to December 15
Office hours: 9:00 A.M. to 9:00 P.M.
Affiliation: HI-FUAJ
Extras: Campground, laundry, bike rentals, meals ($)

A former schoolhouse in the little village of les Aldudes, this place was completely worked over and just opened in June 2000, so we can't yet speak about it or rate it. Tell us what you know. But we can say that this village is quite near that southwestern tip of France where the Mediterranean meets the Atlantic—an interesting place to watch the waves, if nothing else.

Gestalt: All dudes

Party index:

How to get there:

By bus: Contact hostel for transit route.

By car: Take main road into les Aldudes; hostel is on left, 300 yards past entrance to village.

By train: Nearest station is in Osses, 15 miles away; contact hostel for transit route.

MAISON PELAU HOSTEL

Estivade d'Aspe Pyrénées, Lourdios-Ichère, Pyrénées Atlantique, 64570

Phone Number: 05–59–34–46–39

Fax Number: 05–59–34–48–04
Rates: 48 francs per HI member (about $8.00 US)
Credit cards: None
Beds: 25
Private/family rooms: Yes
Kitchen available: Yes
Office hours: Call hostel for hours
Affiliation: HI-FUAJ
Extras: Meals ($), laundry, camping

The best thing about Maison Pelau is its position in the Pyrénées, where ski-hungry Euros congregate each winter for some delightful schussing conditions. (Think of them as Colorado with, oh, a Spanish accent, and you're starting to get the picture.)

Gestalt:
Snow business

Party index:

As usual in France, even this simple hostel serves three meals a day for a reasonable charge. The laundry is handy afterward.

How to get there:

By bus: Take bus from Oloron to APASP-Arros stop.

By car: Call hostel for directions.

By train: Oloron station, 14 miles away, is nearest stop. Call hostel for transit route.

MILLAU HOSTEL

26, rue Lucien Costes, Millau, Aveyron, 12100

Phone Number: 05–65–61–27–74

Fax Number: 05–65–61–90–58
Rates: 51 francs per HI member (about $9.00 US)
Credit cards: None
Beds: 60
Private/family rooms: Yes
Kitchen available: Yes
Office hours: Twenty-four hours
Affiliation: HI-FUAJ
Extras: Meals ($), laundry, bike storage, TV

Located inside a park, this hostel gives you good privacy options: Its lodgings consist of two single rooms, two triple rooms, and four quads. Meals are sometimes available, a kitchen is thankfully opened to hostellers, and the usual common room–television room combo is present. Walking seems to be the prime pastime around these parts, so why not join in?

Gestalt:
Walkabout

Party index:

Having a laundry on premises is a bonus—especially if you've just dribbled some of that local Roquefort cheese on your shirt.

How to get there:

By bus: Take 1 bus to hostel.

By car: Call hostel for directions.

By train: From Millau station, walk ½ mile from hostel.

LOGIS DES JEUNES

Base de Plein Aire, Gelos (Pau), 64110

Phone Number: 05–59–06–53–02

Fax Number: 05–59–11–05–20

E-mail: logis.des.jeunes.pau@wanadoo.fr
Rates: 51 francs per HI member (about $9.00 US)
Credit cards: None
Beds: 40
Private/family rooms: None
Kitchen available: Yes
Office hours: Twenty-four hours
Affiliation: HI-FUAJ
Extras: Laundry, bike storage

This hostel's in a dull building, sure . . . but it's all single rooms—all forty. So that can't be the worst thing in the world.

There is a serious drawback, however—schoolkids. Lots of 'em. For some reason this joint is often packed to the rafters with the little kiddies. We're not guaranteeing you'll be tripping over them, mind you; just be aware of the possibility.

Gestalt: Pau prince

Party index:

Otherwise, staff keeps the place neat and clean, and bathrooms are very good.

How to get there:

By bus: Take 1 bus to Mairie de Gelos stop.
By car: Call hostel for directions.
By train: Pau station, 1½ miles away.

FOYER DE JEUNES TRAVAILLEURS (PÉRIGUEUX HOSTEL)

Rue des Thermes Prolongés, Périgueux, Dordogne, 24000

Phone Number: 05–53–06–81–40

Fax Number: 05–53–06–81–49
E-mail: fjtdordogne@wanadoo.fr
Rates: 51 francs per person (about $9.00 US)
Credit cards: None
Beds: 16
Office hours: 4:00 P.M. to 9:00 A.M.
Affiliation: HI-FUAJ
Extras: Laundry, meals ($)

$

This tiny place is gonna be hard to get into, it's so small—doubly so beacause of the really popular area it's located in. They don't have much in the way of extras, either, just a laundry and meal service. But it's by FAR the cheapest bed you'll find in this town.

Gestalt: Up Périgueux

How to get there:

Party index: 🎉🎉

By bus: Contact hostel for transit route.

By car: From Lyon or Bordeaux, take R89 highway to R21 and continue to Périgueux.

By train: From Périgueux station, walk 1 mile to hostel.

PERPIGNAN AUBERGE DE JEUNESSE

Parc de la Pépiniere, Avenue de Grande-Bretagne, Perpignan, Pyrénées-Orientales, 66000

Phone Number: 04–68–34–63–32

Fax Number: 04–68–51–16–02
Rates: 70 francs per HI member (about $12 US)
Credit cards: None
Beds: 49
Private/family rooms: Yes
Kitchen available: Yes
Season: January 20 to December 20
Office hours: 7:00 to 11:00 A.M.; 4:00 to 11:00 P.M.
Lockout: 11:00 A.M. to 4:00 P.M.
Affiliation: HI-FUAJ
Extras: Breakfast, sheets ($)

Breakfast is included in the price at this nice-looking (if unassuming) hostel, located in an interesting area of a neat city. However, bathroom facilities are of the squat variety and are not for the squeamish.

Gestalt: Perpignan sequitor

Hospitality:

Party index:

The great management and staff keep things humming along, and you'll want to hit the beach nearby—especially during the scorching, relentless summer. (This is among the driest places in France.) For fun, the area is chock-full of summer festivals and tapas bars that reflect nearby neighbor Spain's foodways and folkways more than France's.

We especially liked, er, loved the local factory where you can get a delicious sample of the humble cocoa bean. However, we were a little put off by another store in town that sells nothin' but escargot. Yeah. Snails.

How to get there:

By car: Call hostel for directions.

By train: From Perpignan station, walk ¼ mile to police station; hostel is behind.

POITIERS AUBERGE DE JEUNESSE

1, allée Roger Tagault, Poitiers, Vienne, 86000

Phone Number: 05–49–30–09–70

Fax Number: 05–49–30–09–79
E-mail: poitiers@fuaj.org
Rates: 51 to 68 francs per HI member (about $9.00 to $12.00 US)
Credit cards: Yes
Beds: 132
Private/family rooms: Yes
Kitchen available: Yes
Season: January 3 to December 31
Office hours: 7:00 A.M to 1:00 P.M.; 6:00 P.M to 3:00 A.M.
Affiliation: HI-FUAJ
Extras: Meals ($), store, Internet access

Not on the beaten track, not at all, but this hostel succeeds at providing clean and quite private beds for the weary traveler in southwestern France. And it's so friendly for a French hostel that we had to check our map to make sure we hadn't slipped into Spain or Portugal by accident.

Insiders' tip:
Hit the Futuroscope

Gestalt:
Prêt à Poitiers

Hospitality:

Party index:

Rooms are especially nice at the hostel, uncrowded and with en-suite wash-up facilities; all in all, a congenial and tidy place with just one caveat. Yep, it gets busy (you knew we were gonna say this) with area schoolchildren in spring. The hostel's restaurant meals are a good deal, too.

Afterward check out Poitier's bohemian side (translation: There's a university here.) or the Futuroscope, an IMAX-like movie theater that truly must be seen to be believed.

How to get there:

By bus: From bus station, take 1 or 3 bus to Cap Sud stop.
By car: Call hostel for directions.
By train: Poitiers station, 2 miles; from station, take 1 or 3 bus to Cap Sud stop.

PUICHERIC AUBERGE DE JEUNESSE

2, rue Marcellin Albert, Puicheric, 11700

Phone Number: 04–68–43–73–81

Fax Number: 04–68–43–71–84
Rates: 48 francs per HI member (about $8.00 US)
Credit cards: None

Beds: 10
Private/family rooms: Yes
Kitchen available: Yes
Office hours: Twenty-four hours
Affiliation: HI-FUAJ
Extras: Laundry, meals ($), store, TV, bar, grill

Gestalt:
Tiny taters
Party index:

"Boy, is this place small."

That's what everyone says when they get here to the Languedoc-Pyrénées border and find this joint, which contains a grand total of four bunkrooms: one double room that couples get dibs on, two quad rooms better for traveling families, and one dorm room of seven beds.

Actually, this is a nice change of pace from the usual huge places. Meal service, a laundry, a grill, and an outdoor bar are additional surprising amenities; this must be France. For fun, canoeing and kayaking are popular in the area.

This small town is pretty close to the bigger—and absolutely fascinating—walled city of Carcassone. It's also a good place to sample the local Minervois wines if you have time for a tour of the local vineyards.

How to get there:

By bus: From Carcassonne, take bus to Puicheric stop.

By car: Call hostel for directions.

By train: Lezignan Corbieres station, 9 miles away, is nearest stop; call hostel for transit route.

ROCHEFORT LOGIS D'ÉTAPE

20, rue de la République, Rochefort-sur-Mer, 17300

Phone Number: 05–46–82–10–40

Fax Number: 05–46–99–21–25
E-mail: jeunesserochefort@neotech.fr
Rates: 48 francs per HI member (about $8.00 US)
Credit cards: None
Beds: 50
Private/family rooms: Yes
Kitchen available: Yes
Season: July 1 to August 31
Office hours: 8:00 to 10:00 A.M.; 5:30 to 10:00 P.M.
Affiliation: HI-FUAJ
Extras: Laundry, meals ($), garden, store, camping, TV, bike storage

You can't ask for much more than this, thrashing around the west coast of France: As a hostel, it supplies everything you'll want and more. Nice garden. No stupid rules like a lockout or lights-out time. A really great kitchen where you can cook all those fruits and veggies found at the covered market held every weekday morning. They'll serve you meals to boot!

But the biggest bonus is this one: NO SCHOOL GROUPS ALLOWED. Amen, brother. Gotta give us a few places where quiet is possible.

Note that the office here is located in a different building (#97) than the actual hostel (at #20), where three quad rooms, four dorm rooms of five to eight beds apiece, and one still larger bunkroom handle the hosteller load. Biking trails run nearby, and the beach is about 10 miles distant. Any questions?

Well, yeah, actually one: How come it's open for such a short season? (The answer: Sometimes it will reopen any time of year for special reasons, like big group bookings.)

Best bet for a bite: Covered market nearby

Gestalt: Rochefort motel

Cleanliness:

Party index:

How to get there:

By bus: Call hostel for transit route.

By car: Call hostel for directions.

By train: From Rochefort-sur-Mer train station, walk ½ mile toward HOTEL ROCA FORTIS (following signs). Hostel is adjacent.

AUBERGE QUATRE SAISONS

26, boulevard des Capucines, B.P. 19, Onet le Château, Rodez Cedex 09, Aveyron, 12034

Phone Number: 05–65–77–51–05

Fax Number: 05–65–67–37–97
E-mail: assoc.fjt.gd.rodez@wanadoo.fr
Rates: 85 francs per HI member (about $15 US)
Credit cards: Yes
Beds: 60
Private/family rooms: Yes
Kitchen available: No
Office hours: Twenty-four hours
Affiliation: HI-FUAJ, FJT
Extras: Laundry, meals ($), breakfast, TV, pool table, table tennis, bike storage

This thirty-bed place sits in a functional three-story building with an annex. Breakfast is included, green lawns provide picnicking possibilities, and the game room is well used. Self-serve lunches and dinners can be had for a price.

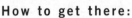

Locals like to fish, so you might try that. We're glad to see that there's one wheelchair-accessible bunkroom in the joint.

Gestalt: Rodez trip

Party index:

How to get there:

By bus: Take 1 or 3 bus to Marché d'Oc or Rosiers Capucines stop.

By car: Call hostel for directions.

By train: Rodez station, 2½ miles away.

FERME ÉQUESTRE AUBERGE DE JEUNESSE

Rodome, 11140

Phone Number: 05–68–20–32–22

Fax Number: 05–68–20–76–10
E-mail: h_val@club-internet.fr
Rates: 44 francs per HI member (about $9.00 US)
Credit cards: None
Beds: 26
Private/family rooms: Yes
Kitchen available: Yes
Season: February 15 to November 15
Office hours: 8:00 A.M. to 10:00 P.M.
Affiliation: HI-FUAJ
Extras: Meals ($), bike storage, camping, garden, table tennis, horseback riding

A smallish hostel, but satisfying if you want to get local, this place is located in an atmospheric (even handsome?) two-story stone house with big windows.

The accommodations consist of three triples, one quad room, and three dorm rooms of five to eight beds each; there are also six campsites for true nature-lovers. Since this is an equestrian farm, horsey activities obviously rule the roost. So, what the heck, give riding a shot. Or ski in the area, or check out the chateaus.

Gestalt: Horse sense

Party index:

How to get there:

By bus: Take bus to Espezel stop.

By car: Call hostel for directions.

By train: Quillan station, 20 miles away, is nearest stop; call hostel for transit route.

AUBERGE LE VÉNASQUE

3, rue de la Résidence, Saint-Gaudens Cedex, 31804

Phone Number: 05–61–94–72–73

Fax Number: 05–61–94–72–74
Rates: 51 francs per HI member (about $9.00 US)
Credit cards: None
Beds: 20
Private/family rooms: Yes
Kitchen available: No
Season: January 2 to December 30
Office hours: Twenty-four hours
Affiliation: HI-FUAJ
Extras: Meals ($), laundry, store, camping, bar

This place is very small. It's equipped with just twenty bunks, a bit of family room space, and a laundry. They also serve meals.

Gestalt: OhmyGaudens

Party index:

How to get there:

By bus: Call hostel for transit route.
By car: Call hostel for directions.
By train: From Saint-Gaudens station, walk ½ mile to hostel.

SAINTES AUBERGE

2, place Geoffroy Martel, Saintes, Charente-Maritime, 17100

Phone Number: 05–46–92–14–92

Fax Number: 05–46–92–97–82
E-mail: saintes@fuaj.org
Rates: 68 francs per HI member (about $12 US)
Credit cards: None
Beds: 70
Private/family rooms: Yes
Kitchen available: Yes
Office hours: Twenty-four hours
Affiliation: HI-FUAJ
Extras: Restaurant ($), breakfast, bike storage, camping, store, TV, game room

Saintes (once known as Xaintes) may not be the most exciting place in France. Okay, that's an understatement. It's just a place to pass through and notice nice churches, maybe. But you probably won't find stimulating nightlife, nature, or culture . . . unless you hit the summertime festival rush, of course.

The hostel is adequate. You might grab one of the two doubles or one triple; otherwise, things are still okay in any of the thirteen quad rooms and two dorms of six beds each. One of the bedrooms is wheelchair accessible, and lots of them have en-suite bathrooms. Twenty-six campsites round out the selection.

Gestalt: Saintes alive

Party index:

Breakfasts are included, and meals are served; there's no kitchen, though. Best bet for social interaction? Hang out in the common room; that might be as good as it gets.

How to get there:

By bus: Take 1 bus toward Abbaye Aux Dames to Centre Commercial Leclerc stop.

By car: Call hostel for directions.

By train: Saintes station, 1 mile away.

AUBERGE DE JEUNESSE VERTE (COUNTRY HOSTEL)

Route du Padu, Stade Al Cartero, Salies-de-Béarn, Pyrénées-Atlantique, 64270

Phone Number: 05–59–65–06–96

Rates: 44 francs per HI member (about $8.00 US)
Credit cards: None
Beds: 20
Private/family rooms: None
Kitchen available: Yes
Office hours: 8:00 A.M. to 7:00 P.M.
Affiliation: HI-FUAJ
Extras: Laundry

This is ultimate rustication: Here's a small hostel that remains open in winter, but it's not heated! Not much else in amenities here, either, though the laundry is a nice surprise.

Gestalt: Salt of the earth

Party index:

Definitely a destination for foodies, Salies-de-Béarn is famous for a couple things: Salt is mined here and used to preserve the famous Bayonne hams. That's one. The other reason is perhaps more decadent: The area is renowned for its chocolate industry. Try some at a local shop. This is also the place where that buttery *Joy of*

Cooking staple, béarnaise sauce, was invented, in case you were wondering.

How to get there:

By bus: From Pau or Biarritz, take bus to Salies.
By car: Call hostel for directions.
By train: Puyos station, 5 miles.

VILLA SALIS HOSTEL

Rue du General Revest, Sète, Hérault, 34200

Phone Number: 04–67–53–46–68

Fax Number: 04–67–51–34–01
Rates: 118 francs per HI member (about $20 US)
Credit cards: Yes
Beds: 80
Private/family rooms: Yes
Kitchen available: No
Season: January 15 to December 15
Office hours: Call hostel for hours
Affiliation: HI-FUAJ
Extras: Breakfast, meals ($), bike storage, camping

Set (heh-heh) in the quiet fishing town of Sète, on a road so rough that buses can't make the trek, this hostel charges you more than most small ones in France. That's because "half-board" is required. What's that mean? Simple. You pay for breakfast and dinner—whether you want 'em or not.

We don't know if this is the best system ever devised, but we'd guess that it ensures that you'll eat something besides the week-old rice and apples rattling around at the bottom of your backpack. Lunch does cost extra, as usual.

KEY TO ICONS

- Attractive natural setting
- Ecologically aware hostel
- Superior kitchen facilities or cafe
- Offbeat or eccentric place
- Superior bathroom facilities
- Romantic private rooms
- Comfortable beds
- Editors Choice Among our very favorite hostels
- A particularly good value
- Wheelchair-accessible
- Good for business travelers
- Especially well suited for families
- Good for active travelers
- Visual arts at hostel or nearby
- Music at hostel or nearby
- Great hostel for skiers
- Bar or pub at hostel or nearby

Gestalt:
Up-Sète

Party index:

All twenty rooms here are quads, but none have en-suite bathroom facilities; twenty campsites provide additional space.

Mostly a fishing town, this is not excitement central. Gazing upward at the volcano that gives the town such dramatic location, or else mucking around the local canals and fishing boats, is about the main pastime.

How to get there:

By bus: Call hostel for transit route.
By car: Call hostel for directions.
By ferry: Near Sète ferry dock.
By train: Steve station, 1 mile away.

FOYER DE JEUNES TRAVAILLEURS

88, rue Alsace Lorraine, Tarbes, 65000

Phone Number: 05–62–38–91–20

Fax Number: 05–62–37–69–81
Rates: 68 francs per HI member (about $12 US)
Credit cards: None
Beds: 58
Private/family rooms: Yes
Kitchen available: Yes
Office hours: Twenty-four hours
Affiliation: HI-FUAJ, FJT
Extras: Cafeteria ($), game room, pool table, bar, TV, bike storage, laundry, store, garden

Tarbes, not far from the shrine village of Lourdes, has a pretty happenin' hostel considering that few hostellers find their way here.

Breakfast is included at this joint, which has ten nice single rooms with bathrooms en suite, eight doubles without en-suite bathrooms, and eight quad rooms. One room is wheelchair accessible, too. Other facilities include a television room, pool table, game room, and laundry.

Gestalt:
Tarbes baby

Party index:

For fun, we'd hang out in the garden or the bar or make the 12-mile trek over to Lourdes. Maybe.

How to get there:

By bus: Take 1 bus to FJT stop.
By car: Call hostel for directions.
By train: Tarbes station, 1 mile away.

FOYER DU ROUERGUE

13, rue Emilie de Rodat, Villefranche-de-Rouergue, Aveyron, 12200

Phone Number: 05–65–45–09–68

Fax Number: 05–65–45–62–26
Rates: 51 francs per HI member (about $9.00 US)
Credit cards: None
Beds: 6
Private/family rooms: None
Kitchen available: Sometimes
Office hours: Twenty-four hours
Affiliation: HI-FUAJ
Extras: Meals ($), bike storage, laundry

One of France's two smallest hostels, this teenie place has just one coed dorm room containing eight plain beds. They offer meals and have a bike shed but not a whole lot more. But at least it's cheap, er, inexpensive.

Gestalt:
Teeny weenie

Party index:

How to get there:

By bus: Call hostel for transit route.
By car: Call hostel for directions.
By train: Villefranche-de-Rouergue station nearby.

NORTHERN ITALY

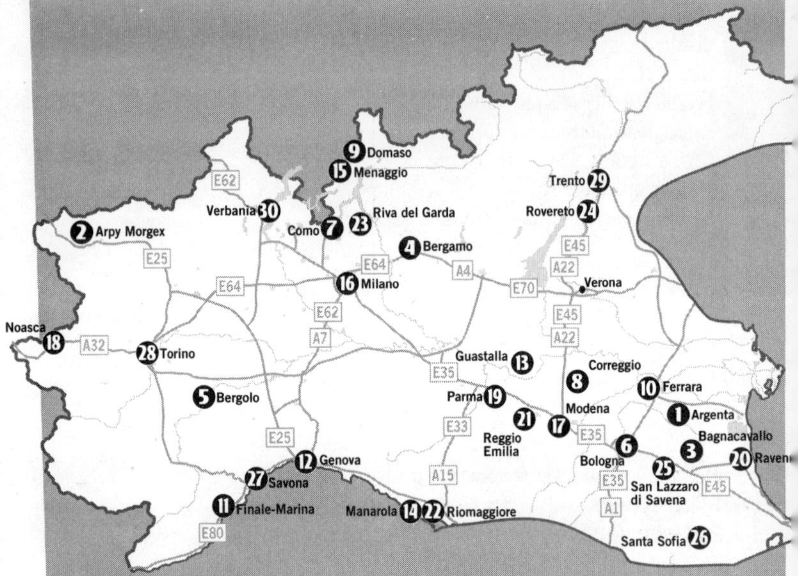

Page numbers follow town names.

NORTHERN ITALY

Northern Italy is, in some ways, the best of Italy—but it's also the least Italian. Swiss, French, German, and other influences all collide to create one damned interesting area.

The Italian Riviera—and its little cousin, the Cinque Terre—is one of Italy's prettiest and most distinctive regions, all big cliffs clinging to the blue Mediterranean. Depending on the town, it's either yachts and jet-setters or humble fisherfolk and quiet local vacationers. (Gee, which one do you think *we* prefer?) You can also find the odd nude beach here by looking and asking around a little. French influences occasionally seep across the border, but the Italians are doing a good job of resisting.

Farther north, the Lakes District rivals this area for beauty, though it's a different kind. Here the enormous lakes—framed by the foothills of the Alps—make for incredible views and boat excursions. Again, the key is to pick carefully; some of these rich-kid lake towns are among Italy's most expensive to visit and dine in, while others have retained some local character. The Alps themselves, of course, loom huge in any tourist itinerary.

Hyperactive Milano and slightly slower Torino and Bologna are antitheses of what you might expect in Italy: They're places where people actually wolf down their lunch standing up so that they can get back to work! Italian fashion reaches its apex (or nadir) in these cities, so for gosh sakes, dress up a little unless you want lots of dirty looks.

Other regions to check out in the vast north include Trentino, the Piedmont, and overlooked but well-fed Emilio-Romagna.

To hit the most and best hostels, we'd hug the coastline on the train coming from France. There are at least four really good ones on the Italian Riviera within an hour of the French border, and they're often quieter than their counterparts in Cannes or Nice. Then we'd scoot up to the lakes district, where two of the three hostels are superb, among the best small ones in all Italy. Reserve a bed there for a couple days and vacuum up the scenery.

Finally, we might venture inland to places like Bologna (for good food) or Gran Paradiso Park (for Alpine views)—both home to good hostels, as well.

OSTELLO DI CAMPOTTO

Via Cardinala 27, 44010 Campotto di Argenta

Phone Number: 0532–808–035

Fax Number: 0532–808–035
Rates: 20,000 lire per HI member (about $11 US); family rooms 22,000 lire (about $13 US)
Credit cards: None
Beds: 52
Private/family rooms: Yes
Kitchen available: No
Season: March 1 to October 31
Office hours: 7:00 to 10:00 A.M.; 5:00 to 11:30 P.M.
Affiliation: HI-AIG
Extras: Breakfast, bar, TV, bike rentals, laundry, store

Located just outside Bologna, this fairly simple country hostel is situated halfway between the palatial city of Ferrara and the final resting place of Dante in Ravenna. The building is of historical interest, and it's a good place for families, with family rooms, kitchen, laundry, and television room. Free breakfast is included with your bed.

Gestalt: Bird brains

Party index:

You can hire a bike right here and explore miles of flat terrain, which includes the Lagoon of Comacchio and the Po River delta—an area often referred to as the Camargue of Italy. (The French equivalent is a flat, swampy region that attracts naturalists). Natural history lesson: Many migrating birds stop off here before embarking farther south; you might get lucky enough to spot bean geese and white egrets, for instance. Plans have even been advanced to convert this rich ecological area—from the point where the Po empties out in Venice all the way back inland to Ravenna—into a national park.

Meantime, enjoy this rustic place.

How to get there:

By bus: From Bologna, take bus to Argenta station and walk 50 yards to hostel.

By car: Call hostel for directions.

By train: Argenta station, 1 mile; call hostel for transit route.

OSTELLO VALDIGNE MONT BLANC (MONT BLANC HOSTEL)

Località Arpy, 11017 Arpy Morgex AO

Phone Number: 0165–841–684

Fax Number: 0165–841–684
E-mail: coserco@tin.it
Rates: 25,000 lire per HI member (about $14 US); doubles 60,000 lire (about $34 US)
Credit cards: None
Beds: 130 beds (summer); 70 (winter)
Private/family rooms: Yes
Kitchen available: No
Season: January 1 to May 3; June 24 to September 3; December 7 to December 31
Office hours: 7:00 to 10:00 A.M.; 3:30 to 11:30 P.M.
Affiliation: HI-AIG
Extras: Meals, bar, TV, game room, bike rental, movies, laundry, shuttle, fax

This lively hostel is tucked up against the borders of Switzerland and France, and mountaineers will find an attractive place to test their survival skills.

Party index:

You'll have the opportunity to partake of all manner of high-altitude activities including mountain biking, rock climbing, whitewater rafting and, of course, alpine and cross-country skiing. It's a happening hostel, too, featuring a bar, movie screenings, a laundry (yay), and more.

An interesting area, this; the 1994 Winter Olympics were just over the border in Albertville, and the famous and ancient St. Bernard Pass isn't too far (by mountain standards). Lots of attention is given to those oversized, slobbering dogs who used to help rescue those lost in the mountains. Try not to imitate them.

How to get there:

By bus: Call hostel for transit route.
By car: Call hostel for directions.
By train: Morgex station, 4½ miles away, is nearest stop; call hostel for transit route.

OSTELLO ANTICO CONVENTO DI SAN FRANCESCO (BAGNACAVALLO HOSTEL)

Via Cadorna, 48012 Bagnacavallo

Phone Number: 0512–249–13

Fax Number: 0512–249–13
Rates: 22,000 lire per HI member (about $12 US); doubles 48,000 lire (about $27 US)
Credit cards: None

Beds: 73
Private/family rooms: Yes
Kitchen available: No
Office hours: 7:00 to 10:00 A.M.; 3:00 P.M. to midnight
Affiliation: HI-AIG
Extras: Laundry, garden, TV, VCR, meals ($), meeting room

Yet another hostel located inside a palace, this one complements the recent closing of an AIG hostel in nearby Rimini. It's extremely well-equiped, despite being in a beautiful former Franciscan convent. There's a garden, of course, but also a television lounge (with its own VCR), a laundry, and meal service. You might just sit outside taking pictures of the hostel all day, it's that nice-looking.

Gestalt: Holy Roller

Party index:

This town, located in grape-growing country just west of coastal Ravenna, is notable mostly for its old San Pietro church. You can't miss it; take a gander inside for fine examples of old fresco work.

How to get there:

By bus: Contact hostel for transit route.
By car: Contact hostel for directions.
By train: From Bagnacavallo station, walk ½ mile to hostel.

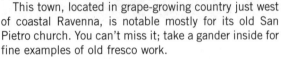

NUOVO OSTELLO DI BERGAMO (NEW BERGAMO HOSTEL)

Via Galileo Ferraris 1, 24123 Bergamo BG

Phone Number: 035–361–724 or 035–343–038

Fax Number: 035–361–724
E-mail: hostelbg@spm.it
Rates: 23,000 lire to 25,000 lire per HI member (about $13 to $14 US); doubles 70,000 lire (about $39 US)
Credit cards: Yes
Beds: 84
Private/family rooms: Yes
Kitchen available: No
Office hours: 7:00 A.M. to midnight
Curfew: Midnight
Affiliation: HI-AIG
Extras: Meals ($), bar, laundry, TV, bike rentals, Internet access, parking, movies, fax

Although Bergamo's hostel sits atop a hill, your room probably won't come with a decent view. Ah, well, that's life. This hostel has recently received a face-lift and has great facilities such as a restaurant and bar, TV, Internet access, and the all-important laundry. Word on the street is that there's also a good grocery store nearby.

Gestalt:
Nice Bergamo

Party index:

Management allows you to use the common facilities during the day, a good thing usually—unless the get-a-lifers are camped out in front of the tube. Other big pluses include some single rooms and lots of en-suite bathrooms, which hostellers really seem to appreciate.

Bergamo itself is quite scenic, with ascending strata of increasingly nice buildings.

How to get there:

By bus: Take 14 bus to Località Monteross and walk to hostel.

By car: Call hostel for directions.

By train: From Porta Nuova station, take 14 bus to Località Monterosso and walk to hostel.

OSTELLO LE LANGHE

Via Roma 22, 12070 Bergolo

Phone Number: 0173–872–22

Fax Number: 0173–872–22
Rates: 18,000 lire per HI member (about $11 US); doubles 40,000 lire (about $24 US)
Credit cards: Yes
Beds: 34
Private/family rooms: Yes
Kitchen available: No
Season: March 1 to October 31
Office hours: 7:00 to 10:00 A.M.; 3:30 to 11:30 P.M.
Affiliation: HI-AIG
Extras: Sports equipment, heating/hot water ($), meals ($), parking, library

Remoteness is the key word at this hostel; the town of Bergolo doesn't even appear on most maps of Italy, it's so small. That might be an advantage for non-Italian hostellers—you might get not just a bed but also a real feel for the local flavor of the Langhe region, a series of rolling hills in Piemonte located midway between Alba and Savona.

Gestalt:
Athletic supporter

Party index:

The hostel is a tidy two-story edifice with a large courtyard. It's a real draw for families and athletes alike, offering sports equipment and playing fields. Mountain trekking and orienteering are the activities that draw the hardbodies. You can also explore the region via horseback or mountain bike.

How to get there:

By bus: From Savona, take Geloso bus line toward Cortemilia; get off in Bergolo and walk 100 yards to hostel. From Acqui Terme, take Francone bus line through Cortemilia to Bergolo and walk 100 yards to hostel.

By car: Call hostel for directions.

By train: Acqui Termi station, 25 miles away, is closest stop; from station, take Francone bus line through Cortemilia to Bergolo and walk 100 yards to hostel.

OSTELLO DI SAN SISTO

Via Viadagola 14, San Sisto 1, 40127 Bologna BO

Phone Number: 051–501–810

Fax Number: 051–501–810
Rates: 21,000 lire per HI member (about $13 US); doubles/quads 44,000 to 48,000 lire (about $26 to $29 US)
Credit cards: None
Beds: 50
Private/family rooms: None
Kitchen available: No
Office hours: 7:00 to 10:00 A.M.; 3:30 to 11:30 P.M.
Lockout: 10:00 A.M. to 3:30 P.M.
Curfew: 11:30 P.M.
Affiliation: HI-AIG
Extras: Meals ($)

This good—though small—hostel, housed in a cute little villa and surrounded by green growing things, is certainly a welcome antidote to the active city of Bologna. Rooms are clean and the design is efficient, though cleanliness sometimes suffers a bit due to popularity.

Best bet for a bite:
Via Drapperie markets

Gestalt:
Bologna pony

Party index:

There are lots of chances to get to know your bunkmates in a highly civilized alfresco ambience; many outdoor tables and picnic tables will enhance your attempts at multilingual conversation.

Bologna is perhaps the queen of all Italian cities in terms of architecture. Many medieval towers poke over the red-tile rooftops of the city, creating a pleasing visual effect. Also pleasing to hostellers are the scads of eateries here, some super-rich and some aimed at lira-pinching students. There are lots of them, helping keep an exuberant vitality going in this place, and the city's justly famous for its rich sauces and food. So dig in.

How to get there:

By bus: Take bus 20/b, 93, 301, or 21/b; all stop near hostel.

By car: Call hostel for directions.

By train: From train station, walk 2 blocks south to via dei Mille/via Imerio, then catch bus 93, 20B, or 301 to San Sisto.

OSTELLO DUE TORRI (TWO TOWERS HOSTEL)

Via Viadagola 5, San Sisto, 40127 Bologna BO

Phone Number: 051–501–810

Fax Number: 051–501–810
Rates: 21,000 lire per HI member (about $13 US); doubles 44,000 lire to 48,000 lire (about $26 to $29 US)
Credit cards: None
Beds: 75
Private/family rooms: Yes
Kitchen available: No
Season: January 20 to December 19
Office hours: 7:00 A.M. to noon; 3:30 P.M. to midnight
Affiliation: HI-AIG
Extras: Restaurant, bar, TV, library, movies, bike rentals, laundry, sports equipment

Strangely, this big hostel is used as an overflow for the smaller San Sisto joint in town that's managed by the same fellow. This place, not as aesthetically pleasing as its sister hostel up the road, nevertheless offers many more amenities—including family rooms that come with breakfast, movies, a laundry, and more. So it's the definite choice if you're coming with the young 'uns.

Check out strada Maggiore and via Zamboni for student eats and other diversions. And the hostel gets its name from two big towers that, well, tower over the city; check 'em out, too. One looks like it'll fall, the other's straight and proud, but both remind you that Italy's a very old place indeed.

Best bet for a bite:
Clorafilla for vegetarian

Gestalt:
My Bologna

Cleanliness:

Party index:

How to get there:

By bus: Take 93, 20B, 21B or 301 bus to San Sisto.

By car: Call hostel for directions.

By train: From train station, walk 2 blocks south to via dei Mille/via Imerio and catch 93, 20B, 21B, or 301 bus to San Sisto.

Ostello Villa Olmo

Como

(photo courtesy of AIG)

OSTELLO VILLA OLMO

Via Bellinzona 2, 22100 Como

Phone Number: 031–573–800

Fax Number: 031–573–800
Rates: 17,000 lire per HI member (about $10 US); doubles 38,000 lire (about $23 US)
Credit cards: None
Beds: 76
Private/family rooms: One
Kitchen available: No
Season: March 1 to November 30
Office hours: 7:00 to 10:00 A.M.; 4:00 to 11:30 P.M.
Affiliation: HI-AIG
Extras: Meals ($), bar, library, bike rentals, laundry, games, lockers, fax

It's likely you won't mind the cramped quarters in this joint, since the friendly managers, who have a facility with languages, have stocked it with many hosteller-friendly extras like a convivial bar, out-of-this-world meals, a laundry, and (gasp) an ironing board.

Other little touches include newspapers, homemade jellies, and travel planning assistance; heck, it's just like being at home—

except that everybody here likes you. Nope, they don't come much friendlier than this team.

Como is the biggest—and thus appears busier—town on Lago di Como, but it still retains the casual, laid-back charm of other towns like Menaggio, Varenna, and Bellagio at the other end of the lake. Still, it ain't half bad and might be the place to stock up on grub before foraying out around the lakes. Use the good boat service to check out additional quaintness.

Gestalt: Merry Como

Hospitality: 👍

Cleanliness: 👍

Party index: 🎉🎉🎉🎉

How to get there:

By bus: Take bus 1, 6, 11, or 14 to hostel.

By car: Call hostel for directions.

By train: From Como station, walk down via Borgovico until it becomes via Bellinzona; bear to the left, following signs to the hostel. Or take bus 1, 6, 11, or 14 to hostel.

OSTELLO CITTA DI CORREGGIO (CORREGGIO HOSTEL)

Corso Cavour, 42015 Correggio

Phone Number: 051–224–913

Fax Number: 051–224–913
Rates: 19,000 lire per HI member (about $12 US)
Credit cards: Yes
Beds: 25
Private/family rooms: Yes
Kitchen available: Yes
Office hours: 7:00 to 10:00 A.M.; 3:30 to 11:30 P.M.
Affiliation: HI-AIG
Extras: Fax, TV, VCR, meals ($)

$

Yet another brooding stone building is the site of this new entry. This hostel isn't all that far from Prato, actually, which just got its own new hostel. So we have a hunch that Italian schoolkids are gonna be your main deal here. It does have some nice touches, though, like a TV lounge with a VCR, some meals for a charge, and a fax service.

Gestalt: Rolling stone

Party index: 🎉

How to get there:

By bus: From Capri station, 4 miles away, take bus to Correggio and walk ⅓ mile to hostel.

By car: Contact hostel for directions.

By train: From Capri station, 4 miles away, take bus to Correggio and walk ⅓ mile to hostel.

OSTELLO "LA VESPA" DOMASO

Via Case Sparse 12, 22013 Domaso CO

Phone Number: 034–497–449

Fax Number: 034–497–575
Rates: 14,000 lire per person (about $8.00 US)
Credit cards: Yes
Beds: 30
Private/family rooms: One
Kitchen available: Yes
Season: April 1 to October 31
Office hours: 8:00 A.M. to midnight
Affiliation: HI-AIG
Extras: Laundry, bike rentals, meals ($), TV, Internet access, videos, games

This amiable hostel straddles the borders of Italy and Switzerland, where the waters of Lago di Como attract hardbodies in search of *ondi perfetti* for their sailboarding pleasure. It's possible to access this hostel by land or water, but no matter how you do it, you'll be charmed by its rustic beauty.

Gestalt:
Great lake

Party index:

Cozy couples might consider reserving far in advance for the only private room here. But if you don't mind being in a bunkroom, this is indeed another—the third, in fact—good lakes region hostel in which to base yourself. And the views of the lake are stupendous.

How to get there:

By bus: Station is 50 meters from hostel.
By car: Call hostel for directions.
By train: Call hostel for transit route.

KEY TO ICONS

- Attractive natural setting
- Ecologically aware hostel
- Superior kitchen facilities or cafe
- Offbeat or eccentric place
- Superior bathroom facilities
- Romantic private rooms
- Comfortable beds
- Editors Choice Among our very favorite hostels
- A particularly good value
- Wheelchair-accessible
- Good for business travelers
- Especially well suited for families
- Good for active travelers
- Visual arts at hostel or nearby
- Music at hostel or nearby
- Great hostel for skiers
- Bar or pub at hostel or nearby

OSTELLO ESTENSE (FERRARA HOSTEL)

Corso Biagio Rossetti, 67, 44100 Ferrara

Phone Number: 051–224–913

Fax Number: 051–224–913
Rates: 20,000 to 23,000 lire per HI member (about $12 to $14 US); doubles 50,000 lire (about $30 US)
Credit cards: Yes
Beds: 84
Private/family rooms: Yes
Office hours: 7:00 to 9:00 A.M.; 3:30 to 11:30 P.M.
Affiliation: HI-AIG
Extras: Meals ($), meeting room, laundry, TV, garden

Facilities at this brick factory-looking building include family rooms, a television lounge, decent garden, meal service, and a laundry.

Ferrara's got more to see than you'd expect in this part of Italy; this snug city, not far from Bologna, was once (a lon-n-n-ng time ago) home to some important dukes (that's dukes, not dudes); as a result, it's got great squares, clocks, palaces, and alleyways. The Po River's deltas are nearby, and the annual Buskers Festival brings singing to the streets. The food isn't bad either.

Gestalt: Brick house

Party index:

How to get there:

By bus: Contact hostel for transit route.
By car: Contact hostel for directions.
By train: From Ferrara station, walk ⅓ mile to hostel.

OSTELLO WUILLERMAN CASTLE (WUILLERMAN CASTLE HOSTEL)

Via Generale Caviglia 46, 17024 Finale-Marina, Savona

Phone Number: 019–690–515 or 0347–241–4683

Fax Number: 019–690–515
E-mail: ostellof@ivg.it
Rates: 20,000 lire per HI member (about $12 US); doubles 44,000 lire (about $26 US)
Credit cards: Yes
Beds: 69
Private/family rooms: Yes
Kitchen available: No
Season: March 15 to October 15
Office hours: 7:00 to 10:00 A.M.; 3:30 to 11:30 P.M.

Curfew: 11:30 P.M.
Affiliation: HI-AIG
Extras: Laundry, meals ($), courtyard, watchdog (friendly), bar, library, bike rentals, games, fax

This vertigo-inducing hostel pretends to be a real castle, and it breaks your back with about 300 steps over which to schlep your pack. But it receives top honors all around for its friendly management and great location.

Gestalt: Stair master

Hospitality:

Cleanliness:

Party index:

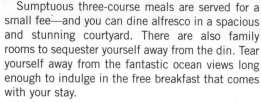

Sumptuous three-course meals are served for a small fee—and you can dine alfresco in a spacious and stunning courtyard. There are also family rooms to sequester yourself away from the din. Tear yourself away from the fantastic ocean views long enough to indulge in the free breakfast that comes with your stay.

Unfortunately, they don't take reservations here; that could be a major downer if you climbed all those stairs only to find the place entirely packed with other, luckier hostellers. Also, the place is short on showers; our advice is to take one at night if you can.

The area's pretty cool. Finale Ligure is one heck of a coastal town to set yourself up in, with superior walking and biking (everything around here's on the side of a hill) as well as shops, restaurants, locals, and a historic quarter. You're also only a couple miles by foot or by bus from Portvecchio's yacht scene or Santa Margherita's gentle waterfront.

How to get there:

By bus: Call hostel for transit route.
By car: Call hostel for directions.
By train: From Finale station, go left on via Mazzini, then left on Gradinata delle Rose and go up, up, up, following signs to hostel.

OSTELLO GENOVA

Via Costanzi 120, 16136 Genova

Phone Number: 010–242–2457
Fax Number: 010–242–2457
E-mail: HOSTELGE@IOL.IT
Rates: 23,000 lire per HI member (about $14 US); doubles 50,000 lire to 60,000 lire (about $30 to $36 US)
Credit cards: None
Beds: 213
Private/family rooms: Yes
Kitchen available: No

Season: February 2 to December 19
Office hours: 7:00 to 11:30 A.M.; 3:30 to midnight
Affiliation: HI-AIG
Extras: Elevator, laundry, patio, TV, meals ($), e-mail, lockers, bar, library, games

An excellent choice for those fond of Northern European efficiency (which is *very* atypical in Italy), this modern hostel fills up its halls with happy hostellers who are treated to big, clean, and comfortable rooms. It's one of Italy's best.

The staff is surprisingly helpful, friendly, and multilingual. Some rooms have showers for those folks who've been slumbering in their clothes during nighttime train rides. Family rooms here can accommodate four and are equally nice. Sheets, towels, and a hot shower are included in your rate. The beds even have individual reading lights, plus there's a television lounge where nobody seemed to want to hang out. Stow your stuff in the hallway lockers.

The hostel is not in Genova's downtown proper but is a short bus ride away. Along the way, be prepared for lots of scenery: The hostel's perched on a hill with splendiferous ocean views. Be careful while in downtown, Genoa, though. It has developed a not-so-savory rep; lots of crime and drugs have made it a dicey destination, so explore the wonderful back alleys with a group rather than hoofing it on your own at night.

Do make a point, though, of trying Genova's world-famous pesto at one of the *casalingas* (homey cafes) sprinkled around the city. You can buy all the Ligurian region's wonderful produce at the Mercato Orientale and tote it back to the hostel in your pack, though, since there's no kitchen, you won't be able to cook any of it.

Gestalt: Super Genova

Safety:

Hospitality:

Cleanliness:

Party index:

How to get there:

By bus: Take 40 bus to top of hill; get off at via Costanzi and walk to hostel.

By car: Call hostel for directions.

By plane: Genova airport, 5 miles away; call hostel for transit route.

By train: From Genoa station, take bus 40 (or 35 for five stops with transfer to 40) to top of hill; get off at via Costanzi and walk to hostel.

OSTELLO PO

Via Lido Po 11, 42016 Guastalla RE

Phone Number: 0522–219–287

Fax Number: 0522–839–228
E-mail: lunetia@tin.it
Rates: 19,000 lire per HI member (about $12 US)
Credit cards: None
Beds: 24
Private/family rooms: One
Kitchen available: Yes
Season: April 1 to October 15
Office hours: 7:00 to 10:00 A.M.; 3:30 to 11:30 P.M.
Affiliation: HI-AIG
Extras: Meals ($), TV, bike rentals, games, garden

On the banks of the famous Po River, this hostel's building used to house workers called *pontieri,* who tended the river. The river at one time played an important role in the ferrying of passengers, goods, and food, as well as serving as an effective means of communication among local communities.

Gestalt:
Po' boy

Party index:

Today the Po hostel is a decent place to bring the family; you can rent bikes to ride along the river's edge, take a breather in the lovely gardens, or play some board games with the kiddies. There's a television to distract them, too.

How to get there:

By bus: Call hostel for transit route.

By car: Call hostel for directions.

By train: Guastalla station, 2 miles away; call hostel for transit route.

OSTELLO 5 TERRE

Via B. Riccobaldi 21, 19010 Manarola

Phone Number: 039–187–920–215

Fax Number: 039–187–920–218
E-mail: ostello@cdh.it
Rates: 25,000 lire per person (about $16 US)
Beds: 48
Private/family rooms: Sometimes
Season: January 1 to January 14; February 16 to November 5; December 6 to 31
Office hours: 7:00 A.M. to 1:00 P.M.; 4:00 P.M. to midnight
Lockout: 2:00 to 5:00 P.M.
Affiliation: None
Extras: Internet access, breakfast ($), meals ($), TV, solarium

Run by a collective of three local guys, this Cinque Terre joint scores big with its emphasis on coastal Italian culture and its easy-to-use facilities.

Best bet for a bite:
On premises

Insiders' tip:
Walk the Lover's Way

What hostellers say:
"G'day mate. I mean, buongiorno."

Gestalt:
Five alive

Hospitality:

Cleanliness:

Party index:

The Cinque Terre region is among Italy's quaintest and prettiest: Vineyards cover the hillsides, and the ocean seems to always be that great shade of blue-green. The hostel takes full advantage, backing up against those hills and overlooking the little town of Manarola with its bundles of pastel houses and little harbor. The rooftop, reached by a cool elevator, is perfect for sunning or hanging with others.

Dorm rooms all contain six sleek beds apiece, and there are lots of quads, too. They contain shelves and lockers for each bunk, plus reading lights and tables. They are among the more spacious ones we've seen, and the mattresses were more than ample enough. The one quad room—with two sets of bunk beds instead of three—is sometimes used as a family room, and sometimes two couples share it. It's got an en-suite bathroom, unlike the rest of the rooms, good for families on the go.

Breakfasts and dinners here are actually good and filling and cheap, for a change, and the dining room is incredibly sociable. (The television that gets lots of channels, including Eurosport and CNN, didn't hurt either.) Other guests hung out at the Internet terminal, e-mailing stuff home like "wow!" while still others spent their days hiking the cliffside trail that links the five villages giving this region its name.

The staff couldn't have been more helpful or knowledgeable, either, and this is part of what makes the place special: real interaction with people who actually grew up here and don't have any attitude. They simply act like who they are: local Italian guys. They close the front desk for random smoke breaks, indulge in long-winded chats with buddies while you're waiting in line, take three-hour lunches—and you don't even mind because they run one heck of a great hostel.

Yeah, this hostel is already one of Italy's best—a place where fun and location intersect to create a truly wonderful experience. Too bad the crowd is almost 100 percent Aussies and Americans, so far. Let's hope some more folks hear about it soon.

How to get there:

By train: From La Spezia or Genova, take local train to Manarola station; walk uphill to town church; follow sign to hostel above and behind church.

OSTELLO LA PRIMULA (LA PRIMULA HOSTEL)

Via IV Novembre 86, 22017 Menaggio CO

Phone Number: 034–432–356

Fax Number: 034–431–677
E-mail: menaggiohostel@mclink.it
Season: March 15 to November 5
Beds: 50
Rates: 17,000 lire per HI member (about $10 US); doubles 38,000 lire (about $23 US)
Credit cards: None
Private/family rooms: Yes
Kitchen available: Yes ($)
Affiliation: HI-AIG
Office hours: 7:00 to 10:00 A.M.; 3:30 to 11:30 P.M.
Extras: Meals ($), bar, library, bike rentals, laundry, games, Internet, fax

Your kids will thank you later in life for taking them to this extremely family-friendly hostel. Not only are you able to stretch your travel dollar safely, but you'll have a fantastic time doing it. You can sample local wines here while washing your stinky socks in the laundry machines—not at the same time, though. Explore the surrounding countryside with some rented bikes available at the hostel.

Hospitality:

Cleanliness:

Party index:

Even if you haven't procreated, you'll probably love recreating at this place. Rooms are spic and span, and some can accommodate family groups. Management speaks English and cooks meals that are, yes, fabulous. (Come to think of it, it seems like every hostel in Italy serves up a great dinner. Well, hallelujah to that.) You can cook your own meals in a kitchen for once, even though you'll have to pay extra to use the kitchen equipment. No sweat. This place rules, and its lakeside town of Menaggio is really nice; you get there by ferry, which keeps the throngs away.

How to get there:

By bus: Call hostel for transit route.

By car: Call hostel for directions.

By train: Take train from Como to Ravenna, then take ferry (one and one-half hours) across lake to Menaggio.

OSTELLO PIERO ROTTA (PIERO ROTTA HOSTEL)

Via Martino Bassi 2, 20148 Milano

Phone Number: 02–392–670–95

Fax Number: 02–330–001–91
Rates: 26,000 lire per HI member (about $16 US), doubles 60,000 lire (about $36 US)
Credit cards: None
Beds: 380
Private/family rooms: Yes
Kitchen available: No
Season: January 13 to December 22
Office hours: 7:00 to 9:30 A.M., 3:30 P.M. to midnight
Lockout: 9:30 A.M. to 3:30 P.M.
Curfew: Midnight
Affiliation: HI-AIG
Extras: Internet access, gardens, TV, lockers, fax, bar

This place obviously has little of the easygoing attitude pervasive at other northern Italian hostels; the no-exceptions lockout and strict lights-out policy could sour your experience. Definitely don't come here expecting lots of warm and fuzzy vibes.

Hospitality:

Cleanliness:

Party index:

We'll concede that the hostel's location is serene, on the outskirts of town, but this could seriously cramp your partying style, since you have to return by the midnight curfew. There's a three-day-max stay, too. Your only consolation? Milano isn't really a destination. It's more of a business center, where fashion, design, and movie powerhouses operate and tourists find little to do. It's a mighty convenient transit hub, however, with lots of high-speed trains going all over Europe and lots of flights heading off to North America.

You are almost always guaranteed a room here, at least, so don't worry too much about being shut out. (You can always call ahead to be sure.) Remember that Milano empties out in August—completely—so that's the worst time to come. Nothing is open. Nothing. DO NOT COME IN AUGUST. There. We warned you.

Still, this is probably the cheapest and most efficient option in one of Italy's most expensive cities. And it's certainly clean and well run (if you like Gestapo tactics), if a tad hospital-like. No, make that dentist-like: a dentist with almost 400 chairs.

How to get there:

By bus: Take 90 or 91 bus to ostello (hostel) stop, then walk 300 yards to hostel.

By plane: Two airports. Milano Linate is 15 kilometers (about 10 miles) from hostel; Milano Malpensa is 40 kilometers (about 25 miles) from hostel. Call hostel for transit routes.

By subway: Take subway to QT 8-MM1 stop and walk 300 yards to hostel; stay to the right and watch for church on left. Hostel is on right.

By train: Centrale station, 2 miles from hostel; call hostel for transit route.

OSTELLO SAN FILIPPO NERI (MODENA HOSTEL)

Via Santa Orsola 48–52, 41100 Modena

Phone Number: 059–222–556

Fax Number: 059–217–149
Rates: 23,000 lire per HI member (about $14 US); doubles 50,000 lire (about $30 US)
Credit cards: Yes
Beds: 82
Private/family rooms: Yes
Kitchen available: No
Office hours: Twenty-four hours
Affiliation: HI-AIG
Extras: TV, Internet access, fax

Best bet for a bite: Farmers' market

Insiders' tip: Renaissance festival in summer

Gestalt: Depeche Modena

Party index:

A pretty good place, here, up in Emilia-Romagna—which, as we keep telling you, is Italy's stomach, so to speak. The hostel has dorms and family rooms, an Internet hookup, a television lounge, and a fax for hosteller use. No meals, however.

This city is world-famous for its balsamic vinegar, made by soaking wine with the pitch of a certain tree; some kinds are so sweet that Italians drink it for dessert! (It's not as weird as you'd think; we've tried it.) But Italians know it for other reasons—the opera singer Pavarotti lives here, and it's home to the headquarters of big-time Italian companies like Ferrari and Lamborghini. Can you smell the bucks?

How to get there:

By bus: Contact hostel for transit route.
By car: Contact hostel for directions.
By train: From Modena station, walk 300 yards to hostel.

CENTRO DI SOGGIORNO PARCO NAZIONALE (GRAN PARADISO NATIONAL PARK HOSTEL)

Frazione Gera Sopra, 10080 Noasca TO

Phone Number: 0124–901–107

Fax Number: 0124–901–107
Rates: 27,000 lire per HI member (about $16 US)
Credit cards: None
Beds: 68
Private/family rooms: Yes
Kitchen available: No
Office hours: 7:30 A.M. to 11:00 P.M.
Affiliation: HI-AIG
Extras: Cafeteria ($), bar, library, TV, movies, games, bike rentals, laundry

A full-service hostel for those who want to bask in all the natural glory of the National Park of Gran Paradiso, this is a great place for outdoor enthusiasts year-round. The hostel's located in a contemporary building, looking very much like the ski lodge that it is, plunked down at the foot of a huge mountain. Both cross-country and alpine skiing are the rules of thumb as far as wintertime activities go, but tours can also be arranged to view the local glaciers.

Gestalt: Park place

Hospitality:

Party index:

Hostellers are well taken care of here, especially those with families: A steady supply of books, movies, games, and bike rentals help fill in the blanks of the day, although you should have no problem deciding what to do. Don't worry about packing tons of food into the park, because cheap and tasty meals are offered in the hostel's cafeteria. You can even get schnockered in the on-premises bar. And kudos for the wheelchair-accessible private room.

Walkers have fantastic opportunities for trekking; you'll be amazed at the abundance of creatures such as the exotic horned ibex—it's related to the deer but looks more like a mountain goat.

Other principal attractions around here include the Paradisia Alpine Garden and the Cascata di Balma, a spine-tingling waterfall near the hamlet of Lillaz.

How to get there:

By bus: Take autolinea Torino-Ceresole Reale to Noasca and walk 50 yards to hostel.

By car: Call hostel for directions.

OSTELLO CITTADELLA

Parco Cittadella 5, 43100 Parma PR

Phone Number: 0521–961–434

Rates: 16,000 lire per HI member (about $10 US)
Credit cards: None
Beds: 50
Private/family rooms: None
Kitchen available: No
Season: April 1 to October 31
Office hours: 6:30 to 10:00 A.M.; 3:30 to 11:30 P.M.
Lockout: 10:00 A.M. to 3:30 P.M.
Curfew: 11:00 P.M.
Affiliation: HI-AIG
Extras: Camping, gardens, meals ($)

Gestalt: Parma chameleon

Party index:

Built smack dab in the middle of the Renaissance, this former fort was also once a prison, of all things; now it confines budget travelers who aren't always pleased with the upkeep. Or the fact that certain items normally gratis—like T.P.—carry an extra charge. (Hot tip: Bring yer own; it's softer anyway.)

Or, worst of all, that management takes so many big groups that individual hostellers often find a three-week backlog before any rooms will become available. If things are really feeling bad and you're stuck in town for the night, pitch that tent in the adjacent gardens for a possibly more pleasant experience.

Some of our hosteller snoops liked the spacious rooms and hot showers, though, which stand head and shoulders above the usual European bathroom facilities. Parma partyers were uniformly disappointed by the ironclad 11:00 P.M. hostel curfew, though, which they claimed put a crimp in their style.

Parma itself is more than just grated cheese and salty ham; it's really a pretty old city, with an old-world look and polite, well-heeled denizens who dress up when they go out. There's lots of walking to be done here, just seeing the sights and reveling in an Italy that hasn't been discovered by tourists yet.

This hostel's in a gorgeous location. Too bad you'll probably never score a room here.

How to get there:

By bus: Call hostel for transit route.

By car: Call hostel for directions.

By train: From train station, take 9 bus to Via Martiri della Liberta; follow signs to park

OSTELLO DANTE

Via Aurelio Nicolodi 12, 48100 Ravenna

Phone Number: 0544–421–164

Fax Number: 0544–421–164
E-mail: hostelra@hotmail.com
Rates: 23,000 lire per HI member (about $14 US); doubles 50,000 lire (about $30 US)
Credit cards: Yes
Beds: 140
Private/family rooms: Yes
Kitchen available: No
Office hours: 7:00 A.M. to noon; 2:00 to 11:30 P.M.
Lockout: Noon to 2:00 P.M.
Affiliation: HI-AIG
Extras: Meals, bar, TV, games, Internet access

If this hostel had been around during Signor Alighieri's time, maybe that darned Dante wouldn't have been so fixated on his beloved Beatrice.

Gestalt:
Divine comedy
Party index:

Despite its sterile-looking exterior, which doesn't appear to exude a lot of warmth, the hostel that carries Dante's name today embodies all that the world has come to associate with Italy. It's brash and lively, and you'll come away with many new *amici*. It's also got a great location for hostellers—a supermarket and park rub shoulders with it—and friendly staff.

Families benefit from the many family-designated rooms and games for the kiddies (or for the kid at heart). Remember to take into consideration, though, that you can only take a shower in the evening for a period of about three hours; that's when the water becomes hot. This place definitely retains the original mission of hostels—it's a clean and simple place to rest your head.

How to get there:

By bus: Take 1 or 11 bus.

By car: Call hostel for directions.
By train: From train station, take 1 bus to via Molinetto.

OSTELLO REGGIO EMILIA (REGGIO EMILIA HOSTEL)

Via dell'Abbadessa 8, 42100 Reggio Emilia RE

Phone Number: 0522–454–795

Rates: 17,000 lire per HI member (about $10 US)
Credit cards: None
Beds: 36
Private/family rooms: None
Kitchen available: Yes
Office hours: 7:00 to 10:00 A.M.; 3:30 P.M. to midnight
Affiliation: HI-AIG
Extras: Meals ($), TV, bike rentals, kitchen, heating/hot water ($)

Party index:

Although this hostel is in the middle of Reggio Emilia's downtown action, it still charges a fee for the privilege of heat and hot water. Oh, well.

At least they make up for it with a decent discount at the eatery next door and a homey, quiet feel; it feels like (and, heck, may in fact be) someone's house. No lockers for storing your stuff, though, which could be a bummer.

Reggio Emilia is well known as the place where Italy's famous tricolor flag was designed. It's known for its incredible ethnic diversity as well. You'll see all that and more, and when you get back to the hostel, crash in front of the tube for a dose of amusing Italian television.

How to get there:

By bus: Take bus to hostel stop, walk 100 yards to hostel.
By car: Call hostel for directions.
By train: From train station, walk ⅓ mile to hostel.

OSTELLO MAMMA ROSA (MAMMA ROSA'S HOSTEL)

Piazza Unita 2, Riomaggiore

Phone Number: 0187–920–050

Rates: 20,000 lire per person (about $12 US)
Beds: 60
Affiliation: None
Extras: Cats

This place is one of the most hotly debated joints in European hosteldom. Simply put, it's scruffy with a capital "S" . . . yet friendly and convivial. If you're a cleanliness freak, keep on truckin'; but if you're into the experience of meeting other folks and seeing the "real" Italy, hang with it awhile.

Gestalt: Mamma mia . . .

Hospitality:

Cleanliness:

The place is easy to find: When you get off the train (and you will—no cars are allowed!), Mamma Rosa finds you almost before you can draw a breath.

Entering her hostel, the first thing you notice is the pervasive odor of cats—specifically, cat fur and urine—that's everywhere; their bathroom is your bathroom and so on. A health inspector from the States would probably pass out at the sight of it, but here in l'Italia it's just business as usual. Bottom line? If this is the kind of thing that can make or break your vacation, then it's probably the only thing you'll remember about Mamma Rosa's.

Rooms are coed, too, which takes getting used to. And the showers are outside the building in roofless cubicles. Dorm rooms, with four to ten bunks apiece, aren't exactly stellar.

If you can stand all that, though, the location's absolutely unbeatable. A more social place you won't find; backpackers love this place, and they love to convene to rave about the awesome Cinque Terre landscape. And, after many liters of vino shared with your fellow hostellers, you probably won't even notice the stench or the other, ahem, amenities—like the lukewarm water that's supposed to be calda but isn't.

How to get there:

By bus: Call hostel for transit route.

By car: Call hostel for directions.

By train: Take train to La Spezia; change to milk train and continue to Riomaggiore. From station, find Mamma Rosa or walk into village and ask for directions.

OSTELLO BENACUS

Piazza Cavour 10, 38066 Riva del Garda, Trento

Phone Number: 0464–554–911

Fax Number: 0464–559–966
E-mail: ostelloriva@anthesi.com
Rates: 20,000 lire per person (about $12 US)
Credit cards: None
Beds: 67
Private/family rooms: None
Kitchen available: No
Season: April 1 to October 31
Office hours: 7:00 to 9:00 A.M.; 3:00 P.M. to midnight
Lockout: Noon to 3:30 P.M.

Curfew: Midnight
Affiliation: HI-AIG
Extras: Laundry, meals ($), bike rentals

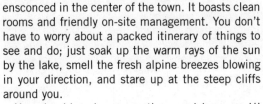

This is another great and newly renovated hostel that serves as a crash pad for windsurfers in the know. Situated on the north shore of Lago del Garda and next to a church, Benacus is pleasantly ensconced in the center of the town. It boasts clean rooms and friendly on-site management. You don't have to worry about a packed itinerary of things to see and do; just soak up the warm rays of the sun by the lake, smell the fresh alpine breezes blowing in your direction, and stare up at the steep cliffs around you.

Gestalt: Cliff notes

Party index:

You should make reservations and have an HI membership card when you check in, though. People love this place, and it's jam-packed with hostellers during the busy summer season. And make sure you've brought your sleep sack or, better yet, sheets.

How to get there:

By bus: Bus stops 100 yards from hostel.
By car: Call hostel for directions.
By train: Rovereto station, 13 miles away, is nearest stop; call hostel for transit route.

OSTELLO CITTÀ DI ROVERETO (CITY OF ROVERETO HOSTEL)

Via della Scuola 16/18, 36068 Rovereto TN

Phone Number: 0464–433–707

Fax Number: 0464–424–137
E-mail: YOUTHOSTROV@TQS.IT
Rates: 20,000 lire per HI member (about $12 US); doubles 56,000 lire (about $33 US)
Credit cards: Yes
Beds: 90
Private/family rooms: Yes
Kitchen available: No
Season: January 1 to February 2; February 25 to December 31
Office hours: 7:00 A.M. to midnight
Lockout: 9:00 A.M. to 5:00 P.M.
Curfew: 11:30 P.M.
Affiliation: HI-AIG

Extras: Meals ($), bar, TV, laundry, library, games, bike rentals, Internet access

This classy joint caters to all travelers, and the friendly family who run it speak a number of languages. Other special amenities include en-suite bathrooms and tasty meals that can become vegetarian upon request. Some rooms even have terraces attached. The town of Rovereto's no big deal, but it's not chopped liver, either, and it's on some train lines, which makes it more attractive.

Hey, this place is clean and affordable; what more could you ask for?

Gestalt:
Rovereto's return

Hospitality:

Cleanliness:

Party index:

How to get there:

By bus: Call hostel for transit route.

By car: Call hostel for directions.

By train: From Verona, take train to Rovereto; from Rovereto station, cross street and walk down via Rosmini, turn right on via Fontana, then go left on Borgo S. Caterina; stay straight on via Garibaldi, make a right on viale della Scuole and you're there.

VILLAGGIO-OSTELLO CENTRO EUROPA UNO (ONE EUROPE CENTER HOSTEL VILLAGE)

Via Emilia 297, Cicogna 40068, San Lazzaro di Savena BO

Phone Number: 051–625–8352

Fax Number: 051–625–8357
Rates: 24,000 lire per Hi member (about $15 US)
Credit cards: None
Beds: 42
Private/family rooms: Yes
Kitchen available: Yes
Affiliation: HI-AIG
Extras: Bike rentals, laundry, camping, sauna, fax, library, sports equipment, meals ($)

Get away from the hordes of college students in Bologna at this relaxing, family oriented hostel, located outside that educated and well-fed city known sometimes as Bologna the Fat. You take city buses 5 miles out into the countryside to get here.

Be aware, though, that you may be accompanied by hordes of schoolchildren or other groups who might make or break your visit. The hostel has been incorporated into a mini–tourist village of which it is just one component. You can avail yourself of the sauna, camping area, bike rentals, and playing fields for sports—but you surely won't be alone.

Gestalt:
Fun in the sun

Party index:

How to get there:

By bus: Take 94, 98, 916, or 101 (extraurbani) bus to hostel.

By car: Call hostel for transit route.

By plane: Borgo Panigale airport in Bologna, 9 miles away; call hostel for transit route.

By train: From Bologna station, 5 miles away, take 94, 98, 916, or 101 (extraurbani) bus to hostel.

OSTELLO SANTA SOFIA

Piazza Matteotti, 47018 Santa Sofia FO

Phone Number: 0543–974–511

Rates: 22,000 lire per HI member (about $13 US)
Beds: 26
Private/family rooms: Yes
Kitchen available: No
Office hours: 7:00 to 10:00 A.M.; 3:00 P.M. to midnight
Affiliation: HI-AIG
Extras: Store, meals ($), TV

Located in central Emilia-Romagna, partway between Florence and the Adriatic coast, this brand-new hostel is popular with day-trippers and youth groups seeking to enjoy the plethora of outdoor activities offered in the area: walking in the National Park of the Casentinesei Forests, for instance, or hiking up either Monte Falterona e Campiglia or Monte Fumaiolo, the birthplace of the Tevere River.

Gestalt:
Sofia city, sweetheart

Party index:

Since this joint is so new and remote, we haven't heard much about it yet. We do know that it's housed in a sizable building—yet, for some reason, contains a small amount of beds.

How to get there:

By bus: From Forli, take Forli-Camaldoli bus line to Santa Sofia, ask for drop-off near ostello (hostel) and walk 100 yards to hostel.

By train: Forli station, 25 miles away, is nearest stop. From station, take Forli-Camaldoli bus line to Santa Sofia; ask for drop-off near ostello (hostel) and walk 100 yards to hostel.

OSTELLO FORTEZZA PRIAMAR

Fortezza Priamar, Corso 17100 Mazzini Savona SV

Phone Number: 019–812–653 or 019–852–485

Fax Number: 019–812–653
E-mail: priamarhostel@iol.it
Rates: 22,000 lire per HI member (about $13 US); doubles 46,000 to 52,000 (about $27 to $31 US)
Credit cards: Yes
Beds: 60
Private/family rooms: Yes
Kitchen available: No
Season: January 15 to December 14
Office hours: 7:00 to 10:00 A.M.; 3:30 to 11:30 P.M.
Affiliation: HI-AIG
Extras: Meals ($), TV, laundry, Internet access, bike rentals, videos, library, fax

There are two excellent hostels in this little-visited town on the Italian Riviera. This is the more charming of the two, housed in an old fort you might actually become lost in. We mean, like, medieval old. Too bad management's so stern and standoffish, because this hostel has potential.

Families will undoubtedly enjoy this place for its history and unique architecture as well as the rooms reserved for family use that come in configurations of two to four beds. These bunks are okay, and bathrooms come en suite. Single travelers will also find it refreshing to find that this hostel has some rooms with just one bed. No lockers, though.

There's not a whole lot to keep you occupied in this primarily industrial city, so head for the nearby beach, where most of the action is. You can use this town as a good base to explore the more glitzy Riviera towns like nearby San Remo or sleepy Ventimiglia—snuggled up against the French border, sure, but undeniably Italian.

Gestalt:
My Savona

Hospitality:

Cleanliness:

Party index:

How to get there:

By bus: Take 2, 7, or 8 bus. Bus stops 100 meters from hostel.
By car: Call hostel for directions.
By train: Call hostel for transit route.

OSTELLO VILLA DE FRANCESCHINI

Via alla Strà 29 (Conca Verde), 17100 Savona SV

Phone Number: 019–263–222

Fax Number: 019–263–222
E-mail: concaverd@hotmail.com
Rates: 18,000 lire per HI member (about $11 US); doubles 40,000 lire (about $24 US)
Beds: 244
Private/family rooms: Yes
Kitchen available: No
Office hours: 7:00 to 10:00 A.M.; 3:30 to 11:30 P.M.
Season: March 15 to October 15
Affiliation: HI-AIG
Extras: Meals ($), bar, TV, games and sports equipment, laundry, bike rentals

Party index:

This is the other, and also good, hostel in Savona. We still can't figure out why there are 300 total hostel beds in a town that most guidebooks give only a brief mention (a sentence is usually all it gets); that's more beds than many big cities get.

But here we are, a monster of a facility ensconced on a pretty big spread of green space outside the city. It's well equipped, with a television room, bar, laundry, and more. The hostel even provides a shuttle bus to escort you to the city center, where all other transportation modalities wait to whisk you away. And look at it this way: Although industrial Savona's pretty darned unexciting, you can usually find room at the inn somewhere near the Italian coast.

How to get there:

By bus: Private bus from hostel to city center and back.
By car: Call hostel for directions.
By train: Call hostel for transit route.

OSTELLO TORINO

Via Albi 1, 11013 Torino

Phone Number: 011–660–2939

Fax Number: 011–660–4445
E-mail: hostelto@tin.it
Rates: 20,000 lire per HI member (about $12 US); doubles 44,000 lire (about $26 US)
Credit cards: None
Beds: 76

Private/family rooms: Yes
Kitchen available: No
Season: February 1 to December 17
Office hours: 7:00 to 10:00 A.M.; 3:30 to 11:30 P.M.
Affiliation: HI-AIG
Extras: Meals ($), laundry, lockers, TV, bar, games and sports equipment, fax, heating and hot water ($ winter)

Some hostellers claim they've seen the silhouette of the Holy One in their sleep sacks while staying here.

Okay, okay, don't get out those pens and pads and start writing nasty letters. We're just kidding. Seriously, though, this lire-stretching and immaculate hostel stands shoulder to shoulder among Torino's posh shops and cafes, definitely not a budget stickler's turf. Thankfully, the hostel serves quite good three-course dinners for about 14,000 lire ($9.00 US) and throws in a free light breakfast to boot. This hostel has a surprisingly good social atmosphere, and people were chatting up a storm when we swung through.

Gestalt: Grand Torino

Safety:

Hospitality:

Cleanliness:

Party index:

Other stuff? Well, there's a laundry—which is fairly expensive at the equivalent of about $6.00 a load, by the way—plus lockers are available to stash your pack. You'll also be grateful for other amenities like graceful balconies with good views and a television room. There are tennis courts and gardens out back, too. Only drawback? The hostel has to charge an extra 2,000 lire (relax, it's only about $1.25 US) for heating in winter.

Torino is a student's paradise; it's a university town full of bookstores in its city center for your perusal. History mavens will enjoy Torino's place in history as the birth of the Risorgimento (the unification of Italy), and a museum showcases memorabilia from this turbulent era. Also, in case you didn't know, Torino is the Detroit of Italy: Fiat pumps out the cars here, enabling workers to abandon the vitality of the city center and move out to the god-awful suburbs.

Mystics may also be drawn to the renowned Shroud of Turin, the cloth that allegedly reveals the visage of Jesus Christ. It was placed on public display for a few months during early 1998, but normally you need very special permission to view it.

How to get there:

By bus: The 52 bus stops 300 meters away.
By car: Call hostel for directions.
By train: From train station, take bus 52 to hostel.

OSTELLO GIOVANE EUROPA (YOUNG EUROPEAN HOSTEL)

Via Alessandro Manzoni, 17 Trento, 38100

Phone Number: 0461–234–567

Fax Number: 0461–268–434
Rates: 22,000 lire per HI member (about $13 US); doubles 50,000 to 60,000 lire (about $30 to $36 US)
Credit cards: Yes
Beds: 68
Private/family rooms: Yes
Kitchen available: No
Office hours: 7:00 A.M. to midnight
Curfew: Midnight
Affiliation: HI-AIG
Extras: TV, bar

This centrally located and newly renovated hostel provides basic accommodation with no frills. You'll be pleased with the clean rooms and super java, though. Rooms are small, containing anywhere from one to six beds each. Sorry to report that meals here are for groups only, and there's no kitchen. Look for a local pizzeria to fill in the gaps, or just stock up on extra rolls from the breakfast that's included with your night's stay.

Party index:

Catholic and Protestant historians alike are drawn to this city, which was the site of the Council of Trent, a restructuring event that succeeded in luring about half of Europe's lapsed Catholics back into the arms of the Church in what's known as the Counter-Reformation.

Big deal? Well, it was back then . . . anyhow, Trento also is a perfect base for exploring the surrounding region, known for its majestic Alpine mountains and the pretty Adige River.

How to get there:

By bus: Call hostel for transit route.

By car: Call hostel for directions.

By train: From Trento station, turn left on via Dogana, then go right on via Romagnosi and left on via Manzoni to hostel.

OSTELLO VERBANIA

Via Alle Rose, 7 28048 Verbania VB

Phone Number: 0323–501–648

Fax Number: 0323–507–877

Rates: 48,000 lire per HI member (about $29 US); doubles 54,000 lire (about $32 US)
Credit cards: None
Beds: 72
Private/family rooms: Yes
Kitchen available: No
Office hours: 7:00 to 10:00 A.M.; 3:30 to 11:30 P.M.
Affiliation: HI-AIG
Extras: Meals ($), bar, TV, library, bike rentals, movies, laundry, games and sports equipment

Like lakes? This hostel is perfectly situated on the shores of Lago Maggiore, a narrow swath of water that pits the upright Alps in neighboring Switzerland against the more rolling terrain of Lombardy. Most hostellers will be attracted to the enchanting Borromean islands that dot the interior of the lake.

Gestalt:
Lombardy popular

Party index:

The hostel itself, though, isn't nearly as exciting. It is reasonably clean and comfortable, a decent enough draw for families with its private rooms, meals, games and sports equipment for the kiddies—as well as movie nights and a library for all ages.

The tiny town of Verbania houses an intriguing museum that highlights the fashion sense of the local peasants. (Gee, we didn't know that these humble farmers and fisherfolk would set about to change the world of fashion.) Fans of flora can skip that and visit the nearby botanical gardens.

How to get there:

By bus: Take the Milano–Novara–Torino line.
By car: Call hostel for directions.
By train: Station in Verbania is 6 miles away.

VENICE AND THE VENETO

Page numbers follow town names.

VENICE AND THE VENETO

There's only one Venice. Soggy, overpriced, overrun with tourists . . . it doesn't matter at all, because this is quite simply the most beautiful city in the world. Too bad nobody local lives there anymore, hardly.

If you're coming in fall or winter, remember that high tides sometimes flood the city silly. They lay down boards to deal with this *acqua alte* (high water) and carry on like nothing's wrong, but it could get mighty uncomfortable if you're wearing nonwaterproof shoes like sneakers. Check conditions ahead of your arrival by calling the tourism office.

The Veneto is the region surrounding Venice. During old times, cities like Verona or Vicenza were controlled by the Venetians, and they built some beautiful places indeed—on higher ground than their muggy flagship city. We've also included the Adriatic Sea region here, which bumps up against Eastern Europe and has a distinctly un-Italian flavor as a result.

OSTELLO EKAR (EKAR HOSTEL)

Costalunga Ekar 1, Asiago, Vicenza, 36012

Phone Number: 0424–455–138

Fax Number: 0424–455–138
Rates: 23,000 lire per HI member (about $14 US); doubles 60,000 lire (about $36 US)
Credit cards: None
Beds: 130
Private/family rooms: Yes
Kitchen available: No
Season: January to February; May 20 to September 10; December
Office hours: 7:00 A.M. to 11:30 P.M.
Affiliation: HI-AIG
Extras: Meals ($), bar, TV, game room, sports, bike rentals, breakfast

Visitors and residents alike gush incessantly about this fantastic region, thought of as a veritable garden of Eden. And this hostel helps hostellers enjoy the area with an efficient and clean establishment containing tons of great amenities like a bar, bike rentals, free breakfasts, meal service, and more. The facility itself is rather nondescript and resembles a postmodern three-story apartment building; the good stuff is hidden inside.

For starters, hikers can traverse more than 300 trails, which extend all directions from the hostel. Other activities in the area include golf and tennis. Or taste the incredibly scrumptious local cheese, which isn't too soft and isn't too hard—it's somewhere in between, one of the tastiest in Italy. And that's saying something.

Party index:

How to get there:

By bus: Bus stops 100 meters from hostel; call hostel for transit route.

By car: Call hostel for directions.

By train: Bassano del Grappa station, 15 miles away, is nearest stop; call hostel for transit details.

OSTELLO ROCCA DEGLI ALBERI (CASTLE IN THE FOREST HOSTEL)

Castello degli Alberi, Porta Legnago, 35044 Montagnana PD

Phone Number: 0429–810–76 or 0498–070–266

Fax Number: 0429–810–76 or 0498–070–266
Rates: 17,000 lire per HI member (about $10 US); doubles 40,000 lire (about $26 US)
Credit cards: None
Beds: 48
Private/family rooms: One
Kitchen available: No
Season: April 1 to October 15
Office hours: 7:00 to 10:00 A.M.; 3:00 to 11:30 P.M.
Lockout: 10:00 A.M. to 3:00 P.M.
Affiliation: HI-AIG
Extras: Camping, bike rentals, TV, gardens

If you're into jousting or courtly love poetry, this medieval town's right up your alley. And the hostel contributes to the knights-of-the-round-table gestalt, since it's located inside one of two castles in this walled city.

Gestalt: Friendly host

Party index:

Be prepared for a haunting ambience, though. The castle's age and atmosphere might give you the creeps, but think of all the stories you'll have to tell when you get home of strange apparitions that followed you into the bathroom and such.

Anyhow, this hostel is usually pretty quiet and empty, which almost guarantees you a bed, albeit a soft one. But

Ostello Rocca degli Alberi

Montagnana

(photo courtesy of AIG)

make sure to call ahead anyway, as it sometimes attracts little ghoulies of a different kind in the form of schoolchildren on class trips. Also call ahead to reserve the one nice private room for couples, a bit extra but worth it. A television room, some good gardens, and bikes for rent add to the fun.

How to get there:

By bus: Bus stops 200 yards from hostel; call hostel for transit route.

By car: Call hostel for directions.

By train: From Montagnana station, walk ⅓ mile to hostel.

OSTELLO CITTÀ DI PADOVA (CITY OF PADUA HOSTEL)

Via Aleardo Aleardi 30, 35122 Padova

Phone Number: 049–875–2219

Fax Number: 049–654–210
Rates: 23,000 lire per HI member (about $14 US); doubles 50,000 lire (about $30 US)
Credit cards: Yes
Beds: 112
Private/family rooms: Yes
Kitchen available: No
Season: January 7 to December 24
Office hours: 7:00 to 10:00 A.M., 2:30 to 11:00 P.M. (Monday to Friday); 7:00 to 10:00 A.M., 4:00 to 11:00 P.M. (Saturday to Sunday)
Lockout: 10:00 A.M. to 4:00 P.M.
Curfew: 11:00 P.M.
Affiliation: HI-AIG
Extras: Meals ($), bar, TV, movies, laundry, bike rentals, breakfast, store, lockers

Hospitality:

Cleanliness:

Party index:

This hostel is a mixed bag, to be sure. It's got beautiful tile flooring and includes a restaurant that serves out-of-this-world pasta dishes, sure. The common area is big, roomy, and friendly. Rooms are okay, if crowded. There's also a laundry, especially appreciated in Italy, where self-serve laundries are notoriously expensive and bothersome. Management couldn't be friendlier or more helpful to wayward hostellers.

Another bonus is Padova's proximity to Venice, which is just half an hour away by train. You can see all the sights you want to see there, then hop the train back for a night of peace and quiet—and better food. Venice is so expensive and the trains so cheap that you'll probably spend less this way anyhow. And this town has its own lesser known streets and sights to entice.

All isn't picture-perfect here, though: One downside is that the hostel neighborhood is a little marginal, so be careful about going out alone at night. Also, a five-day maximum stay is imposed, which could be considered bad by some but a good idea by others. Finally, the place could be cleaner. Must be the crowds. Get our drift? If you're coming, reserve early, it remains a popular and sometimes packed place.

How to get there:

By bus: Take 3, 8, 12, 18, or 22 bus to hostel stop and walk 250 yards to hostel.

By car: Call hostel for directions.

By train: From Padova station, walk 1 mile down corso Garibaldi to via Settembre; turn right onto XX Settembre and follow to via Seminaro, make a left and immediate right. Hostel is at Aleardi.

OSTELLO IMPERINA (IMPERINA HOSTEL)

Località Le Miniere 32020, Rivamonte Agordino, BL

Phone Number: 0437–624–51

Rates: 25,000 lire per HI member (about $15 US)
Credit cards: None
Beds: 44
Private/family rooms: None
Kitchen available: No
Office hours: 7:00 to 10:00 A.M., 3:30 to 11:30 P.M.
Affiliation: HI-AIG
Extras: Bar, TV

Better brush up on your German if you plan on staying in this neck of the Dolomites. And this tiny hostel—which is a refurbished *baita* (an Alpine wooden building once used for hay stacking and barnyard animals)—brings to mind the sort of structure you would expect. Think Heidi, plus her grandfather and assorted goats. Just kidding.

Gestalt: Yodel-lay-hee-hoo

Party index:

Most hostellers who make their way here are yearning to *schuss* down the Dolomites' famous slopes. A word of advice, even if you're here in the summer: Pack warm and waterproof clothing, as the weather here changes rapidly. And be sure to stick to well-marked trails.

How to get there:

By bus: Take Belluno–Agordo bus line and stop at Le Campe, about 1.5 km (9/10 mile) away.

By car: Call hostel for directions.

By train: Belluno station is 35 km (about 21 miles) from hostel.

OSTELLO TERGESTE

Viale Miramare 331, 34136 Trieste TS

Phone Number: 040–224–102

Fax Number: 040–224–102
Rates: 20,000 lire per HI member (about $12 US)
Credit cards: None
Beds: 74

Ostello Tergeste

Trieste

(photo courtesy of AIG)

Private/family rooms: None
Kitchen available: No
Season: March 1 to December 31
Office hours: 7:00 to 10:00 A.M.; noon to midnight
Lockout: 9:00 A.M. to noon
Curfew: 11:30 P.M.
Affiliation: HI-AIG
Extras: Meals ($), bar, parking, TV, bike rentals, garden, free lockers

Bugged by bugs? Then don't come to this modern hostel that overlooks the Adriatic Sea. If it's great views and beaches you crave, though, and you're fascinated by the triumvirate of languages (German, Italian, and Slavic) spoken in the city, maybe you can overlook the unclean and somewhat broken-down facilities. We'd pass it up for a good hotel instead.

There are no more than four bunks to a room; there are family rooms, too. None of them are good. Rooms are derelict, beds are rusty, and the lockers are broken. We're just telling it to you straight.

Wanna forget your bed? Party hearty at an on-site bar that sometimes showcases live music but usually just blasts yucky Top 40 hits from the States. And give a pat to the convivial canine. Remember that you're just 15 feet from the beach yet 8 long miles from the center of downtown Trieste. Hey, at least you're practically in the former Yugoslavia. Now there's something to write home about. (Actually, the beach here is good, and the old town's pretty nice, too.)

But that bar . . . well, it's upstairs and the general public uses it. A lot. Occasional parties keep it rockin' into the wee hours; at least the hostel check-in desk also stays open those nights.

Gestalt: Seasick

Cleanliness:

Party index:

How to get there:

By bus: Take bus 36 to hostel. Exit before hill and walk along waterfront following signs to hostel.

By car: Call hostel for directions.

By train: Take bus 36 from train station to hostel. Exit before hill and walk along waterfront, following signs to hostel.

OSTELLO SAN SALVARO (SAN SALVARO HOSTEL)

Località San Salvaro, 35044 Urbana (San Salvaro)

Phone Number: 042–981–076

Fax Number: 0498–070–266
Rates: 17,000 lire per HI member (about $10 US); doubles 40,000 lire (about $24 US)
Credit cards: None
Beds: 24
Private/family rooms: Sometimes
Kitchen available: No
Office hours: 7:00 to 10:00 A.M.; 3:30 to 11:30 P.M.
Affiliation: HI-AIG
Extras: Bike rentals

A pretty simple place, this is, in the inland Veneto. You're probably only going to find school groups getting out to this whitewashed old building, so look sharp if you come. They don't serve meals yet, but they do rent bikes; go figure. At least that's in keeping with the ecologically minded managers, who earned this place a "Green Hostel" stamp from Italy's national hostel association.

Gestalt: Green machine

Party index:

How to get there:

By bus: Contact hostel for transit route.

By car: Contact hostel for directions.

By train: From Montagnana station, 4 miles away, contact hostel for transit route.

VENICE

You're gonna come here, so deal with the facts: First, the only way to get around is by boat or by foot. When you arrive at Santa Lucia train station, the first thing you want to do is grab a *vaporetto* (commuter boat) downtown. Take the number 82 line to get to the center fast if you must, but we prefer the number 1 boat—it's superscenic and gets you right into the sights at once.

To walk around, get a great map and watch for little bridges and side canals; when you get lost (you will), ask locals to point you back toward San Marco plaza at the center of it all, or else just find signs and troop off again. Quite convenient are the many smaller picturesque gondolas: They appear to have been built for tourists, but actually they ferry residents across the bigger canals all day long for a pittance. Avoid the rip-off gondola tours and buy a regular commuter ticket on a cross-city boat instead; it's just as good.

There's a surprising and serious lack of hostel beds here, though. The only big and legit one is the huge HI joint—and it's not even in Venice proper, but on another island. Three little places rent out dorm beds, but they only partly resemble true hostels. Lots of religious organizations in Venice maintain dorms as well, but their strict curfews and no-unmarried couples rules kept 'em out of this book.

VENICE HOSTELS at a glance

	RATING	PRICE	IN A WORD	PAGE
Casa Gerotto		30,000 lire to 50,000 lire	decent	p.261
Ostello Santa Fosca		23,000 lire	quiet	p.262
Ostello Venezia		27,000 lire	okay	p.262
Archie's Hostel		21,000 lire	relaxed	p.261

ARCHIE'S HOSTEL

Rio Terra Santo Leonardo, Cannareggio 1814b, Venezia

Phone Number: 041–720–884

Rates: 21,000 lire (about $13 US) per person; doubles 46,000 lire (about $27 US)
Kitchen available: Yes
Affiliation: None

This family run hostel is certainly for people who appreciate it for what it is and don't ask it be super clean or efficient. If you want bathroom floors on which you could eat a meal and sparkling kitchens, go elsewhere.

The best things about it? No lockout and a friendly familia. The worst things? No breakfast and not very close to the center of action.

Gestalt: Archie's bunkers

Hospitality:

Cleanliness:

Party index:

How to get there:

By boat: From Venezia train station, call hostel for transit route.

CASA GEROTTO

Campo S. Geremia 283, Venezia

Phone Number: 041–715–562

Fax Number: 041–715–361

Rates: 30,000 to 50,000 lire per person (about $18 to $30 US); doubles 80,000 to 130,000 lire (about $47 to $77 US)
Curfew: 12:30 A.M.
Affiliation: None

$

This little hostel, which also doubles as a nice hotel, offers both bunks and private rooms, giving hostellers the best of both worlds. However, it's possible that the hostel section might close down; check ahead for availability. And, bully for you, showers are included in the rate. They're pretty nice for hostel showers, that's for sure.

Although it boasts a location near the train station, where you'll almost surely arrive, it's not central to the rest of the medieval action for which Venice is justly famous. You might enjoy this location, though, in a quiet Venetian suburb if you need to get in late or get out early.

Gestalt: Venetian blinds

Hospitality:

Cleanliness:

Party index:

How to get there:

By boat: From Venezia station, call hostel for transit route.

OSTELLO SANTA FOSCA

Santa Maria dei Servi, Cannaregio, 2372 Venezia

Phone Number: 041–715–775

Rates: 23,000 lire per person (about $14 US)
Private/family rooms: Yes
Season: July 5 to September 18
Office hours: 7:00 to 9:00 A.M.; 6:00 to 11:30 P.M.
Lockout: 9:00 A.M. to 6:00 P.M.
Curfew: 11:30 P.M.
Affiliation: None
Extras: Game room

Party index:

College students will certainly appreciate this summer-only hostel for its relaxed 'tude and lots of diversions to keep them happy, like the omnipresent game of foosball. But you can't hang around here forever.

A former convent, the hostel has both dorm rooms and doubles; thumbs down, though, to the super long lockout that lasts from nine in the morning till six at night. Sure, Venice is one great town, but sometimes we the jet-lagged need to kick back for a few minutes, too.

How to get there:

By boat: From train station, walk left along the main street over three bridges. Turn left over bridge at the P. S. Fosca and left along canal.

OSTELLO VENEZIA (VENICE HOSTEL)

Fondamenta delle Zitelle, Guidecca 86, 30123 Venezia

Phone Number: 041–523–8211

Fax Number: 415–235–689
Rates: 27,000 lire per HI member (about $16 US)
Credit cards: Yes
Beds: 260
Private/family rooms: None
Kitchen available: No
Office hours: 7:00 A.M. to midnight
Season: Closed January 16 to January 31
Affiliation: HI-AIG
Extras: Breakfast, meals ($), bar

This optimally placed former warehouse with a view of San Marco—from across the canal on the island of Guidecca, you understand—really packs 'em in and always seems booked full. Venice is probably the biggest destination for tourists in Italy, the more so in the summer, so reserve way in advance if you want to score a bunk in this somewhat strict hostel.

Still, it's fairly new and friendly and—best of all—efficient. Just remember that you'll have to take a little boat out to a remote island from central Venice, then haul your carcass and your backpack up steep flights of stairs. (Some hostellers compared it to Alcatraz. We can see why: You'll never escape late at night.)

Other complaints have been lodged about the plumbing: Specifically, the showers. They have a tendency to run on the lukewarm side. Of course, being that the hostel is located next to really prime real estate, it gets supercrowded, and with crowds comes a lot of noise. Bring your earplugs to drown out the cacaphony of sounds made by those who are sleeping and those who aren't.

Gestalt:
Blue lagoon
Party index:

Meals are served here, but, for some reason, wine and other spirits are banned. That definitely could be a bummer if you're looking to imbibe.

This island-bound Venice hostel is definitely an option. Just don't expect peace and quiet.

How to get there:

By boat: From Venezia train station, take vaporetto number 82 or number 2 (2,500 lire, about half an hour). Get off at Zitelle and walk to the right to hostel.

OSTELLO VILLA FRANCESCATTI

Salita Fontana del Ferro 15 (Veronetta) 37129 Verona VR

Phone Number: 045–590–630

Fax Number: 045–800–9127
Rates: 23,000 lire per HI member (about $14 US); doubles 52,000 lire (about $31 US)
Credit cards: None
Beds: 120
Private/family rooms: Yes
Kitchen available: No
Office hours: 7:00 A.M. to 11:30 P.M.
Affiliation: HI-AIG
Extras: Breakfast, meals ($), laundry, camping, TV, videos

This hostel is one of the best in Europe, say some. Maybe *the* best, say some. (Us? We're too cool to award such an honor to any one hostel.) It oozes charm and good vibes, from the camper-friendly garden to the frescoed walls and exposed-beam ceilings.

It's in a palazzo (palace) that was once a monastery complex, its construction dating back to the Renaissance—that's the 1500s. Amazing, say some, that it holds up to such stampedes of hostellers; others feel it's kinda run down and ready to fall apart any minute.

Gestalt: My Verona

Cleanliness:

Party index:

Anyway, as you're hopping from room to room, keep in mind that the floors are all original: Yeah, that's right, you're walking on 500 years' worth of history. So don't even think about spilling your Yoo Hoo.

The good vibes here are real and contagious; you can join in a chorus of singers around a piano at night or explore the grottos behind the garden. Breakfast is free, they serve other meals for a charge, and there's a laundry. All in all, it's a beautiful and dreamy place to stay. The only complaint we've heard is that the bathrooms sometimes get a little grungy.

Verona itself is a superb base for day trips to surrounding areas like Trento and Lago di Garda if you want to escape the frenzy of having to stay in a highly touristed lake area. And this beautiful old city has its own charm that captivates many a traveler; try walking downtown to the central piazza around dinnertime for fun. There's also a ruined Roman arena here, right downtown, that sometimes hosts rock-and-roll sessions in summertime. Cool, huh?

Venice, of course, also beckons: It's an hour or more away by train. That might be too far for a day trip, especially with such a great hostel to chill out in for a day or two between Italy's heavyweight destinations, but you could try it. Lotsa folks do.

Definitely worth a night on almost any Italian itinerary!

How to get there:

By bus: Bus stops 200 yards from hostel; call hostel for transit route.

By car: Call hostel for directions.

By train: Porta Nuova station, 2 miles away; call hostel for transit route.

OSTELLO OLIMPICO (VICENZA HOSTEL)

Viale Giuriolo 9, 36100 Vicenza VI

Phone Number: 0444–540–222

Fax Number: 0444–547–762
Rates: 23,000 lire per HI member (about $14 US); doubles 50,000 lire (about $29 US)
Private/family rooms: Yes
Office hours: 7:00 to 9:30 A.M.; 3:30 to 11:30 P.M.

Affiliation: HI-AIG
Extras: TV, bike rentals

$

This new place is quite good, and it's set in a beautiful yellow villa pretty close to the center of town. The amenities here didn't include a laundry or meal service at press time, but those may come later. Rooms are comfortable, and there's both a TV lounge and the option of renting a two-wheeler to tool around on.

Vicenza is today an industrial city, true, but it's also a showpiece for Veneto's own (Andreas) Palladio, whose architecture has been copied the world over. The city's central square, dwarfed by a Palladio basilica, is the logical place to start; then check out some of the many palaces in the area. Then check out the Rotunda and everything else around here.

Best bet for a bite: Brek

Gestalt: Olympic heights

Hospitality:

Cleanliness:

Party index:

How to get there:

By bus: Contact hostel for transit route.

By car: Contact hostel for directions.

By train: From Vicenza station, walk 1 mile to hostel, or contact hostel for transit route.

FLORENCE AND TUSCANY

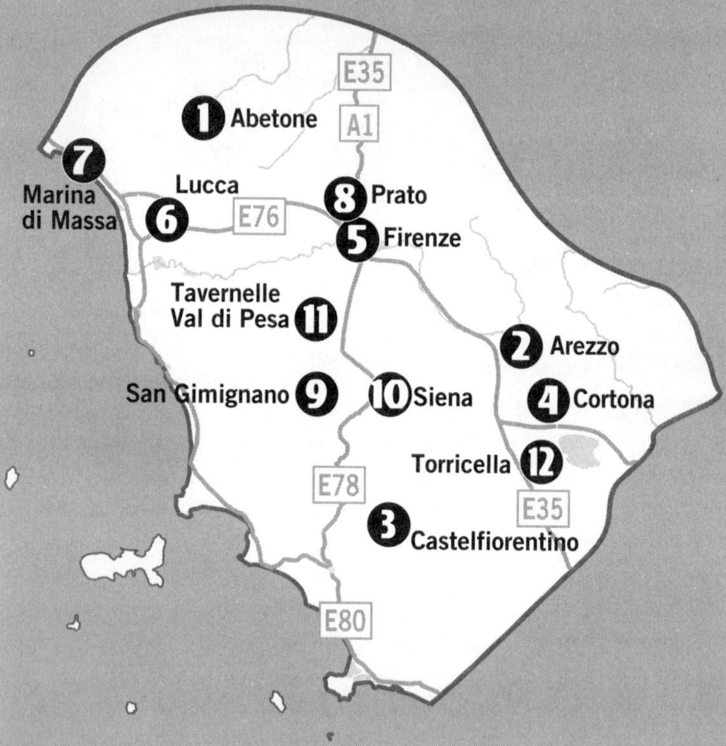

Page numbers follow town names.

FLORENCE AND TUSCANY

Everybody wants to go to Tuscany, and it's not hard to see why. This huge region (for Italy) contains just about everything you could want to write home about in a fairly compact area: hills, farms, churches, city squares—and, oh yeah, some of the finest artistic treasures of Western civilization. A spate of recent movies and books about Tuscany haven't hurt, either.

The upshot? You won't be alone here, especially in summer, unless you get off the main tourist path and hit the backroads. But you probably won't mind; your jaw will be too wide open to care.

The countryside sure is beautiful around here, an earthy brown-red soil set against the green of (usually) grapes. The local people have a true appreciation for the earth and one another. (Once in a while, of course, you'll run into foreigners buying into the Tuscan dream too. This can be good or bad, depending on the attitudes of the foreigner in question.)

And the cities! These might be Europe's best. We're talking Florence, Siena, Orvieto, Cortona . . . just saying the names is giving us goose bumps. Make sure you like churches, though, and stone—and public squares made of churches and stone. You won't see too much green park space in Italy; it's all about the people.

To hit the most and best hostels, we'd hit Florence and then a few select hill towns. Florence (Firenze in Italian, but you knew that, right?) actually has more than a couple decent hostels in which to lay your head, a welcome change from the usual motley crew of hostels in a European city.

Among the hill towns, Cortona, Arezzo, and San Gimignano have the best hostels—and all are fabulous travel destinations, too! Siena and Orvieto are just two of the many other Tuscan towns that deserve a look, though the hostel situation isn't as great in those places. Make 'em a day trip from Florence, maybe.

OSTELLO RENZO BIZZARRI (RENZO BIZZARRI HOSTEL)

Strada Statale dell'Abetone Pistoia, 51021 Abetone PT

Phone Number: 0573–601–17

Rates: 18,000 lire per HI member (about $11 US); doubles 36,000 lire (about $22 US)
Credit cards: None
Beds: 64
Private/family rooms: Yes

Kitchen available: No
Season: December 12 to April 30; June 15 to September 30
Office hours: 7:00 to 10:00 A.M.; 3:30 P.M. to midnight
Affiliation: HI-AIG
Extras: Breakfast, meals ($), TV, movies, bar, bike rentals, laundry

This skier's hostel straddles the border of Tuscany and Emilia-Romagna and is a chalet with a spectacular mountain view. The communal bar and television room keep things humming along for the younger set, while the laundry and family room are welcomed with open arms by older folks with kids.

Party index:

However, this area's attractions aren't just limited to winter sports; it's an all-seasons kinda place. If you need to keep up your museum-church-fresco quota, you're very close to Modena and Lucca for history and culture.

How to get there:

By bus: Abetone bus station is 50 yards from hostel.
By car: Call hostel for directions.
By train: Nearest station in Pistoia, 25 miles away; call hostel for transit route.

OSTELLO VILLA SEVERI

Via F. Redi 13, Arezzo

Phone Number: 0575–299–047

Fax Number: 0575–299–047
Rates: 20,000 lire per person (about $12 US)
Beds: 68
Season: May 1 to October 31
Office hours: 9:00 A.M. to 1:00 P.M.; 6:00 to 11:30 P.M.
Lockout: 2:00 to 5:30 P.M.
Curfew: 11:30 P.M.
Affiliation: None
Extras: Meals ($)

The goal of this hostel remains unclear. It wants to be all things to all people and ends up confusing independent travelers. At the time of our visit, it was playing host to an American university student group *and*, get this, refugees from Kosovo as well as a few stragglers from the backpacker set. Outside the hostel was a whole different story: Homeless people had set up camp in a grove of trees. Management seemed fairly oblivious to this arrangement and may have encouraged it. So be prepared for strangeness. The hostel itself is in a villa within a city park. Getting there on foot is not recommended. Try to be patient, and wait for the infrequent city buses.

Bathrooms, which have earned high kudos in the past, were nothing spectacular. Water temperature remained tepid despite repeated attempts to increase heat. Bunkrooms, though spacious, remained dark (but that's okay in the baking mid-Italian sun); each one had a balcony.

Gestalt:
Arezzo development

Party index:

One caveat, though: Cigarette smoke is pervasive and will hunt you down and find you! If you have allergies or just can't stand smoke, stay elsewhere.

In short, call this hostel a few days before arriving to make sure it's not booked. You may be unpleasantly surprised otherwise.

How to get there:

By bus: Take 4 bus to one stop after Ospedale Civile.

By car: Call hostel for directions.

By train: From via Guido Monaco station (right side), take 4 bus to one stop after Ospedale Civile.

OSTELLO CASTELFIORENTINO (CASTELFIORENTINO HOSTEL)

Viale Roosevelt 26, 50051 Castelfiorentino

Phone Number: 057–164–002

Fax Number: 057–164–002
Rates: 25,000 lire per HI member (about $15 US); doubles 60,000 lire (about $36 US)
Credit cards: None
Beds: 84
Private/family room: Yes
Kitchen available: No
Office hours: 7:00 to 10:00 A.M.; 3:30 to 11:30 P.M.
Affiliation: HI-AIG
Extras: Meals ($), garden, TV

Situated in stunning Tuscan countryside near better-known Certaldo, this is definitely off the beaten track; as such, you'll get a much better local experience. The place has a garden, a television lounge, and a supply of double and quad rooms for families.

Gestalt:
Tuscan son

Party index:

How to get there:

By bus: Contact hostel for transit route.

By car: Contact hostel for directions.

By train: From Castelfiorentino station, walk ½ mile to hostel.

OSTELLO SAN MARCO

Via Maffei 57, Cortona, 52044

Phone Number: 0575–601–392

Fax Number: 0575–601–392
Rates: 19,000 lire per HI member (about $12 US)
Credit cards: None
Beds: 80
Private/family room: Yes
Kitchen available: No
Season: March 15 to October 15
Office hours: 7:00 to 10:00 A.M.; 3:30 P.M. to midnight
Affiliation: HI-AIG
Extras: Breakfast, meals ($), bar, TV, bike rentals, laundry, fax

This steep hill town is one of the lesser known towns of its ilk, completely romantic and medieval and still slightly undiscovered. It's been a mecca of sorts for University of Georgia students contemplating art, Italian, and other creative endeavors during their summer months abroad.

Best bet for a bite:
Trattoria Etrusca

Insiders' tip:
Lots of Georgians here

Gestalt:
Full Cortona

Hospitality:

Cleanliness:

Party index:

The hostel here, tucked in a typical slanting and narrow hill-town street, is fantastic and oozes medieval charm. Eating in the dining room, you'll feel like a Guelph or a Ghibelline in such a cavernous space. (Your companions might be Aussies or Americans, who seem to fill this place all the time, but deal with it.) The dining room's got arched ceilings with chandeliers primed for a swashbuckler's sabre—one of the most interesting hostel dining rooms in Europe, we'd wager.

Hostellers feel cozy in the dorm rooms, which are kept quite clean; sheets and showers are included in your rate. So's a free breakfast. Just repeat this mantra, so common in Italy: You can't take your showers late at night, because there's no hot water then.

Of course there's a bar here, plus a television room and one extremely coveted double room. Laundry and bikes for rent are other welcome touches, though tour groups occasionally overwhelm the place.

And why not? You're so high in the air that you'll feel like a bird when you hike to the edge of town and stare out at miles of fields. Also check out local churches like San Marco and the piazzas where locals and schoolkids gather for the daily lunchtime chat.

How to get there:

By bus: From bus stop, walk up via Margherita and look for hostel sign.

By car: Call hostel for directions.

By train: From Cortona-Terontola or Camucia station, take shuttle bus to Cortona. From bus stop, walk up via Nazionale to via Margherita, turn right, and walk uphill to hostel on left.

FLORENCE

Firenze's wonders can't be overstated, and although you're going to have to wait in line to experience them, the place is really something. The art hanging indoors and the architecture standing outdoors rival anything else in the world. A few words here can't possibly do it all justice, so just go see it. Parts of the city are gorgeous, parts are somewhat dirty and noisy, but you probably won't care. Simply dive in and try to ignore the press of the crowds.

Getting to Florence is easy; walking downtown is, too. Streets radiate outward from the extremely convenient train and bus stations—which, for once, are actually located near the action, across from a great church and just ten minutes' walk from some of the most amazing buildings and paintings in Italy. Get a really good map and use it; the streets can be a bit maddening here. Also watch yourself late at night in dim alleys, and take advantage of lots of American-geared services around town: stores, Internet places, cafes, and the like.

The hostel situation is amazingly good here, too. This city has six decent hostels, not a really bad one in the bunch, and we can honestly say that this came as a real surprise. Most aren't central, but a fifteen-minute walk will usually get you right into town.

In short, Firenze's one of a kind. A bit of a madhouse, but we love it.

FLORENCE HOSTELS at a glance

	RATING	PRICE	IN A WORD	PAGE
Archi Rossi		20,000 lire to 40,000 lire	sociable	p.272
Pensionato Pio X		25,000 lire to 30,000 lire	roomy	p.276
Ostello Villa Camerata		25,000 lire	huge	p.274
7 Santi Ostello		30,000 lire to 50,000 lire	new	p.277
Ostello Santa Monaca		25,000 lire	crowded	p.273

OSTELLO DI ARCHI ROSSI

Via Faenza, 94r, Firenze

Phone Number: 055–290–804

Rates: 20,000 to 40,000 lire per person (about $12 to $24 US)
Credit cards: None
Beds: 87
Private/family rooms: Yes
Kitchen available: Sometimes
Office hours: 7:30 to 9:30 A.M.; 3:30 to 11:30 P.M.
Lockout: 11:00 A.M. to 2:30 P.M.
Curfew: 12:30 A.M.
Affiliation: None
Extras: Movies, patio, snack shop ($), breakfast ($), lockers, laundry

This fairly new hostel—where guests attempt to draw their own *Last Supper* on its walls with the hostel crayons—has already made quite an impression on legions of enthusiasts. It isn't as grungy as many backpacker-type places in Europe, and isn't a twenty-four-hour party. All in all, it's not a bad option.

The entranceway could easily pass for that of a museum or nice hotel. Inside, it's just as nice: Bunks come five or six to a dorm room, often with en-suite bathroom, though they say you should get here by 9:00 A.M. if you want any hope of getting a bed. We'd take it one step further and advise you to get your butt over there as early as possible. Don't count on calling; they don't take reservations. The ten private rooms with en-suite bathrooms are especially in demand.

Best bet for a bite:
Giardino di Barbano for pizza

Gestalt:
Archi's bunks

Safety:

Hospitality:

Cleanliness:

Party index:

The hostel provides free hot showers, sheets, and blankets; a towel rental will cost you all of 1,000 lire (about 60 cents US). They don't serve meals, but guests have access to a teeny microwave and refrigerator. No stovetop here. Showering and other stuff you do in the bathrooms will be enhanced by the superclean facilities. And people love the nice outdoor terrace as a gathering place.

The staff are very nice and do speak some English. The best thing about this hostel is its location: It's only five minutes from the train station and ten or fifteen minutes by foot to such sites as San Lorenzo, Il Duomo, and some nice shopping areas. There's easy access to both the local orange buses that zip (okay, crawl) around Florence and the blue SITA buses, which go off to day trips in the surrounding countryside.

Just bring earplugs to block out the delightful street sounds at night—this is just 2 blocks from Florence's main train station, so it ain't superquiet even if it is superconvenient for arrivals and departures. All in all, a good retreat from the hectic hustle and bustle of Florence.

How to get there:

By bus: From bus station, walk left around corner to train station and cross through station onto via Nazionale. Walk to via Faenza; turn left. Hostel sign is neon blue. Or take via Val Fonda, turn corner at via Cennini, and follow it to via Faenza; cross street. Hostel is on right, marked by blue sign.

By car: Call hostel for directions.

By train: From Firenze station, exit left onto via Nazionale and walk to via Faenza; turn left. Hostel sign is neon blue. Or take via Val Fonda, turn corner at via Cennini and follow it to via Faenza; cross street. Hostel is on right, marked by blue sign.

By plane: Airport outside Florence. From airport, take bus to train station stop and walk up via Val Fonda to via Cennini; turn corner and follow via Cennini to via Faenza, then cross street. Hostel is on right, marked by blue sign.

OSTELLO SANTA MONACA (SANTA MONACA HOSTEL)

Via Santa Monaca, 6 50124 Firenze

Phone Number: 055–268–338

Fax Number: 055–280–185
E-mail: info@ostello.it
Web site: www.ostello.it
Rates: 25,000 lire per person (about $15 US)
Credit cards: Yes
Office hours: 6:00 A.M. to 1:00 P.M.; 2:00 P.M. to 1:00 A.M.
Lockout: 9:30 A.M. to 2:00 P.M.
Curfew: 1:00 A.M.
Beds: 140
Private/family rooms: None
Kitchen available: Yes
Affiliation: None
Extras: Lockers, laundry

This hostel, located away from the madding crowds on the other side of the Arno, provides quiet seclusion and clean bathrooms, to boot.

Though not affiliated with HI, it still follows some of the stricter rules, like a lockout and a curfew that's not too unreasonable. You can't make a reservation here, but you can put yourself on a waiting list during the morning office hours.

Dorms border on the claustrophobic with a minimum of eight bunks and a maximum of twenty bunks. Ouch. No lockers, either, so if you're sleeping by a door you'd be smart to chain your stuff to something. It's tight as a tick here, but at least it's clean.

Best bet for a bite: Sugar Blues

Insiders' tip: Internet café just down street

Hospitality: 👍

Cleanliness: 👍

Party index: 🎉🎉🎉🎉

You're bound to run into people you've seen scrambling all over Europe in other hostels. You'll look at your traveling partner and say, "Hey, wasn't that the guy who put his foot in my face as he climbed to the top bunk at the Young & Happy in Paris?" or "Wasn't she the loud American who wouldn't shut up?" Yep, they be the ones, but you might be happy when it turns out to be someone you yukked it up with or thought was cute. Anyhoo, this place attracts Americans like the Super Bowl does football fans.

Some detractors have objected to noisy rooms and small dorm rooms with too many bunks. And although the kitchen is free for use, alas, there are no utensils. Still, most agree that it's a pretty decent place to rest your head in this culture-permeated town. Good thing the hostel has struck up a deal with a nearby eatery for meals.

How to get there:

By bus: Call hostel for transit route.
By car: Call hostel for directions.
By plane: Airport outside Florence; call hostel for transit route.
By train: Call hostel for transit route.

OSTELLO VILLA CAMERATA (FRIENDSHIP VILLAGE HOSTEL) 👍

Viale Augusto Righi 2/4, 50137 Firenze FI

Phone Number: 055–601–451

Fax Number: 055–610–300 or 055–600–315
Rates: 25,000 lire per HI member (about $15 US); doubles 52,000 lire (about $31 US)
Credit cards: None
Beds: 322
Private/family rooms: Yes (not in summer)
Kitchen available: No
Office hours: 7:00 A.M. to midnight
Lockout: 9:00 A.M. to 5:00 P.M.
Curfew: Midnight
Affiliation: HI-AIG

Ostello Villa Camerata
Firenze
(photo by Martha Coombs)

Extras: Meals ($), bar, library, movies, laundry, Internet access, TV, campground, parking

This exceptionally popular hostel asks that you reserve months in advance with a letter and credit card deposit, or several weeks ahead if you fax. Bottom line: Don't just show up expecting a bed.

Lots of folks like this huge hostel for its cleanliness, fabulous gardens, and belly-busting pasta-and-salad meals. Dorm rooms are fairly standard, although the family-room wing does contain quads with their own bathrooms. The dining room is a very sociable and popular place for exchanging addresses and stories, as are the handsome marble front porch, the Internet room, and about anywhere else here. One of the best places in Italy to hook up with others for ride-sharing, we'd say.

Bet bet for a bite: In town

Gestalt: Candid camerata

Hospitality:

Cleanliness:

Party index:

There's a TV, too—but you have to ask the staff to change the channels. Humbug. (We noticed the same staff occasionally flipping to a naughty channel late at night. Is this really what our money should be paying for?)

The big minus here is the usual story: This is quite a jaunt from town, although greenery is on all sides and you're in a handsome villa. You have to take the bus for almost half an hour from the Duomo to get out here, and then—if it's late at night—walk a poorly lit half-mile-long driveway with woods on both sides. A little creepy feeling, although in summer things should be hopping enough to make you feel safe. There's a busy campground here as well.

Oh, and keep in mind that you might occasionally be sharing bunkrooms with schoolchildren who could seriously cramp your style—as will the great distance from town, the hot-and-cold staff, and the awful 9:00 A.M. lockout that boots you out to the bus stop for the day.

How to get there:

By bus: From Firenze station, exit track 5 and take bus 17A or 17B to hostel.

By car: Call hostel for directions.

By plane: Call hostel for transit route.

By train: From Firenze station, exit track 5 and take bus 17A or 17B to hostel; walk through gates and follow signs.

PENSIONATO PIO X (POPE PIUS X HOSTEL)

Via dei Serragli, 106, Firenze

Phone Number: 055–225–044

Rates: 25,000 to 30,000 lire per person (about $15 to $18 US)
Beds: 46
Curfew: 12:30 A.M.
Affiliation: None
Two-day minimum stay required

This is another great and friendly hostel for the Firenze-bound hosteller, across the river in staid but tried-and-true Oltrarno's residential neighborhood.

Once again, plan ahead and you'll probably snag a bunk in a room that's big but limited to just four hostellers. Pay extra for a bath in your room, but showers are included with the rate. The staff is pretty friendly, although you can only stay for up to five nights.

Watch out, though, late sleepers—you have to check out by 9:00 in the morning. Yikes!

Gestalt:
X marks the spot

Party index:

How to get there:

By bus: Take 36 or 37 bus to first stop after crossing river.

By car: Call hostel for directions.

By train: From Firenze station, exit by track number 16, turn right and walk to P. della Stazione. Go straight down via degli Avelli, with church Santa Maria Novella on immediate right. Cross P. Staz. Maria Novella and continue straight down via dei Fossi, over the Ponte alla Carraia bridge, and down via dei Serragli. Or take 36 or 37 bus to first stop after crossing river.

7 SANTI OSTELLO (7 SAINTS HOSTEL)

Viale dei Mille, 11, Firenze

Phone Number: 055–504–8452

Fax Number: 055–505–7085
E-mail: 7santi@eidinet.com
Web site: www.eidinet.com/7santi
Rates: 30,000 to 55,000 lire per person (about $18 to $33 US); doubles 70,000 to 85,000 lire (about $41 to $50 US)
Private/family rooms: Yes
Kitchen available: No
Affiliation: None
Extras: Breakfast, bar, TV, laundry, fax, e-mail

Part of a convent beside the Church of the Sette Santi (Seven Saints), this new hostel touts its central location and super amenities as reasons to pay extra cash for a night's stay. To be sure, it's a big and attractive place.

Gestalt:
Santi clause

Hospitality:

Cleanliness:

Party index:

Singles, doubles, and bunks in quad to six-bedded dorm rooms are priced according to a fairly complicated structure based on size and bathroom availability. Suffice to say that at press time, this was the most expensive hostel in town by a long shot—but also the one with the most amenities. They include telephones on each floor, a sports field, a laundry, and fax and e-mail service. Breakfast was included for free at last report.

So take your pick: Save a buck and stay somewhere else, or open up your wallet and ratchet up the experience.

How to get there:

By bus: Take 11 or 17 bus to Sette Santi stop; walk ½ mile to hostel.

By train: From Santa Maria Novella station, take 11 or 17 bus to Sette Santi stop; walk ½ mile to hostel.

OSTELLO IL SERCHIO

Via del Brennero, 673, 55100 Lucca

Phone Number: 0583–341–811 (or 0586–862–517)

Fax Number: 0583–341–811
Rates: 19,000 lire per HI member (about $11 US); doubles 42,000 lire (about $25 US)
Credit cards: None
Beds: 90
Private/family rooms: Yes
Kitchen available: No
Season: March 10 to October 31
Office hours: 7:00 to 10:00 A.M.; 3:30 to 11:30 P.M.
Affiliation: HI-AIG
Extras: Breakfast, meals ($), bar, library, parking

Gestalt: Lucca blue
Party index:

A blocky, uninteresting hostel with large, ten-bed rooms, this place consistently produces unhappy campers who were drawn to Lucca for a gander at its famous walls but didn't like this place. Maybe crowding is only a problem in summer, however; other times you might find you have more than ample room to spread out your stuff.

The joint does cater to families with private rooms and a library/reading room. Breakfast is also included with your bed; just don't count on beauty and grace from this too-modern facility.

At least Lucca is nice to walk around—not as touristed as, say, San Gimignano and a little easier to get to. This town's got a train station, reachable from Pisa.

How to get there:

By bus: Call hostel for transit route.

By car: Call hostel for directions.

By train: From Lucca station, take 1A bus to via Brennero, then walk up via Brennero to hostel.

OSTELLO APUANO (APUANO HOSTEL)

Via le delle Pinete 237, Partaccia, I-54037 Marina di Massa E Carrara MS

Phone Number: 0585–780–034

Fax Number: 0585–748–58
Rates: 14,000 lire per HI member (about $8.00 US)
Credit cards: Yes
Beds: 200
Private/family rooms: Yes (not available July and August)
Kitchen available: Yes
Season: March 16 to September 30
Office hours: 7:00 A.M. to 11:30 P.M.
Affiliation: HI-AIG
Extras: Meals ($), bar, gardens, camping, bike rentals, games, sports equipment, fax, TV, laundry, library

Tuscany is not usually thought of as a beach bum's haven, but here it is; a hostel that's a stone's skip away from the beach.

This hostel, in a really nice villa, is located in a town that attracts working-class families on holiday, so summers are nutso. Yet the place is well equipped to handle the crush, offering a bar, sports stuff, bikes for hire, gardens, and a campground. All of which serve to distribute hostellers evenly around the facility. Note that there's an additional charge for heat and hot water here, although the basic rack rate is pretty cheap.

You're only a short hop from Pisa, but we'd say there are better beaches in Italy, even on this part of the coast. Stay here only if you really want to see the area.

Gestalt:
Coast is clear
Party index:

How to get there:

By bus: Take Avenza Mare line to Marina di Massa bus station, then walk 200 yards to hostel.

By car: Call hostel for directions.

By train: Carrara station, 2 miles away; call hostel for transit route.

VILLA FIORELLI (PRATO HOSTEL)

Parco di Galceti, 59100 Prato

Phone Number: 0574–697–611

Fax Number: 0574–697–6256
Rates: 25,000 lire per HI member (about $11.00 US); doubles 60,000 lire (about $35 US)

Credit cards: None
Beds: 52
Private/family rooms: Yes
Kitchen available: No
Office hours: 7:00 to 10:00 A.M.; 3:30 to 11:30 P.M.
Affiliation: HI-AIG
Extras: Meals ($), meeting room, garden, laundry

A new hostel just north of Florence, this one has smartly located itself in an old villa in a park. You're just a short train ride from Florence's wonders, if that city's full up, and the facilities here are good—laundry, lush grounds and so forth.

Best bet for a bite: Lo Scoglio

Gestalt: Prato party

Party index:

The walled city of Prato's a working-class town, but there's always been enough money around here (thanks to Florence) to pay for nice buildings. Check out the cathedral and castle for starters, then head for a series of smaller churches with impressive artwork inside.

How to get there:

By bus: From Prato station, take 13 bus and walk 50 yards to hostel.

By car: Contact hostel for directions.

By train: From Prato station, take 13 bus and walk 50 yards to hostel.

SAN GIMIGNANO HOSTEL

Via delle Fonti 1, San Gimignano

Phone Number: 0577–941–991

Rates: 21,000 to 24,000 lire per person (about $13 to $15 US)
Beds: 75
Private/family rooms: None
Kitchen available: No
Season: March 1 to October 31
Office hours: 7:00 to 9:00 A.M.; 5:00 to 11:30 P.M.
Lockout: 9:00 A.M. to 5:00 P.M.
Curfew: 11:30 P.M.
Affiliation: None
Extras: Breakfast, meals ($), bar

This place is off the beaten track, but it can get crowded anyway because it's located in one gr-r-r-r-r-eat Tuscan hill town behind an incredibly big and old tree.

One of three hostels owned by a small private chain based in Tavernelle, it gets so-so reviews from our hostel snoops. Some loved the sociable atmosphere (and the housekeeper Sabatino is a hoot if you speak Italian).

Gestalt:
Kids on the hill

Party index:

Rooms are huge and barren, resembling barracks—worn linoleum and metal bunks are the rule, though they've got great views of the town and the pines. Cleanliness is so-so, and the huge unisex bathrooms have seen better days. The dorms don't have much privacy at all, so we'd say they're ideal for groups who don't care about comfort and want a super location. There's no kitchen, but they do serve meals. They're super ecoconscious here, at least, recycling and keeping a tight leash on water use.

You also don't have to worry about getting locked out after midnight—staff provide a key so that you can come and go as you please. Not that there's much nightlife here, but you could wander these old alleyways forever staring up at the famous medieval towers that still stand. (There used to be lots more, by the way.) It won't be long before you, too, will be spouting stuff like "the medieval Manhattan" and other tourist-office blather that turns out, on closer inspection, to be absolutely true.

How to get there:

By bus: Take SITA bus to Tavernelle; transfer at Poggibonsi and continue to San Gimignano.

By car: Call hostel for directions.

By train: Call hostel for transit route.

OSTELLO DELLA GIOVENTÙ GUIDORICCIO

Via Fiorentina 89, Siena

Phone Number: 0577–522–12

Fax Number: 0577–561–72
Rates: 30,000 lire per person (about $18 US)
Beds: 110
Private/family rooms: None
Kitchen available: No
Office hours: 7:00 to 9:00 A.M.; 3:00 to 11:30 P.M.
Lockout: 9:00 A.M. to 3:00 P.M. (weekdays); 9:00 A.M. to 4:30 P.M. (weekends)
Curfew: 11:30 P.M.
Affiliation: None
Extras: Bar, breakfast

Positive, friendly vibes don't always emanate from this hostel, but if all you need is a clean place to shower, then it'll do. It's another in the local three-hostel chain based in Tavernelle.

Bunkrooms are as standard as standard could be. The family rooms are a bit better, although they don't have private bathrooms, just a sink. The huge common room and bar are quite popular with hostellers, if spartan. We might be able to overlook the lax security and party atmosphere. Unfortunately, it's also rather far from the town center, and there are lots more budget-oriented pensions and the like closer to town. So you might decide to save your bus money. To add insult to injury, the breakfast that's included with your hefty rate is a measly piece of stale bread.

Best bet for a bite:
Forno Independenza for pizza

Gestalt:
Burnt Siena

Hospitality:

Cleanliness:

Party index:

But Siena! Now this is one of the greatest cities in all Italy, especially July 2 and August 16, when the annual Palio pits the city's neighborhoods—each symbolized by an animal or other totem—in a much-beloved horse race. Most tourists rush through town heading for Florence, but don't make that mistake. Getting around town is easy via the many city buses or sloping alleyways. A healthy student population keeps things interesting.

What to see? The fan-shaped Campo is one of Europe's most famous public spaces, and the food here is getting more interesting. For breakfast head for one of the local coffee bars, where you line up and drink standing up—then order the famous local panforte (literally, strong bread), which is kinda like fruitcake. For lunch, grab pizza or a picnic and sit right down on the campo dodging pigeons and looking cool, like the gaggles of Italian guys who never seem to have anything but time on their hands.

KEY TO ICONS

- Attractive natural setting
- Ecologically aware hostel
- Superior kitchen facilities or cafe
- Offbeat or eccentric place
- Superior bathroom facilities
- Romantic private rooms
- Comfortable beds
- Editors Choice Among our very favorite hostels
- A particularly good value
- Wheelchair-accessible
- Good for business travelers
- Especially well suited for families
- Good for active travelers
- Visual arts at hostel or nearby
- Music at hostel or nearby
- Great hostel for skiers
- Bar or pub at hostel or nearby

How to get there:

By bus: From bus, take stop after huge sign entrance to Siena.
By car: Call hostel for directions.
By train: From station, walk to P. Gramsci and take 15 bus to hostel. Or from P. Matteotti, take 15 bus to hostel.

OSTELLO DEL CHIANTI

Via Cassia, Tavernelle Val di Pesa, 50028

Phone Number: 055–807–7009

Fax Number: 055–805–0104
Rates: 23,000 to 26,000 lire per person (about $14 to $16 US)
Credit cards: None
Beds: 80
Private/family rooms: None
Kitchen available: No
Season: March 1 to October 31
Office hours: 6:00 to 8:00 P.M.
Affiliation: None
Extras: Breakfast, meals ($), library, information desk, bar, laundry

A bit remote, situated in a so-so town on the Via Cassia (old road to Siena, that is), this hostel is very good—especially considering the pricey region it's in. It's the flagship hostel in that three-hostel chain we keep mentioning, and it's by far the best of the bunch. Add that superb location and you've got one of the special places in France and Italy.

A brand-new building was opening in 1999, and it looked even better than the original one. New wooden bunks were the stars, and many of the three-bed and five-bed dorm rooms were going to have their own bathrooms and desks. A really active and friendly staff helps visitors educate themselves by offering an itinerary that includes wine and olive oil–making demonstrations and tours of the area. After all, this is Chianti—say Key-auntie—a region famous for vino. You're just a hop from Barberino and other cutesy-dootsie Chianti towns. Definitely use the excellent and efficient tourist office at the hostel itself.

Best bet for a bite:
Supermarket in town

Insiders' tip:
Walk 15 miles to San Gimignano

Gestalt:
Tavernelle on the green

Party index:

Breakfast is free and great—coming soon, a buffet with muesli and yogurt and stuff that you *never* find in Italian hostels. (See, the Italians believe that coffee equals food for breakfast.) This helps alleviate the pain of buying local groceries and meals a bit. They don't serve dinner at the hostel yet but might begin by the time this book hits the stands; let's hope they do it right. Staff can also recommend some superific walking tours through the vineyards and olive groves that give this area its picturesque quality. Do that rather than stick around the boring town of Tavernelle.

Though it's not supereasy to get here by public transportation, it can be done from Florence by taking buses heading to Siena; they run several times a day. This place is probably best for families with cars, but anyone will enjoy it. It's that good.

How to get there:

By bus: From Florence or Siena, take SITA bus to Tavernelle.

By car: Call hostel for directions.

By train: Poggibonsi station, 5 miles away, is nearest stop; call hostel for transit route.

OSTELLO TORRICELLA (TORRICELLA-LAKE TRASIMENO HOSTEL)

Via Del Lavoro 10, 06060 Torricella di San Feliciano PG

Phone Number: 075–843–508

Fax Number: 075–843–508
Rates: 20,000 lire per HI member (about $12 US); doubles 50,000 lire (about $30 US)
Credit cards: None
Beds: 88
Private/family rooms: Yes
Kitchen available: No
Season: March 1 to October 31
Office hours: 7:00 A.M. to 1:00 P.M.; 3:00 P.M. to midnight
Affiliation: HI-AIG
Extras: Breakfast, meals ($), laundry, games and sports equipment, bar, bike rentals, fax

Gestalt: Tower room
Party index:

If you're heading for the biggest lake in central Italy, you'll be rewarded with a decent hostel that commands a view of the surrounding area.

History afficionados will be thrilled to discover this area, known for three major Roman battles that took place here. One was the famous battle of 217 B.C. between the Romans and Hannibal's army, which ended in a victory for the Carthaginians.

It's likely you won't be fighting any battles over space here, since the town of Torricella isn't readily found on many maps and isn't a big destination. There's an abundance of beds, and breakfast is included for free. You can also pay extra for dinner.

Explore the countryside with bikes that you can rent, or shoot some hoops around the hostel. Families will especially like this quiet spot for its private rooms. Otherwise, though, we gotta be honest—the area's kinda blah.

How to get there:

By bus: Take ASP bus to Torricella stop, then walk 100 yards to hostel.

By car: Call hostel for directions.

By train: From Torricella station, walk 100 yards to hostel.

ROME AND CENTRAL ITALY

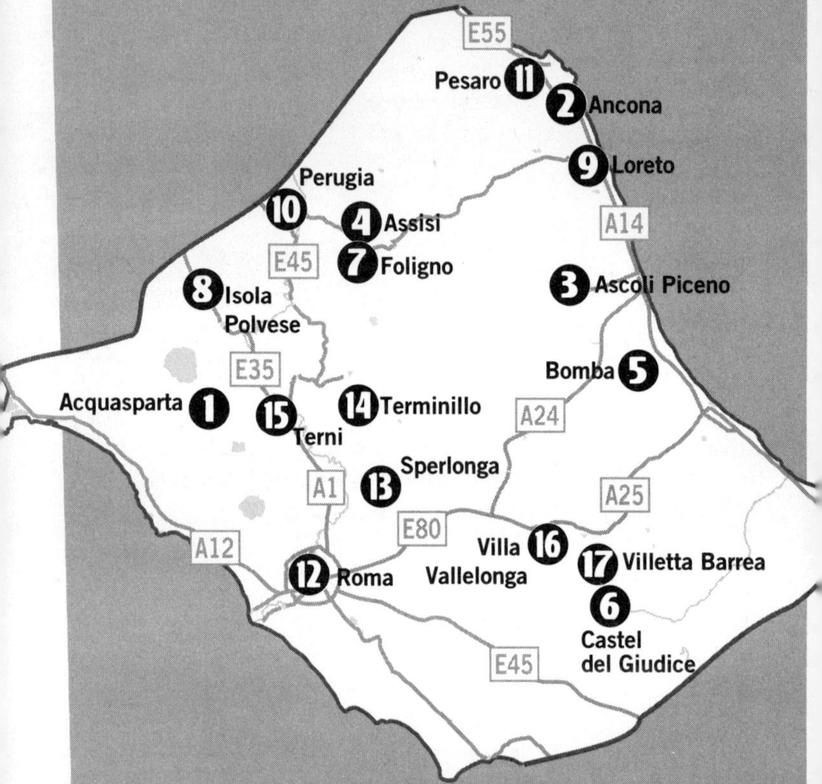

Page numbers follow town names.

ROME AND CENTRAL ITALY

The central Italian landscape, like Tuscany above it, is brown and green: the brown of dusty hills and earth mixing nicely with the green of vines and crops.

A number of regions organize what seems, at first, a random landscape. The Lazio is the region surrounding Rome, and all roads lead back to the capital (as well as the Vatican). Umbria is becoming better known as an alternative to touristed Tuscany, while the Marches—another region of former hill kingdoms bordering the ocean—still retain much of their original feel. Finally, Abruzzo is still a kind of ham to many people, and that means the tourists won't be stepping all over you there.

The hostels here are so-so. In Rome they're just adequate, with a few stinkers; nothing spectacular. To hit the best of the rest, you'll have to make a detour to out-of-the-way places like Ascoli Piceno (where?), Pesaro, and Terminillo. Your reward? Actual local culture, minus the tourists, plus great bunks. So give it a go.

Transportation can be frustrating, though, unless you look at it as one of life's fun challenges. You're nuts to drive a car anywhere near Rome, but it's possible to get around—slowly—in the countryside. Trains sometimes run where you want them, and cheaply, though only on a few routes. All go through Rome first, of course, but few are timely. Buses fill in the gaps and even cost less.

When in Rome, simply do as the Romans: Take the Metro subway, which goes everywhere. Just be careful of thieves, who run rampant in stations. They're unlikely to hurt you, but they want those cameras and lire badly.

OSTELLO SAN FRANCESCO (ACQUASPARTA HOSTEL)

Via San Francesco 1, 05021 Acquasparta

Phone number: 0744–943–167

Fax Number: 0744–944–168
Rates: 25,000 lire per HI member (about $15 US)
Credit cards: None
Beds: 120
Private/family rooms: Yes
Kitchen available: No
Office hours: 7:00 to 10:00 A.M.; 3:30 to 11:30 P.M.
Affiliation: HI-AIG
Extras: Meals ($), breakfast, meeting room, Internet access

Kudos to these guys for wiring up the place with an Internet terminal. The hostel, in a blockish two-story villa somewhere in Umbria, isn't too far from places like Assisi, Perugia, and Spoleto (though most of those have good hostels already). It's better than those places, though, if you want to hike—this is in a wilder place.

Gestalt: Aqua Velva

Party index: 🎉

How to get there:

By bus: Contact hostel for transit route.
By car: Contact hostel for directions.
By train: From Acquasparta station walk ⅓ mile to hostel.

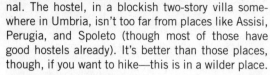

OSTELLO ANCONA MARCHE (ANCONA HOSTEL)

Via Lamaticci, 60126 Ancona

Phone number: 0717–501–026

Fax Number: 0717–501–026
Rates: 23,000 lire per HI member (about $14 US)
Credit cards: None
Beds: 56
Private/family rooms: Yes
Kitchen available: Yes
Office hours: Twenty-four hours
Affiliation: HI-AIG
Extras: Breakfast ($), TV, Internet access

If you're here, it's probably for one reason: to catch a ferry to Greece or Turkey. The hostel here isn't all that great, but it is a cheap sleep. (It could be cheaper: They charge for breakfast, and there's an extra heating charge, too.) The hostel, inside a pinkish building on a sloping street, at least stays open all night and all year long.

Gestalt: Greece is the word

Party index: 🎉🎉🎉

What to do in Ancona? Well, there's an old port area; this is basically a working port town, with onward ferry connections to Greece, Croatia, and Albania. There is some new life in the downtown area, and you'll find some interesting sights in the alleys, but you'll likely still use this solely as a jumping-off sleep before heading to Greece. Okay, there's a Roman arch, some pretty good cathedrals, and churches, and a nice stone duomo (dome). There's also the smell of salt air and stinky fish on the docks, if that gets you going. Not the greatest place, but adequate. See ya in Greece.

How to get there:

By bus: Contact hostel for transit route.
By car: Contact hostel for directions.

Ostello Dé Longobardí
Ascoli Piceno

(photo courtesy of AIG)

By train: From Ancona Centrale station, take ATMA bus and walk 200 yards to hostel.

OSTELLO DÉ LONGOBARDI (LONGOBARDI HOSTEL)

Via Soderini 26 Palazzetto, Longobardo, 63100 Ascoli Piceno AP

Phone number: 0736–259–007

Rates: 18,000 lire per person (about $11 US)

Credit cards: None
Beds: 30
Private/family rooms: None
Kitchen available: Yes
Office hours: 7:00 A.M. to midnight
Affiliation: HI-AIG
Extras: Meals ($), tours, movies, TV, fax service, parking

$

When you have tired of the tourist grind that can leave a unpleasant taste in your mouth from towns like Venice, Rome, and Florence, settle into Ascoli Piceno, a delightful burg that has all the aforementioned great medieval architecture and, gasp, amiable citizens who really like you. They really do!

Gestalt:
Tower of power
Party index:

Add a laid-back hostel in a medieval tower that almost always has enough room, and you have the fixings for a stress-free excursion. Other pluses include free tours of the well-preserved medieval architecture in a town where you don't have to overextend your hamstrings (it's in a valley), a nice central location, and no daytime lockout.

Do yourself a huge favor and take the detour from the overtouristed hill towns of Tuscany to this little hamlet, which owes its existence to a helpful woodpecker that supposedly (this is the legend) led villagers to the town site.

How to get there:

By bus: Call hostel for transit route.
By car: Call hostel for directions.
By train: From train station at P. del Popolo, take via del Trivio to P. Ventido Basso, then via Soderini to Longbardo.

OSTELLO DELLA PACE (PEACE HOSTEL)

Via di Valecchie 117 Assisi, 06081 PG

Phone number: 075–816–767

Fax Number: 075–816–767
Rates: 22,000 lire per HI member (about $13 US); doubles 56,000 lire (about $33 US)
Credit cards: Yes
Beds: 70
Private/family rooms: Yes
Kitchen available: No
Season: January 1 to January 9; March 1 to December 31
Office hours: 7:00 to 10:00 A.M.; 3:30 to 11:30 P.M.
Lockout: 9:00 A.M. to 3:30 P.M.

Ostello Della Pace
Assisi

(photo courtesy of AIG)

Curfew: 11:30 P.M.
Affiliation: HI-AIG
Extras: Meals ($), breakfast, laundry, bike rentals, library, games, bar

Assisi is known to all as the home of St. Francis, founder of the simple-living movement—and what better location to situate two hostels that prove you don't need to overpamper yourself to enjoy traveling. What's more, this incredible hostel offers spiffy big rooms and squeaky-clean bathrooms—and a free shower and breakfast (not at the same time, silly) are always included in your rate. Simply put, it's one of the best small hostels in Europe.

Great management keeps this place clean and happy, making it a clear pick over the unkempt independent hostel also in town. Besides, you can catch a shuttle bus from the train station to the hostel and be treated to a stunning view of the surrounding area along the way.

The hostel grounds are nice and rustic. Even better are the views from the quiet country road

Best bet for a bite:
Giuseppe's meals on-site

Insiders' tip:
Internet place in bar

What hostellers say:
"Molto bene!"

Gestalt:
Assisi chair

Hospitality:

Cleanliness:

Party index:

where the hostel sits—miles of olive groves on one side (come in late fall and you can watch workman raking ground for the best ones), splendid views of the domed basilica of Santa Maria degli Angeli on the other, and all the while the hilltop town of Assisi looms practically right on top of you. Really, it feels that way. Walking to town is easy (though uphill) too.

Bunkrooms are nice, and family rooms are palatial for a hostel—complete with views. The real star is the dining room, where filling breakfasts and delicious homemade dinners bring guests together like nowhere else. The crowd is surprisingly American, so that's not necessarily good if you don't want to meet others of your ilk. But it can be nice to hear English once in a while, too.

And the owners know more about hostelling than we ever thought possible. Even the lockout's shorter than usual, and it gives you a chance to explore cool Assisi (say a-seezy), with its double basilica (damaged during an earthquake but reopened to the public in 2000) plus a ruin believed to be an ancient Roman temple of Minerva.

How to get there:

By bus: Take bus to P. Unita and walk downhill to hostel.

By car: Call hostel for directions.

By train: From Assisi station, take a right to junction, then a left onto via San Pietro; hostel is on left, on hill. Or take SITA bus toward town and ask driver for drop-off at hostel della Pace; walk to hostel.

OSTELLO FONTEMAGGIO

Via Eremo delle Carceri 8, Fontemaggio (Assisi) PG

Phone number: 075–813–636

Fax Number: 075–813–749
Rates: 17,000 lire per person (about $10 US)
Affiliation: None
Extras: Camping, restaurant

Gestalt:
Meatballs

Party index:

Here you have a varied lodging choice. This complex of hotel, campground, and hostel has received complaints of uncleanliness and crowding in the dorms. You might relieve yourself of these problems by pitching a tent in the verdant campground, but as a hostel it's not a top pick, especially since the HI-AIG joint in Assisi is excellent.

This hostel is closer to the city than its HI counterpart, sure, but it might not be a good choice if it's law and order (or cleanliness) that you seek.

How to get there:

By bus: Call hostel for transit route.
By car: Call hostel for directions.
By train: Call hostel for transit route.

OSTELLO ISOLA VERDE (GREEN ISLAND HOSTEL)

Via Lago, 66042 Bomba CH

Phone number: 0872–860–475 or 0872–860–568

Fax Number: 0872–860–568
Rates: 20,000 lire per HI member (about $13 US); private/family rooms 25,000 to 30,000 lire (about $15 to $18 US)
Credit cards: Yes
Office hours: 7:00 A.M. to midnight
Beds: 44
Private/family rooms: Yes
Kitchen available: No
Affiliation: HI-AIG
Extras: Restaurant ($), bar, TV, bike rentals, movies, games, and sports equipment, breakfast ($)

This hostel provides inexpensive respite from the strenuous hiking in Abruzzo National Park, Italy's get-back-to-nature spot with tons of outdoor activities. There are also great little undiscovered (by Americans, at least) towns with lots of budget food options.

The Bomba Lake hostel has lots of amenities that'll help stretch a lire: movies and TV for those less inclined to don hiking boots; sports and games, too, for kids and adults alike. You won't have to worry about fixing dinner here, since there's an on-site restaurant-bar combination.

Gestalt:
La Bamba
Party index:

Besides the obvious outdoorsy activities, the Abruzzo region contains many ruins for archeology hounds to check out. And summertime brings lots of interesting cultural events like regional festivals featuring local produce. This is one town that hasn't (yet) succumbed to the world-weary attitude of bigger, more-well-known tourist areas, and the locals still carry a refreshingly cheery and helpful demeanor. God bless 'em.

How to get there:

By bus: Bus stop is 1 mile from hostel; call hostel for transit details.
By car: Call hostel for directions.
By train: From Lago di Bomba station, walk 150 yards to hostel.

OSTELLO LA CASTELLANA (LITTLE CASTLE HOSTEL)

Via Fontana Vecchia 1, 86080 Castel del Giudice

Phone number: 0865–946–222

Fax Number: 0865–946–222
Rates: 22,500 lire per HI member (about $14 US)
Credit cards: None
Beds: 60
Private/family rooms: Yes
Kitchen available: No
Office hours: 7:00 A.M. to midnight
Affiliation: HI-AIG
Extras: Meals ($), bar, TV

Gestalt: Ski school
Party index:

Families who ski together can hostel together at this well-located ski lodge. Positioned on the River Sangro, it's a good getaway from the cities if you want to try your hand at canoeing or kayaking or even cast your lure for a few trout.

There's no kitchen, but no worries: The hostel gives you a free breakfast, serves hearty meals for a charge, and runs a smart little bar, too. The television room provides distraction and relaxation after a day of hitting the slopes.

Fungi fanatics might do a little snuffling around for the rare and delicious truffles—both white and black varieties, which are treated like gold around here. You might want some instruction before you set out, though; they're not easy to harvest. (Hint: Bring a pig or specially trained dog. Your own nose is unlikely to detect those subterranean suckers.)

How to get there:

By bus: La Sangritana line is 200 meters from hostel.
By car: Call hostel for directions.
By train: Castel di Sangro station is 15 km (about 9 miles) away.

OSTELLO FULGINIUM (FULGINIUM HOSTEL)

Piazza San Giacomo 11, Foligno, Perugia, 06034

Phone number: 0742–352–882

Fax Number: 0742–340–545
Rates: 15,000 lire per person (about $9.00 US)
Season: March 1 to August 31
Curfew: 11:00 P.M.

Affiliation: None
Extras: Breakfast

Avoid the overpriced hotels in Spoleto if you're in town for the annual summer arts festival and stay in this hostel, about 15 miles away, instead. Take a bus from festival town to get here.

Pluses at this place include free showers as well as a breakfast to get your motor runnin'. Not much else to say. Spoleto itself is another one of those Italian hill towns; the festival brings opera, classical music, and other fancy stuff to town each year to great effect.

Party index:

How to get there:

By bus: Call hostel for transit route.
By car: Call hostel for directions.
By train: Call hostel for transit route.

OSTELLO Il POGGIO (ISOLA POLVESE HOSTEL)

06060 Isola Polvese

Phone number: 075–843–508

Fax Number: 075–843–508
Rates: 20,000 lire per HI member (about $12 US); doubles 50,000 lire (about $30 US)
Credit cards: None
Beds: 76
Private/family rooms: Yes
Kitchen available: No
Season: March 1 to October 31
Office hours: 7:00 to 10:00 A.M.; 3:30 to 11:30 P.M.
Affiliation: HI-AIG
Extras: Laundry, meeting room, garden, meals ($), breakfast

Gestalt: Garden party

Hospitality:

Cleanliness:

Party index:

Now this is great: a hostel located on a little island in Umbria's Lake Trasimeno. If only it were a bit easier to reach. You gotta take a boat from a tiny train station, but it can be done.

Facilities in the rustic place include a laundry, meals, double rooms for families, and plenty of grounds to ramble around on. You're surrounded by water, of course, but the island's also quite green. Extremely relaxing as a getaway.

How to get there:

By bus: Contact hostel for transit route.
By car: Contact hostel for directions.
By train: From Torricella station, take lake ferry to island.

OSTELLO LORETO (LORETO HOSTEL)

Via Aldo Moro, 60025, Loreto AN

Phone number: 071–750–1026

Fax Number: 071–750–1026
Rates: 23,000 lire per HI member (about $14 US); doubles 54,000 to 70,000 lire (about $32 to $41 US)
Credit cards: None
Beds: 150
Private/family rooms: Yes
Kitchen available: No
Office hours: Twenty-four hours
Affiliation: HI-AIG
Extras: Meals ($), bar, TV, laundry, sports equipment, movies, Internet access, fax, parking, gardens

Party index:

Loreto gets its name from the laurel grove that supposedly received the entire house of the Virgin Mary when it was beamed up from the Holy Land by the angels. Hence, the town now sees its fair share of religious pilgrims looking to view the Santa Casa as well as its basilica.

Holy hostellers can stay at this full-service hostel in Loreto and pair up with secular travelers as well. This hostel offers many amenities, including on-site parking for those who have opted to pay the

KEY TO ICONS

- Attractive natural setting
- Ecologically aware hostel
- Superior kitchen facilities or cafe
- Offbeat or eccentric place
- Superior bathroom facilities
- Romantic private rooms
- Comfortable beds
- Editors Choice Among our very favorite hostels
- A particularly good value
- Wheelchair-accessible
- Good for business travelers
- Especially well suited for families
- Good for active travelers
- Visual arts at hostel or nearby
- Music at hostel or nearby
- Great hostel for skiers
- Bar or pub at hostel or nearby

outrageous car rental fees in Italy. It also has a lovely garden in which to stretch out and take a breather. As per usual, meals are whipped up for a fraction of the cost of big-city restaurant eats, and you can do your laundry conveniently while grabbing a vino at the hostel bar.

How to get there:

By bus: Bus stops about 50 yards from hostel; call hostel for transit route.

By car: Call hostel for directions.

By train: Loreto station, 1 mile away; call hostel for transit route.

CENTRO INTERNAZIONALE DI ACCOGLIENZA PER LA GIOVENTÙ (INTERNATIONAL WELCOME CENTER HOSTEL)

Via Bontempi 13, Perugia

Phone number: 075–572–2880

Fax Number: 075–572–2880
E-mail: ostello@edisons.it
Rates: 16,000 lire per person (about $10 US)
Credit cards: None
Beds: 80
Private/family rooms: No
Kitchen available: Yes
Season: January 16 to December 14
Office hours: 7:30 to 9:30 A.M.; 4:00 to 11:00 P.M.
Lockout: 9:30 A.M. to 4:00 P.M.
Affiliation: None
Extras: Library, TV

Party index:

Overall, this hostel receives kudos from most people. A few took exception to a lack of good upkeep, but you can't beat the small, very private dorms—usually they're quad rooms—that are furnished with extras like night tables and comfortable bunks.

Since there's a rather lengthy maximum stay of three weeks, you'll have plenty of time to meet 'n' greet your bunkmates, many with whom you will undoubtedly swap stories in the absolutely wonderful and roomy cucina (kitchen), television room, or library. There's a great balcony, too. You also don't have to wander too far to the action, since this hostel is located right in downtown Perugia.

The city itself has tons of cheap stuff to do, courtesy of a thriving student population that speaks lots of languages. Hooray! Definitely one of the more multiethnic places in Italy. And when you're hungry, go to one of the famous chocolatiers who handcraft treats like world-famous baci (hazelnut and chocolate); this is the chocolate epicenter of Italy.

How to get there:

By bus: Call hostel for transit route.

By car: Call hostel for directions

By train: From station at P. Matteotti, walk up via de' Fari, take right on corso Vannucci, and continue to P. IV Novembre. Take P. Dante, walking away from the Il Duomo, continuing past P. Piccinino and take a right fork (via Bontempi) to hostel. Or call hostel for directions.

OSTELLO ARDIZIO (ARDIZIO HOSTEL)

Strada Panoramica dell'Ardizio, Pesaro, Fosso Sejore, 61100

Phone number: 0721–557–98

Rates: 14,000 lire per person (about $8.00 US)
Beds: 88
Season: May 1 to October 31
Affiliation: None
Extras: Meals ($), tennis courts

Don't forget your swimsuit and trashy summertime novel when you blow into this atypical beach town with an attitude on the Adriatic. Just be prepared for a not-so-warm welcome from the locals, who (we've heard) tend toward the snooty side.

Cleanliness:

Party index:

The hostel here is exceptionally clean and orderly, so don't shake out your beach towel on your bunk or in the bathroom. You also should absolutely reserve a space well in advance if you plan on visiting during those busy summer months. (Geez, how many times have we said that?)

Besides playing beach blanket bingo with the volleyball-spikin' ragazzi, you can don your best duds for the evening ritual of the *passagiata*—the evening walk. Food options tend toward the run-of-the-mill pizza places, though at least they're not as bad as the American pizza megachains that serve bad pizza at inflated prices. Or you can meet your five-a-day requirement of fruits and veggies at the daily public market (which is closed on Sunday).

While here, take advantage of the hostel's tennis courts, available free of charge.

How to get there:

By bus: Take AMANUP bus toward Fano from P. Matteotti, or walk along via 24 Maggio from station. Get off bus at CAMPING NORINA sign on beach to left. Walk away from bar, take road away from highway to grassy area; follow yellow sign to hostel.

By car: Call hostel for transit route.

By train: Call hostel for transit route.

ROME

Chances are, if you've come to Italy, you're going to end up in Rome sooner or later. We've just got two words to say before we leave you off here.

Good luck.

Seriously, though, if you're flying into Rome, don't even try to deal with the chaos while jet-lagged. Instead, we'd recommend that you grab a train straight from the airport (which is south of the city) and head away to Naples, one of its associated islands, or the beautiful Amalfi coast—somewhere south of Rome on the blue ocean where we could catch up on sleep and prepare mentally for the cauldron that is Rome.

Once there, you'd have to be nuts to rent or drive a car—and we're pretty crazy when it comes to driving. But this is one place where we threw up our hands and cried uncle. Use the bus system, which may be hard to understand at first but does the job. Taxi drivers appear to be insane but are savvy. The two Metropolitan (subway) lines are also very useful.

Coming by train? Be extra careful around the Stazione Termini, the train station where most Roman hostellers first arrive. This area—as well as several of the busiest tourist areas in the city, like the Spanish Steps—is notorious for thieves and pickpockets.

So don't wear that expensive camera around your neck, don't flash too much cash, don't wear shorts that advertise your greenhorn status, don't walk alone down teenie alleys at night, and don't pay attention to the hordes of kids who'll do anything—even toss a baby in your face—to occupy you for just the moment it takes to snatch your wallet. Our advice: Wear a money belt.

Other advice? Aw, you know. When in Rome . . .

ROME (ROMA) HOSTELS at a glance

	RATING	PRICE	IN A WORD	PAGE
Fawlty Towers		25,000 lire to 30,000 lire	good	p.300
Pensione Ottaviano		25,000 lire to 30,000 lire	tiny	p.303
Pensione Sandy		25,000 lire to 30,000 lire	small	p.304
M&J's Place		20,000 lire to 30,000 lire	mediocre	p.301
Foro Italico		25,000 lire to 30,000 lire	plain	p.301
Pensione Alessandro		15,000 lire to 20,000 lire	cheap	p.302

FAWLTY TOWERS

Via Magenta 39, Roma

Phone number: 064–450–374 or 064–454–802

E-mail: gi.costantini@agora.stm.it
Web site: www.enjoyrome.it/ftytwhtl.htm
Rates: 25,000 to 30,000 lire per person (about $15 to $18 US); doubles 90,000 to 125,000 lire (about $53 to $75 US)
Private/family rooms: Available
Checkout: 9:00 to 10:00 A.M.
Affiliation: None
Extras: Terrace, Internet access

No, there's no bumbling bellhop named Manuel here or owner Basil Fawlty finding himself constantly in compromising positions. This happenin' hostel just borrowed its name from the popular British comedy starring that ex-Monty Python guy John Cleese.

You're the only one who might find yourself in a compromising and unpleasant situation, though, if you don't reserve your bed well in advance. Otherwise you can look forward to camping out at the front door by 7:00 A.M. at the latest if you really want a short-notice bed. It's that popular, especially in the summer, and deservedly so.

Hostellers love the supersocial terrace that assists in bonding fellow bunkmates. Rooms are accommodating and mostly small, some even equipped with a refrigerator. (There are also dorms, which are okay.) A wide collection of guidebooks and maps keeps travelers occupied when they're not out seeing the carnival that is Roma.

And you're right behind the train station, too.

Gestalt:
No Fawlty

Party index:

How to get there:

By bus: Hostel is within walking distance.
By car: Call hostel for directions.
By train: Train station adjacent to hostel.

KEY TO ICONS

- Attractive natural setting
- Ecologically aware hostel
- Superior kitchen facilities or cafe
- Offbeat or eccentric place
- Superior bathroom facilities
- Romantic private rooms
- Comfortable beds
- Editors Choice Among our very favorite hostels
- A particularly good value
- Wheelchair-accessible
- Good for business travelers
- Especially well suited for families
- Good for active travelers
- Visual arts at hostel or nearby
- Music at hostel or nearby
- Great hostel for skiers
- Bar or pub at hostel or nearby

M&J'S PLACE

Via Solferino, 9, Roma

Phone number: 04–462–802

Rates: 30,000 lire per person (about $18 US); doubles 80,000 to 100,000 lire (about $47 to $59 US)
Private/family rooms: Yes
Affiliation: None
Extras: Radio, TV, refrigerator, bar, ceiling fans

This hostel has it all for young backpackers in the way of varied amenities: TV, on-site bar, refrigerator, and much-needed ceiling fans.

It's certainly a convivial place, although it gets cramped during the summer high season and reports of poor upkeep tend to mar its reputation when compared with the other independent hostels in town. Come here if you don't mind a little grunge and are seeking travel buddies.

Best bet for a bite: Bar across from Termini

Hospitality:

Party index:

How to get there:

By bus: Call hostel for transit route.
By car: Call hostel for directions.
By train: Hostel is a few blocks north of Termini.

OSTELLO FORO ITALICO (ITALIAN FORUM HOSTEL)

Viale delle Olimpiadi 61, 00194, Roma RM

Phone number: 063–236–267

Fax Number: 063–242–613
Rates: 25,000 to 30,000 lire per HI member (about $15 to $18 US); doubles 60,000 lire (about $35 US)
Credit cards: None
Beds: 334
Private/family rooms: Yes
Kitchen available: No
Office hours: 7:00 to 9:00 A.M.; 2:00 P.M. to midnight
Lockout: 9:00 A.M. to 2:00 P.M.
Affiliation: HI-AIG
Extras: Meals ($), breakfast, bar, Internet access, fax, TV

This hostel's architecture is spookily reminiscent of the somber era of *i fascisti*—and it's no accident. It was originally built as a dormitory for Mussolini's charges. Later, it was converted to a hostel, but the gray concrete exterior, too-wide hallways, gang-style showers (slowly being converted to regular ones), and really blah location beside an expressway in the 'burbs remind you of its former life.

Best bet for a bite:
Back in town

What hostellers say:
"Where's the city?"

Gestalt:
Facist architecture

Hospitality:

Cleanliness:

Party index:

Dorms and bathrooms are mostly way too big and institutional; expect groups and potentially noisy nights here, at undoubtedly the least homey or Rome's half-dozen hostels. After a couple of days using transit to get all the way back to town, you'll also start wondering why the heck they picked a place so darned far away from the action. Oh, well. At least the three-night maximum stay ensures that you won't have to deal with the place for too long; for once, this rule is a blessing.

There's a vending machine in the lobby where you can purchase tickets for Rome's buses or Metropolitan subway, which makes planning a visit downtown a snap (though the trip is time-consuming). If you're driven to drink by the boring neighborhood, they also run a small cafeteria/bar downstairs with local characters dishing up light meals, snacks, drinks, coffees, and mineral water. There's a garden out back, a famous sports complex nearby, and the premier's villa next door, which should make you feel a little better.

And, actually, the staff is as professional and friendly as can be—some of them even speak other languages. Maps on the wall help guide you around what can be an intimidating city. And that basement eatery isn't bad at all; during out visit, a Lithuanian women's chorus down there practiced beautifully sad songs that echoed through the halls.

See? We find the good side of everything.

How to get there:

By bus: Take Metro Linea A to Ottavino, exit onto via Barletta, and take bus 32 (from the middle of the street) to Cardorna. Get off before Stadio del Nuoto.

By car: Call hostel for directions.

By train: Call hostel for transit route.

PENSIONE ALESSANDRO (ALESSANDRO'S HOME HOSTEL)

Via Vicenza 42, Roma

Phone number: 064–461–958

E-mail: p.alessandro@iol.it

Rates: 15,000 to 30,000 lire per person (about $9.00 to $18.00 US)
Beds: 53
Family/private rooms: Yes
Kitchen available: Yes
Affiliation: None
Extras: TV, coffee

$

Gestalt: Chaosissimo
Cleanliness:
Party index:

A young staff and laid-back atmosphere make up—partly—for the tight fit in the dorm rooms here, the stuffy dorms, the chaotic streetside location, and lack of cleaning. It's incredibly cheap, which is why people land here. You can avail yourself of cooking facilities as well as the free-flowing coffee.

However, lack of a curfew could mean people traipsing in at all hours of the night and making your attempts at sleep futile. Caveat emptor.

Legend has it that management encourages travelers to get to know one another over glasses of vino. That's not enough to keep us coming back, though.

How to get there:

By bus: Call hostel for transit route.
By car: Call hostel for directions.
By train: Call hostel for transit route.

PENSIONE OTTAVIANO (OTTAVIANO HOME HOSTEL)

Via Ottaviano 6, Roma

Phone number: 063–973–7253 or 063–973–8138

E-mail: gi.costantini@agora.stm.it
Rates: 25,000 to 30,000 lire per person (about $15 to $18 US); doubles 60,000 to 90,000 lire (about $35 to $53 US)
Private/family rooms: Yes
Affiliation: None
Extras: TV, lockers, e-mail

This independent hostel sits close to St. Peter's a mere block from the Vatican.

Yes. *That* Vatican.

Run by the same folks who own Fawlty Towers and Pensione Sandy, it's close to the action. It's also clean and has private rooms and tidy bathrooms.

Some of the rooms even have their own refrigerators, so you can store all of that San Pellegrino mineral water we all love so well. Access all of Rome's wonders from the Metro stop a short stroll away; just don't expect too much in the way of scintillating conversation. The ambience is rather bland, and common space is almost a nonentity. The crowd is almost 100 percent Aussie and American.

No matter. It's a good inexpensive bunk in a town where decent beds are normally outrageous. You're welcome to use the hostel's e-mail facilities, too, to keep in touch with your envious pals back home.

Best bet for a bite: Natural foods store near Vatican

Gestalt: Straight Pope

Party index:

How to get there:

By bus: Call hostel for transit route.
By car: Call hostel for directions.
By train: Call hostel for transit route.

PENSIONE SANDY (SANDY'S HOME HOSTEL)

Via Cavour 136, Roma

Phone number: 064–884–585

E-mail: gi.costantini@agora.stm.it
Web site: www.enjoyrome.it/sandyhtl.htm
Rates: 25,000 to 30,000 lire per person (about $15 to $18 US)
Beds: 30
Affiliation: None

Bring your Tiger Balm to soothe your back after you schlep your backpack up the four flights of stairs to reach this small hostel. But once there, you'll be welcomed into a warm (not in winter—there's no heat!) and hoppin' scene. Beds are cots rather than bunks, but

KEY TO ICONS

- Attractive natural setting
- Ecologically aware hostel
- Superior kitchen facilities or cafe
- Offbeat or eccentric place
- Superior bathroom facilities
- Romantic private rooms
- Comfortable beds
- Editors Choice Among our very favorite hostels
- A particularly good value
- Wheelchair-accessible
- Good for business travelers
- Especially well suited for families
- Good for active travelers
- Visual arts at hostel or nearby
- Music at hostel or nearby
- Great hostel for skiers
- Bar or pub at hostel or nearby

at least you'll only be sharing your room with two to four other folks.

It's not as clean as Fawlty Towers, but it's really close to the Coliseum: just a couple blocks. In fact, you're central to a lot of the sites that attracted you to the "mother of civilization" in the first place, like the Santa Maria Maggiore church. However, since you're also painfully close to the Stazione Termini—Rome's main station and a noted home of lowlifes, pickpockets, and worse—you'll want to watch yourself after dark.

Party index:

How to get there:

By bus: Take 9, 16, 27, 70, 71, or 204 bus.
By metro: Take Linea B; cavour colosseo.
By train: Stazione Termini near hostel.

MARINA DEGLI ULIVI (SPERLONGA HOSTEL)

Contrada Fiorelle, 04029 Sperlonga

Phone number: 0771–549–296

Fax Number: 0771–549–296
Rates: Contact hostel for rates
Credit cards: None
Beds: 60
Private/family rooms: Yes
Kitchen available: No
Season: Contact hostel for current season
Office hours: 7:00 to 10:00 A.M.; 3:30 P.M. to midnight
Affiliation: HI-AIG
Extras: Garden

Beach access is the key here, as you're out on a windblown point of land halfway between noisy Rome and grimy Naples. The place is freshly opened, so we can only report that there's a garden and decent family rooms so far. Hopefully meal service will come soon. A nice hill town, Sperlonga's draw is the nearby grotto—a pool of water undercutting a cave where the emperor Tiberius took dips—and old streets.

Gestalt: Sand castle

Party index:

How to get there:

By bus: Take Rome-Naples bus line to Sperlonga depot and walk 100 yards to hostel.

By car: Contact hostel for directions.

By train: From Rome, take local southbound (toward Naples) train to Fondi station; change to bus for Sperlonga and continue to hostel.

OSTELLO DELLA NEVE (SNOW HOSTEL)

Anello di Campoforogna, 02017, Terminillo RI

Phone number: 0746–261–169

Fax Number: 0746–261–169
Rates: 19,000 lire per HI member (about $11 US); doubles 42,000 lire (about $25 US)
Beds: 120
Private/family rooms: Yes
Kitchen available: No
Season: December 1 to May 15; June 15 to August 31
Office hours: 7:00 A.M. to midnight
Affiliation: HI-AIG
Extras: Meals ($), bar, TV, games

This really nice hostel plays up its main reason for existence in its name: Called the Snow Hostel and located northeast of Rome in the alleged geographical center of Italy, this place is probably the best *indoor* lodging accommodation in the area.

Among its features are family rooms, a bar, a television room, games for the kids, and a series of hiking trails maintained by both the hostel staff and a local government-operated School of Forestry.

The chief benefit here is that you're very close to Rome, yet miles away in terms of ambience—no smog, crime, traffic, and so forth. Might be a good day off from the grind.

Gestalt:
Snow business
Party index:

How to get there:

By bus: Call hostel for transit route.
By car: Call hostel for directions.
By train: Call hostel for transit route.

OSTELLO DEI GARIBALDINI (COLLESCIPOLI/TERNI HOSTEL)

Corso dei Garibaldini 61, 05033 Collescipoli (Terni)

Phone number: 0744–800–467

Fax Number: 0744–800–467
Rates: 20,000 lire per HI member (about $11 US); doubles 50,000 lire (about $28 US)
Credit cards: None
Beds: 37

Private/family rooms: Yes
Kitchen available: No
Office hours: 7:00 to 10:00 A.M.; 3:30 to 11:30 P.M.
Season: Contact hostel for current season
Affiliation: HI-AIG
Extras: Breakfast, meals ($)

This new Umbrian place occupies a stone building in an unknown town, with meal service and other perks to come. Collescipoli is just a suburb of Terni, itself a relatively uninteresting place—think Akron with an Italian accent. (Aw, c'mon, Akron, we're just kidding.) The surrounding area has some waterfalls and parks, and the town has an annual late-April festival called Cantamaggio (singing-in of May, or something like that) that's fun to see.

Gestalt:
Terni, Terni, Terni

Party index:

How to get there:

By bus: Contact hostel for transit route.
By car: Contact hostel for directions.
By train: From Terni station, contact hostel for transit route.

OSTELLO TRE CONFINI (VILLA VALLELONGA HOSTEL)

Via Aia Canale, 67050 Villa Vallelonga

Phone number: 0863–949–373

Fax Number: 0672–597–005
E-mail: treconfini@hotmail.com
Rates: Contact hostel for current rates
Credit cards: None
Beds: 48
Private/family rooms: Yes
Kitchen available: Yes
Office hours: 7:00 A.M. to 11:00 P.M.
Season: February 1 to 28; April 1 to September 30; December 1 to 31
Affiliation: HI-AIG
Extras: Meals ($), laundry, sports facilities, Internet access, TV, VCR, bike rentals

Gestalt:
This old house

Hospitality:

Party index:

So far this new one looks good—the management appears friendly, and the sleekly designed hostel is decked out with Internet access, television lounge, VCR, and a laundry, among other perks. Also note the proximity of ski slopes and

Abruzzo Park. There's a bear museum nearby (yes, a bear museum) if you're hankering to know more about the locals.

How to get there:

By bus: Contact hostel for transit route.

By car: Contact hostel for directions.

By train: Avezzano station, 16 miles away, is nearest station; contact hostel for transit route.

OSTELLO DELL'ORSO

Via Roma, 67030 Villetta Barrea
Phone number: 064–871–152
Fax Number: 064–880–492
Rates: Contact hostel for current rates
Credit cards: None
Beds: 35
Private/family rooms: Yes
Office hours: 7:00 to 10:00 A.M.; 3:30 to 11:30 P.M.
Affiliation: HI-AIG

Gestalt:
Ski? Do!
Party index:

This brand-new, two-story place is less than 2 miles from Villa Barrea, in beautiful Abruzzo National Park. It's a bit like a hotel, though it's so new we don't quite know what to expect when it's fully open. Hiking trails, ski trails, and waterfalls abound in the area, however.

KEY TO ICONS

- Attractive natural setting
- Ecologically aware hostel
- Superior kitchen facilities or cafe
- Offbeat or eccentric place
- Superior bathroom facilities
- Romantic private rooms
- Comfortable beds
- Editors Choice Among our very favorite hostels
- A particularly good value
- Wheelchair-accessible
- Good for business travelers
- Especially well suited for families
- Good for active travelers
- Visual arts at hostel or nearby
- Music at hostel or nearby
- Great hostel for skiers
- Bar or pub at hostel or nearby

How to get there:

By bus: Contact hostel for transit route.

By car: Contact hostel for directions.

By train: Nearest station is at Castel di Sangro, 16 miles away; contact hostel for transit route.

NAPLES AND SOUTHERN ITALY

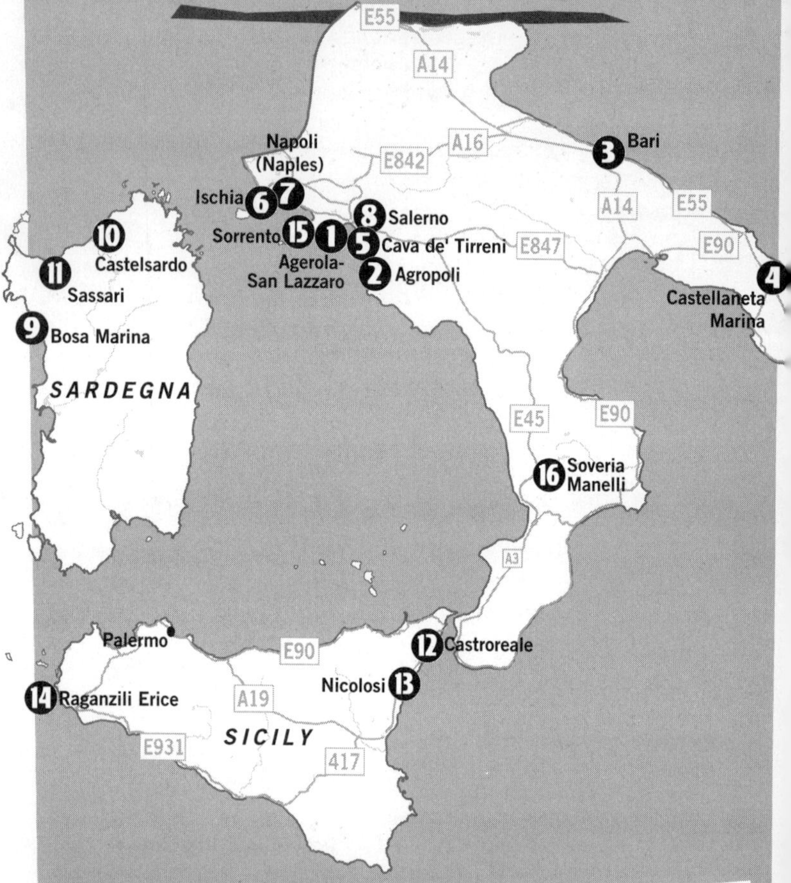

Page numbers follow town names.

NAPLES AND SOUTHERN ITALY

Southern Italy is the most Italian part of the country: slow-moving, hot, at times frustrating; yet there's a warmth and genuineness of character here that permeate daily life. Everything stops for a talk, and you've got to like a people who consume almonds, olives, olive oil, lemons, fish, and fruit in such quantities: a nice antidote to the cream sauces of northern Italy and France.

Your wallet will really appreciate the region's low prices, too. They're among the cheapest on the Continent and look especially good if you've already drained those crucial funds on expensive pizza and coffee in, say, Venice or Paris.

Getting around here, though, can be a bit of an adventure. Public transit moves like a glacier, *if* you can figure it out. Don't count on zipping through this region in a couple days, because the Italian transportation system doesn't work that way, bucko. Accept it and sink into the slower rhythms of life.

Also, this is the part of Italy where safety becomes more and more a concern. Certain streets in Naples can be dangerous any time of day or night, and the same is true of cities in Sicily. Car drivers are occasionally carjacked on remote winding roads down here, an unfortunate development to be sure, and women are likely to be stared at, harassed, even sometimes followed home. So look sharp.

Where to go? Sicilians may be the friendliest people on the planet. If you're in southern Italy, come here first. Naples is pizza capital of the world, and full of things to see and do. The heel and toe of Italy—Puglia and Calabria—aren't nearly as well known, and they make good off-the-beaten-track visits to places where the tourist dollar doesn't rule the world yet.

Finally, a ferry ride to Sardegna (Sardinia)—where Spanish, Italian, Portugese, and other influences all combine to spice up life on this big, beautiful, rocky island—is a special treat, although (again) it'll take awhile to get around.

Hostel quality is a little bit hit-or-miss, however. The joint outside downtown Naples is superb, so by all means book this hostel bed—before you get to Italy if necessary. That way you can stop worrying about the possibility you'll get shut out and end up sleeping in the city's mean streets. Sardinia also has some interesting bunks in beautiful settings.

OSTELLO BEATA SOLITUDO (BLESSED SOLITUDE HOSTEL)

Piazzo Generale Avitabile, 80051 Agerola-San Lazzaro, NA

Phone Number: 081–802–5048

Fax Number: 081–802–5048
E-mail: paolog@ptn.pandora.it
Rates: 16,000 lire per person (about $10 US)
Credit cards: None
Beds: 16
Private/family rooms: No
Kitchen available: Yes
Season: January 1 to September 14; October 1 to December 31
Office hours: 7:00 to 10:00 A.M.; 3:30 to 11:30 P.M.
Affiliation: HI-AIG
Extras: TV, camping, laundry

Gestalt: Quiet riot

Party index:

A small hostel with an enchanting view of the Gulf of Salerno, Agerola aims to please, with its nice airy kitchen and picnic table for informal dining. They do charge for heat and hot water here, but they partly make up for it with a television room and a nice campground.

The biggest draw here is the great beaches, popular with Italians on holiday. Hostel staff helps plan day trips to Sorrento as well as to the Grotto dello Smeraldo, a cave of greenish water where local tour guides will help you try to spot famous international celebrities in the stalactites and stalagmites.

How to get there:

By bus: Bus stops 50 yards from hostel; follow signs to hostel.
By car: Call hostel for directions.
By train: Gragnano station, 10 miles away; call hostel for transit route.

OSTELLO LA LANTERNA (LANTERN HOSTEL)

Località San Marco Via Lanterna 8, 84043, Agropoli SA

Phone Number: 0974–838–364

Fax Number: 0974–838–364
E-mail: lanterna@cilento.peoples.it
Rates: 16,000 lire per HI member (about $10 US); doubles 34,000 lire (about $20 US)

Beds: 56
Private/family rooms: Yes
Kitchen available: No
Season: March 15 to October 30
Office hours: 7:00 to 10:00 A.M.; 3:30 to 11:30 P.M.
Affiliation: HI-AIG
Extras: Restaurant ($), bar, TV, library, tours

Gestalt: Green lanterna

Party index:

The town of Agropoli is unique because of the presence of Cilento National Park, which includes some areas of human habitation in this swath of public land.

Although within the city limits of Agropoli, this new hostel is a rustic cabin surrounded by a grove of shade trees. Looking like something from a spaghetti western movie set, it's filled with rooms of only two to four beds, each neat and tidy, and hostellers can avail themselves of meal service for a small fee. Other goodies here include a television room, a bar, a little library, and both walking and bicycle tours of the area—a nice option.

Nearby are the ancient ruins of Paestum (which used to be the capital of Greater Greece, called Poseidonia). This is a great place for history-lovin' solar babies who can both tour the well-preserved Doric ruins (Temple of Poseidon) and catch some rays on the beach. Sundown is the best time for temple viewing and evening contemplation, we'd say.

How to get there:

By bus: From Palese bus stop, walk 100 yards to hostel, following signs.

By car: Call hostel for directions.

By train: From Palese station, turn right and walk 1 mile along tracks; via Lanterna is first left.

OSTELLO DEL LEVANTE (BARI HOSTEL)

Lungomare Starita, 70123, Bari

Phone Number: 080–549–2823

Fax Number: 080–549–2823
Rates: Contact hostel for rates
Credit cards: None
Beds: 600
Private/family rooms: Yes
Kitchen available: No
Season: January 1 to August 31; October 1 to December 31
Office hours: 7:30 A.M. to 1:30 P.M.; 3:30 to 11:30 P.M.
Affiliation: HI-AIG

Extras: Meals ($), TV, meeting room

This one just opened, and we can't say much about it—yet. We do know this, though: It's a fine-lookin' yellow palace right beside the water, and it's absolutely huge. Six hundred beds! And they'll need 'em too, 'cause zillions of backpackers pour through this port town on the way to Greece each summer.

Gestalt: Bari early

Party index:

How to get there:

By bus: Contact hostel for transit route.

By car: Contact hostel for directions.

By ferry: Contact hostel for transit route.

By train: From Bari station, walk 1 mile to hostel.

VILLINI PARADISO (CASTELLANETA MARINA HOSTEL)

Via Zond 2, 74010 Castellaneta

Phone Number: 099–843–3200

Fax Number: 099–843–0046
Rates: 25,000 lire per HI member (about $15 US); doubles 60,000 lire (about $35 US)
Credit cards: Yes
Beds: 100
Private/family rooms: Yes
Kitchen available: Yes
Office hours: Twenty-four hours
Affiliation: HI-AIG
Extras: Bike rentals, laundry, TV, meals ($)

This new hostel is situated right by the beaches of Puglia, way down there in southern Italy's bottom. It's a bit hard to find, but once here you can take advantage of good facilities—double rooms, a hosteller kitchen, a laundry, a television lounge, and so forth. Plus the beach of course.

You get here by bus or train from the largely overlooked port city of Taranto, in the "arch" of Italy's foot. Why come all this way? Well, believe it or not, Rudolph Valentino was born here; a small museum commemorates this entirely random fact.

Gestalt: Paradiso lost

Hospitality:

Party index:

How to get there:

By bus: Contact hostel for transit route.

By car: Contact hostel for directions.

By train: Taranto station, 20 miles away, is nearest station; contact hostel for transit route.

OSTELLO BORGO SCACCIAVENTI (CAVA DE' TIRRENI HOSTEL)

Piazza San Francesco, 84103 Cava de' Tirreni

Phone Number: 089–466–631

Fax Number: 089–466–631
Rates: Contact hostel for rates
Credit cards: None
Beds: 220
Private/family rooms: None
Kitchen available: No
Office hours: 7:00 to 10:00 A.M.; 3:30 P.M. to midnight
Affiliation: HI-AIG
Extras: Meeting room, garden, TV

An old stone building set in the foothills above the Gulf of Salerno, this place is a good—if hard-to-get-to—base for exploring the Amalfi Coast. Hardy types will hit the mountains, while others will simply head for the coastal beaches. Not often do you get to sleep with such great views of beautiful coastline.

Gestalt: Gulf course

Party index:

How to get there:

By bus: From Cava de' Tirreni station, walk ½ mile to hostel or take 4 or 9 bus to hostel.

By car: Contact hostel for directions.

By train: From Cava de' Tirreni station, walk ½ mile to hostel or take 4 or 9 bus to hostel.

OSTELLO IL GABBIANO (ISCHIA HOSTEL)

S.S. Forio-Panza 162, 80075 Forio d'Ischia

Phone Number: 081–909–422

Fax Number: 081–909–422
Rates: 23,000 lire per HI member (about $14 US)
Credit cards: None
Beds: 100
Private/family rooms: Yes
Season: April 1 to September 30
Office hours: 7:00 A.M. to 12:30 A.M.
Affiliation: HI-AIG

Extras: TV, gardens, pool

This new, three-story palace has a pool right out front and plenty of double rooms. What else do you want? The amenities are a bit slim—no kitchen, of course—but you're near the beach, so that makes up for it.

Gestalt: Beach ball

Hospitality:

Cleanliness:

Party index:

Ischia's an amazingly beautiful island, full of fruit, flowers, trees, and rocks—all of it surrounded by blue, blue water. It's quite a nice change from snooty-nosed (and more expensive) Capri nearby. Get there from Naples' Molo Beverello dock, on the waterfront in front of Nuovo Castle.

How to get there:

By bus: Contact hostel for transit route.

By car: Contact hostel for directions.

By ferry: Docks from Naples 1 mile away; contact hostel for transit route.

By train: Contact hostel for transit route.

OSTELLO MERGELLINA

Via Salita della Grotta a Piedigrotta 23, 80122 Napoli

Phone Number: 081–761–2346 or 081–761–1215

Fax Number: 081–761–2391

Rates: 24,000 lire per HI member (about $14 US); doubles 60,000 lire (about $35 US)

Credit cards: None

Beds: 200

Private/family rooms: Yes

Kitchen available: No

Office hours: 6:30 A.M. to 12:30 A.M.

Curfew: 12:30 A.M.

Affiliation: HI-AIG

Extras: Meals ($), TV, laundry, Internet access, garden, bar, parking, fax

Definitely one of the better city hostels in Italy, the Mergellina provides clean and comfortable beds in small dorms that come with their own bathrooms. Sheets and shower are included with your bed; so is breakfast. Unbelievably, this is still the one and only true hostel in Naples. So thank goodness it's such a good place.

Though remote—it sits on a hillside a mile or more outside central Naples—it's a superb sleepover if you want to avoid downtown's craziness and catch a hydrofoil or ferry to some really beautiful offshore islands. The hostel is also close to the tombs of Virgil and Leonardo. How's that for some history?

Other amenities include meal service, a nice garden, a laundry, a television room, and—yes—Internet access for e-mailing your buddies back home and making them green with envy. That's how good this place is.

Gestalt:
Naples for days
Party index:

How to get there:

By bus: Call hostel for transit route.

By plane: Capodichino airport, 3 miles away; call hostel for transit route.

By subway: Take subway to Mergellina stop; from station, walk under tracks and follow signs to hostel.

By train: From Mergellina station, walk 200 yards to hostel.

OSTELLO IRNO (IRNO HOSTEL)

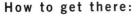

Via Luigi Guercio 112, Salerno, 84100

Phone Number: 089–790–251

Fax Number: 089–405–792
Rates: 15,000 lire per person (about $9.00 US)
Credit cards: None
Beds: 100
Private/family rooms: No
Kitchen available: No
Office hours: 7:00 to 11:00 A.M.; 3:30 P.M. to 12:30 A.M.
Lockout: 11:00 A.M. to 3:30 P.M.
Curfew: 12:30 A.M.
Affiliation: HI-AIG
Extras: Tours, meals ($), TV, movies, games, library, bike rentals, bar

This hostel received mixed reviews in terms of cleanliness. Some feel it's passable, while others found it absolutely disgusting; you be the judge.

Judging from our snoops, migrant workers appeared to be a problem here, and at last report cleanliness was seriously suffering. Deplorable was the word. Theft was also a problem at the hostel, so if you really feel you need to stay here, look sharp!

Gestalt:
Salerno-no
Party index:

Among the supposed pluses here are tours with a local hiking club, a library, movies, and some meal service. But it looks too questionable for now. We wouldn't stay here until things shape up.

How to get there:

By bus: Bus stops 50 yards from hostel.

By car: Call hostel for directions.

By train: From Salerno station, walk to via Torrione and turn left. Walk parallel to train tracks to via Mobilio, continue 300 yards, and climb second stairway on right; via Luigi Guercia is at top.

OSTELLO MALASPINA

Via Sardegna, 1–08013, Bosa Marina (Sardegna), NU

Phone Number: 0785–375–009

Fax Number: 0785–375–009
Rates: 18,000 lire per HI member (about $11 US)
Credit cards: None
Beds: 63
Private/family rooms: None
Kitchen available: No
Office hours: 7:00 A.M. to 1:00 P.M.; 3:30 P.M. to midnight
Affiliation: HI-AIG
Extras: Restaurant ($), bike rentals, movies, laundry, TV, bar, fax, gardens

One of only two legitimate hostels on Sardinia, this brand-new joint boasts an irresistible location close to the beach with tons of amenities. A bonus for you, the hosteller, is the fact that the town of Bosa is still undiscovered by the mainstream tourist public. You'll get a real chance to mingle with the locals and pick up some Sardo lingo.

Gestalt:
Sardinia tin

Party index:

Unfortunately, you'll need to call ahead in the summer, perhaps a week or more, to ensure that you get a bed. Germans and other Euros go absolutely nuts on the island during that season. And Sardinia's definitely not cheap.

Summer also means that once you do get a bed, the dorms will be full—meaning that you'll feel packed like a, well, sardinia.

But this hostel's still got a lot going for it: movies, laundry, bike rentals, even a room that's wheelchair accessible. Yay!

In Bosa, the main attraction is the old city known as Sa Costa—its medieval character is positively beguiling. Again, as in Alghero, you can play cultural detective by figuring out which buildings were built by the Catalans and which were later Italian-built. More *nuraghe* (stone) settlements dot the outlying area, providing you with hours of head-scratching enjoyment as to what became of those mysterious people.

How to get there:

By bus: From Olbia, take Doppio bus to Bosa Marina and walk to hostel.

By car/ferry: Call hostel for directions.

By train: From Bosa Marina station, walk ½ mile to hostel.

OSTELLO GOLFO DELL'ASINARA (GULF OF ASINARA HOSTEL)

Via Sardegna 1, Località Lu-Bagnu, 07031 Castelsardo, Sardegna

Phone Number: 079–474–031 or 079–587–008

Fax Number: 079–587–142
Rates: 19,000 to 23,000 lire per HI member (about $11 to $14 US); doubles 52,000 lire (about $31 US)
Credit cards: Yes
Beds: 110
Private/family rooms: Yes
Season: May 1–September 30
Office hours: 7:00 A.M. to midnight
Affiliation: HI-AIG
Extras: Laundry, TV, garden, restaurant ($), VCR, bike rentals, sports facilities

This new hostel's located on a beach in Sardegna, which gives it immediate caché, and it's so well equipped that you might stick around for a few days. The rooms aren't too big—doubles, triples, and quads—and they serve meals here. Check out the laundry, garden, beach, and restaurant as well. Then rent a bike and head for the hills.

Gestalt: Sardinia can

Hospitality:

Cleanliness:

Party index:

How to get there:

By bus: Contact hostel for transit route.

By car: Contact hostel for directions.

By ferry: Contact hostel for transit route.

By train: Nearest station is Sassari, 20 miles away; contact hostel for transit route.

OSTELLO DEI GIULIANI

Via Zara 1, Localita Fertilia, Sassari (Sardegna), 07040

Phone Number: 079–930–353

Fax Number: 079–930–353
Rates: 14,000 lire per HI member (about $8.00 US)
Credit cards: None
Beds: 50
Private/family rooms: None
Kitchen available: No
Office hours: 7:00 to 10:00 A.M.; noon to 2:30 P.M.; 3:30 P.M. to midnight
Lockout: 9:00 A.M. to 12:30 P.M.; 2:30 to 5:30 P.M.
Curfew: 11:30 P.M.
Affiliation: HI-AIG
Extras: Meals ($), sports

Rumors that this hostel was named for New York City mayor Rudy Giuliani aren't necessarily true. Seriously, though, this is a drop-dead beautiful area with a decent hostel. Of course, it goes without saying that you should book way-y-y in advance to even think of bunking here in the summer months.

Gestalt: Rolling stones

Party index:

The best thing about this hostel? The meals for sure, which are scrumptious and inexpensive and prepared by the Mamma who runs this tight ship.

You'll be fascinated with the decidedly different culture in nearby Alghero, which you need to take a short bus ride to get to. Catalan Spanish is more likely to be spoken here than Italian, and the architecture reflects the Spaniards' culture, which once dominated the island.

This part of the island of Sardinia is rife with mysterious *nuraghe,* stone dwellings that were constructed by a population who left no clues about their remarkable civilization. Unfortunately, the nuraghe sites have been left to ruin and not much has been done to preserve them. Still, it's one heady place to come for a getaway.

Note: At press time, AIG was considering moving this hostel to a new location; all this information may have changed by the time you get to Alghero and Fertilia.

How to get there:

By bus: From Alghero, take AF bus to Fertilia; from bus stop, walk along via Parenzo to via Zara and turn right.

By car/ferry: Porto Torres ferry, 23 miles away, is nearest stop; call hostel for transit route.

By train: From Alghero station, 4½ miles away, take AF bus to Fertilia; from bus stop, walk along via Parenzo to via Zara and turn right.

SICILY (SICILIA) HOSTELS at a glance

	RATING	PRICE	IN A WORD	PAGE
Ostello Etna	—	25,000 lire	active	p.322
Ostello Delle Aquile	—	13,000 lire	small	p.321
Ostello Amodeo	—	25,000 lire	unknown	p.322

OSTELLO DELLE AQUILE (EAGLE'S NEST HOSTEL)

Salita Federica II d'Aragona, 98053 Castroreale Centro, Messina (Sicily)

Phone Number: 090–974–6398

Fax Number: 090–974–6446
Rates: 13,000 lire per HI member (about $8.00 US)
Credit cards: None
Beds: 24
Private/family rooms: None
Kitchen available: Yes
Office hours: 7:00 to 10:00 A.M.; 3:30 to 11:30 P.M.
Season: April 1 to October 31
Affiliation: HI-AIG

Ever fantasize about sleeping in a medieval castle with an exquisite view of the Tyrrhenian Sea? Now's your chance at this antiquated and small hostel in a suburb of Messina. It's supercheap, too.

One downside to this arrangement is that there are no private rooms per se, so you'll definitely be sharing your snoozing space with others. Be sure to make use of the kitchen here.

Gestalt:
Young'uns and Messina

Party index:

How to get there:

By bus: Call hostel for transit route.

By car/ferry: Milazzo ferry, 12 miles from hostel, is nearest stop; call hostel for directions.

By train: Barcellona station, 7 miles away; call hostel for transit route.

OSTELLO ETNA

Via della Quercia 7, 95030 Nicolosi CT (Sicily)

Phone Number: 095–791–4686

Fax Number: 095–791–4701

Rates: 25,000 lire per HI member (about $15 US)
Credit cards: None
Beds: 78
Private/family rooms: Yes
Kitchen available: No
Office hours: 7:00 A.M. to 1:00 P.M.; 3:00 to 11:00 P.M.
Affiliation: HI-AIG
Extras: Meals ($), laundry, bar, TV, library, movies, games, fax

Test your fate at this remote hostel with the unpredictable and potentially hazardous Mount Etna in its backyard. Yep, that's right: an active volcano . . . which you can actually ski down! (When it's not exploding, that is.) How's that for derring-do?

The place provides a comfortable setting in the midst of this thrill-a-minute landscape, with enough basic amenities for families and others who don't like to rough it too much. They serve meals as well as vino on the premises for a charge, like most other Italian hostels, and maintain a reading room and another common room for mingling or television viewing. Movie nights are popular, and games are provided for the young and young at heart. Laundry facilities help you get all that volcanic ash out of your togs.

Nearby is the city of Catania, which will cheer hostellers with calmer sight-seeing ambitions—plenty of churches, frescoes, piazzas, and the like to fill a few days of aimless strolling.

Gestalt:
Joe vs. the Volcano

Party index:

How to get there:

By bus: Take the Catania-Nicolosi line; from Nicolosi bus station, walk 300 yards to hostel.

By car/ferry: Call hostel for transit route.

By train: Catania Centrale station, 8 miles from hostel; call hostel for transit route.

OSTELLO G. AMODEO (AMODEO HOSTEL)

Strada Provinciale 31, Trapani 91100, Raganzili Erice TP (Sicily)

Phone Number: 0923–552–964

Fax Number: 0923–539–398

Rates: 25,000 lire per HI member (about $15 US)
Credit cards: Yes
Beds: 52
Private/family rooms: Yes
Season: January 1 to November 11; December 4 to 31
Office hours: 7:00 to 10:00 A.M.; 3:30 P.M. to midnight
Affiliation: HI-AIG
Extras: Meals ($), breakfast, bar, TV, camping, garden

The twin towns of Erice and Trapani have been relatively unscathed by tourism and therefore offer a glimpse into actual Sicilian day-to-day life. Easter would be an excellent time to drink in the local culture, although rooms are hard to come by then. Trapani celebrates this important holiday with an exceptionally long procession of the Passion and Crucifixion of Christ, an event not for the restless.

Gestalt:
Rock me Amodeo

Party index:

The hostel is no exception to the call-ahead rule, as it's relatively small, though it can provide accommodations for families and couples. Breakfast is offered in a bed-and-breakfast type of deal for a few extra lire. Other facilities include a bar, television room, gardens, and a convenient laundry.

Perched high on a hill from which you can gaze down at the Egadi Islands, the hostel certainly has a jaw-dropper of a location. Erice at one time hosted fertility rituals performed by worshippers of the goddess Venus Erycina. Since that time the region has been dominated by a variety of peoples, the French Normans as well as Arabs.

Most hostellers set themselves up here to embark on day trips to the Egadi, a trio of lightly populated islands where it's not uncommon to have access to a solitary beach and take a long dip au naturel.

How to get there:

By bus: Call hostel for transit route.
By car: Call hostel for directions.

PENSIONE LINDA

Via Degli Aranci 125, Sorrento

Phone Number: 081–878–2916

Rates: 45,000 lire per person (about $27 US); doubles 70,000 lire (about $41 US)
Credit cards: None
Private/family rooms: Yes
Office hours: Call hostel for hours
Affiliation: None

This hotel/hostel is extremely small, and if it weren't for the signs, it would be extremely difficult to find. But it's worth the search, especially considering that the HI-AIG joint in town recently closed. This is a much cheaper town than Naples and makes a good budget base for the stunning (and stunningly expensive) Amalfi Coast.

Best bet for a bite:
On way to beach

Insiders' tip:
Beaches cost money

Gestalt:
Lovely Linda

Safety:

Hospitality:

Cleanliness:

Party index:

The staff here is an older married couple who will do their best to make sure you are comfortable. Their English is limited, but if you know a little Italian or carry a phrase book or dictionary, you'll be fine.

This place is clean, and the spacious rooms have balconies. The double beds here are big enough for three. However, if you request a room for three or four people, don't be surprised if you see a children's bunk bed placed in the room to accommodate the extra people. If no one minds sleeping on top, this shouldn't pose a problem.

Anyway, with the beach just a ten-minute walk away, you probably won't be spending much time in your room. There's also Sorrento's old city to explore, and views of the coast from ridgetops to find.

How to get there:

By bus: Call hostel for transit route.

By car: Call hostel for directions.

By train: From Sorrento station, turn left onto main road, via Degli Aranci. Follow it around curves and up a slight slope until it merges with another street. Continue walking to signs on right; hostel is on second floor.

OSTELLO LA PINETA (PINE GROVE HOSTEL)

Località Bivio Bonacci, 88049, Soveria Manelli CZ

Phone Number: 0968–666–079

Fax Number: 0968–666–079
Rates: 18,000 to 20,000 lire per person (about $11 to $12 US)
Credit cards: Yes
Beds: 52
Private/family rooms: None
Kitchen available: No
Office hours: 7:00 to 10:00 A.M.; 3:30 to 11:30 P.M.
Affiliation: HI-AIG
Extras: Meals ($), TV, camping, sports equipment, bike rentals, bar

Housed in a building that looks like biomedical experiments are being conducted in it, this hostel in the toe of the "boot" of Italy is primarily a ski hostel. Yes, they do get snow down here.

Gestalt:
Pine soul

Party index:

The hostel comes pretty well equipped, offering meal service, a television room, campground, and sports equipment (including but not limited to bicycles) for rent and loan. There are no family rooms here, however; it's bunks all the way, baby.

Fans of rail travel can take a day trip from Cosenza to San Giovanni in Fiore. While the final destination isn't so hot, the ride is fantastic—lots of pristine scenery can be viewed out the train's window. Be sure to sample the exotic local Calabrian cuisine, which includes chocolate-covered figs and the like.

How to get there:

By bus: Call hostel for transit route.
By car: Call hostel for directions.
By train: Call hostel for transit route.

PAUL AND MARTHA'S PICKS

THE TOP 10 HOSTELS IN FRANCE

THE TOP 10 HOSTELS IN ITALY

ABOUT THE AUTHORS

Martha Coombs is a translator, writer, and photographer who works in North America and abroad.

Paul Karr is an award-winning writer, writing coach, and author or co-author of more than a dozen travel guidebooks. He contributes regularly to magazines, and writes screenplays when he's not traveling. He has twice been named a writer-in-residence by the National Parks Service. You can contact him directly at this e-mail address:

Atomev@aol.com